CONSULTANTS REFERENCE GUIDE

by
Charna Klein

with
Mardell Moore

The Scarecrow Press, Inc.
Metuchen, N.J., & London
1989

British Library Cataloguing-in-Publication data available.

Library of Congress Cataloging-in-Publication Data

Klein, Charna
    Consultants reference guide / by Charna Klein with
Mardell Moore.
        p.   cm.
    ISBN 0-8108-2256-3
    1. Consultants--Handbooks, manuals, etc. I. Moore,
Mardell. II. Title.
HD69.C6K54   1989
658.4'6--dc20   89-39476

PREFACE/ACKNOWLEDGMENTS

The Consultants Reference Guide is the culmination of many years of work.

In doing this work we are grateful for the help of the following persons: Joseph Memmel for his role in the initial stage of the project, Judith Winter for editorial assistance and consultation, Robert Wall for his dedicated computer assistance and consultation, and the many librarians who helped locate sources at the Seattle Public Library and University of Washington Library.

Charna Klein
Mardell Moore
Consultant Services Northwest, Inc.

TABLE OF CONTENTS

INTRODUCTION

ABOUT CONSULTANTS

The Consultants Reference Guide is the only business guide designed specifically for all five types of consultants:

- independent practitioners (the one-person firm),
- consultants in small-group practice,
- consultants in larger, established firms,
- in-house consultants (with or without the title),
- would-be consultants (who are gathering expertise while waiting to set up shop).

Have you ever wondered how you could simply and quickly find information about a given business subject, topic, problem, or need? Have you ever wandered around a library not knowing where to look for something yet knowing it's there...somewhere...if you could only find it? Have you ever felt -- what's the use in trying to find it -- it's too much trouble?

The Consultants Reference Guide:

- Helps you find what you're looking for
- Tells you what to expect in a work
- Helps you to evaluate books you'll want
- Rates works in terms of practical value
- Provides a handy library reference and searching tool
- Provides easy access indexes to pertinent publications
- Assists your professional development and business success

Consulting is a way of life, a special style of working, and has its own information needs. Today's consultant may be an expert. More likely, however, the consultant is an eclectic synthesizer of a variety of kinds of knowledge and skills. This is similar to the "ronin" of Feudal Japan. "Ronin" means "wave-people" and refers to persons

who left their allotted stations in life in order
to flow with life -- to be willing and able to
take on a variety of roles as their circumstances
required. Today's ronin is the consultant whose
characteristic job strategy is to work
autonomously, with self-direction, creativity, and
a love of variety. Rather than moving up the
"ladder of success" hierarchically, ronin move
laterally, picking up a variety of knowledge and
skills as they go.

Our need for knowing where to find needed,
relevant information is increasing at an
astounding rate. Yet we often do not know where
to turn for obtaining the information we need, or
we simply feel it would be too difficult to
warrant the time and effort involved. It's for
these reasons that the Consultants Reference
Guide (CRG) was produced. With the CRG, you can
find what you're looking for, quickly and easily.

When coming to this place in writing this
narrative, I (Charna Klein) wanted a statistic on
information overload -- something like I
remembered hearing -- such as there will be x
billions of paper per year in the year 2000, or
there is ten times the amount of paperwork now as
in 1970. Seemingly it would be an easy task to
find such a well-known statement. Not having the
statement ready at hand, however, I called the
largest library in a four-state area, with four
million volumes and put the question to a
reference librarian. She said she'd call me back
with the information. Two days later, I was told
that the staff of reference libraries had been
unable to find the information I had requested.
However, they had used a computer database to come
up with 29 references to articles. I could come
in and pick up the list. I felt discouraged,
overwhelmed, flabbergasted. Luckily I wasn't in a
hurry for a change. Even if I were to research
all sources, there was no guarantee the needle in
this haystack of paper would be found. The fact
that it took a staff of professional librarians
two days to come up with a non-answer did impress
me -- with the very point I am making here -- that
we suffer from information overload.

    This story speaks to the need for information
aids such as the Consultants Reference Guide.
Its purpose is to help you sift through the
"paperstack" to find what you're looking for.

    When I was in the process of becoming a
consultant, much of the field seemed mysterious,
and I did not know how to find the information I
needed.   I would have welcomed the Consultants
Reference Guide. Later I realized that other
aspiring and practicing consultants have similar
needs for information and information tools. I've
chosen selected references to meet these needs.
You'll probably want some of them for your office
bookshelf. Some others may be too expensive for
you to purchase and can be used in a library.

    In attempting to meet the needs of the
consultant library user, librarians need a ready
reference guide to get them going. The
Consultants Reference Guide takes over and points
to what's available, reference works that are key
resources, and others that discuss subject area,
approach or idea. There is simply too much
material in a library and often too little time
for the librarian to take the patron to the
sources, describe them, how to use them, and their
relevance. In addition, librarians can use the
CRG to assess the strengths and weaknesses of
their collection, and to select material.

ABOUT THE REFERENCE SOURCES

    The literature on consulting is comprised
largely of handbooks or manuals on how to become
and succeed as a consultant. The CRG classifies
and abstracts these publications and other
information sources that are important to
consultants as business owners and managers.

    Some subject areas were chosen not only for
their relevance to all readers, but also as
specific content areas represented by consultants
in a variety of specialties: accountants,
computer consultants, business management and
organization development consultants, marketing

consultants, higher education and health
consultants, information consultants, career
development consultants, etc.

The emphasis is on ways of doing business
that can be used regardless of field of expertise.
Product-specific industries have been left out in
favor of types of industries.

Subject Coverage:

Overall, publications abstracted in the CRG
cover four basic subjects, described below:

1. Business Management -- Resources useful
in planning and conducting these and other
critical business functions:

- Accounting
- Advertising and public relations
- Entrepreneurship
- Law
- Marketing and selling
- Preparing business plans and
  proposals
- Negotiating and writing contracts
- Handling money, taxes and financial
  transactions
- Choosing and using accountants, legal
  advisors and consultants
- Managing employees, resources, and
  organizational culture, structure,
  process and change
- Selecting, purchasing and using
  office technology, computers, and
  telecommunications equipment

2. The Consulting Marketplace

- The major markets within which
  today's professional consultants
  operate
- The profit-oriented marketplace
- The nonprofit marketplace
- Useful planning and marketing
  resources
- Key contacts

3. The Product Creation Marketplace

   - Businesses and organizations involved
     in helping consultants to package
     their expertise and skills into
     marketable, salable consulting
     products
   - Key contacts and resources helpful in
     creating and producing publishable
     consulting products in print,
     graphic, computer and audio-visual
     forms

4. "How To" Skills

   - How to perform important business
     management and consulting tasks
   - How to succeed and excel as the
     owner/manager of a professional
     consulting practice
   - How to select, market and sell your
     consulting services
   - How to create, produce, package,
     publish, protect, market and sell
     your consulting products

Selection Considerations:

   Abstracts of approximately 400 important
publications commonly found in public and
college/university libraries are provided in the
CRG. The base from which the publications were
searched included current bibliographic databases
and bibliographies, reference books, and library
card catalogs. Reference librarians and subject
specialists were consulted as well. Upon
examination of individual publications,
approximately half were rejected due to outdated
or irrelevant content, repetition of sources, lack
of practical value, or poor quality.

   Most of the works included in the CRG can be
classified as: information sources, resource
guides, directories, key contacts sources,
handbooks and guides, how-to materials and self-
help resources. You'll find these types in every
chapter.

I have included some older titles that are
out of print since they are available in library
collections. Dictionaries, almanacs,
encyclopedias and magazines have been excluded.
However, some periodical indexes and current
awareness services have been included.

Since no directory like this can be
inclusive, you'll find that if you review the
sections important for you, it will give you an
idea of the kinds of books to look for.

HOW TO USE THIS GUIDE

Organization of Chapters:

The CRG is organized into 25 chapters, each
covering a defined subject area. In cases where
particular works could be categorized in more than
one chapter, they have been placed in the chapter
judged of greatest relevance to the reader. Refer
to the subject index to find items which may be in
different chapters. A subject index, a title
index, and an author index follow the chapters.

Consultants are usually self-starters who
just need guidance and direction. For example,
the consultant in private practice who needs to
know how to get started in business, needs
information about finance, accounting, law,
equipment, marketing and sales. That information
can be found in three ways: 1) use the chapter
headings to identify the chapter on
Entrepreneurship, which describes publications
dealing with that subject; or 2) consult chapters
which specifically deal with finance, accounting,
law, computers, and marketing; or 3) search for
particular subjects in the subject index, or
particular titles or authors in the title or
author index.

Format of Abstracts:

Each reference work is thoroughly abstracted
including these fields: title, subtitle, date,
frequency, edition, author(s), editor(s), pages,

source, publisher, phone, cost, rating,
publication type, inclusion(s), descriptor(s),
identifier(s), summary, and relevance. Those
fields needing explanation are described below:

Source - This field is used only when the
publisher is different from the sponsoring
organization or source.

Rating - Ratings given to publications are
excellent, very good, and good. Publications with
ratings of lower value are not included in the
CRG. Rating criteria used were:

1. Practical value
2. Useful features and inclusions
3. Coverage scope (breadth, depth, etc.)
4. Graphic quality
5. Datedness (not outdated)
6. Convenience and ease of use

Publication Type - This describes the work as
a textbook, manual, handbook, guide, sourcebook,
resource guide, directory, primer, etc.

Inclusion(s) - This field is for features and
aids included in the work, such as index,
bibliography, appendix, illustrations, charts,
advertisements, etc.

Descriptor(s) - This field identifies main
subjects covered in a publication, and forms a
basis for the subject index.

Identifier(s) - This field is for distinguishing
information such as a former title, identifying
organization or term of publication, and is
usually a proper name, abbreviation or acronym.

Summary - This field includes a description
of the publication, including critical
characteristics, breadth of coverage, major
content categories, listing patterns,
representative examples, general quantity
indicators and boundaries of contents, format and
arrangement, emphasis, perspective or slant, and
additional pertinent information.

Relevance - This field contains evaluative statements regarding the intended audience and uniqueness, usefulness and appropriateness of the publication to consultants. It may also include how the publication can be used to: identify markets, market potential, market resources, and market segments, pinpoint marketing efforts and tasks, select marketing vehicles, gain market leverage, and importantly, develop basic awareness, skills, management and know-how.

Where irrelevant or unknown, some field information may not be included. In cases when an earlier edition of a work has been abstracted, information in the edition, pages, and cost fields will be given for the most recent edition. Author or editor field information may also have changed and been cited. Cost and publisher information may have changed since abstracting; it would be advisable to check the latest edition of Books In Print before ordering publications. Some works have hard and soft cover versions; usually the hardback version is cited. Quoted passages within the abstracts are taken from the work in which the citation appears and are usually from the preface or introduction.

SAMPLE ABSTRACT:

The following sample abstract contains all fields with the field names listed. Many fields are optional depending on their relevance for the work being abstracted. Actual abstracts in the CRG leave out field names for the imprint (including fields from title through cost) and include field names for the remainder of the abstract. When in doubt, the user should keep in mind or refer to this sample abstract regarding the order of fields in the imprint. Please note that SOURCE appears prior to PUBLISHER, ISBN appears before ISSN, and AUTHOR(S) precedes EDITOR(S) information.

TITLE: THE GO-GETTER
SUBTITLE: How to Be an Entrepreneur
DATE: 1989

```
FREQUENCY:          Annual
EDITION:            First
AUTHOR(S):          Joe Gogo
EDITOR(S):          Gladys Wendt
PAGES:              300
SOURCE:             National Coming and Going
                    Society
ISBN:               0-01398-22-123
ISSN:               0-1521-51-4

PUBLISHER:          The Revolving Door Press
                    P.O. Box 000
                    New York, NY 00000
PHONE:              (001) 999-9999
COST:               $29.95

RATING:             Excellent
PUBLICATION TYPE:   Abstracts

INCLUSIONS:         Index; bibliography

DESCRIPTORS:        Entrepreneur;
entrepreneurship; business basics; financing;
venture capital

IDENTIFIER:         Former title: Got to Get Up
and Go
```

SUMMARY: This is a collection of
abstracts on entrepreneurial publications....

RELEVANCE: We recommend this
work...just see for yourself how helpful it
can be in getting your business off the
ground. Annual updates make it especially
relevant.

CHAPTER 1

ACCOUNTING

This chapter contains:

- introductory accounting books

- advanced financial accounting

- budgeting and management control

- auditing

- financial statements and analysis

- accounting for governmental and nonprofit organizations

- accounting systems in specific businesses

- surveys of accounting practices

- accounting services

- accounting bibliographies

- accounting index

- taxation

- directory of accountants

ACCOUNTANTS' HANDBOOK
1981
Sixth
Seidler, Lee - Carmichael, Douglas
2064, 2 volumes
0-471-05505-0
John Wiley and Sons, Inc.
605 Third Avenue
New York, NY 10158
(212) 850-6418
Order: 1 Wiley Dr.
Somerset, NJ 08873
(201) 469-4400
$95.00

Very good
Handbook

INCLUSIONS: Index; bibliographies; charts;
tables; sample forms

DESCRIPTORS: Accounting; taxation;
depreciation

SUMMARY: This work is organized into 45
sections. Each is written by a specialist in a
particular field of accounting. The areas covered
are: nature and elements of accounting, accounting
concepts and principles, accounting boards and
organizations, financial statements, SEC reporting
and requirements, cash flow analysis; evaluating
internal controls, sales and receivables,
inventories and purchases, real estate and
construction, fixed assets, depreciation,
intangible assets, accounting for income taxes,
computing earnings per share, reporting
operations, correcting for inflation and value
changes, liabilities, leases, pension and
retirement plans, mergers, data processing
systems, payroll, cost analysis, partnerships,
estates and trusts, nonprofit enterprises, state
and local accounting, and bankruptcy.

RELEVANCE: This work is written for the
accountant as a reference source when dealing with
any of the 45 topics included. This work is
advanced in content and style.

ACCOUNTANTS' INDEX
1988
Quarterly, plus one cumulative annual volume
36th supplement
Pierce, Linda
Varies
0748-7975
American Institute of Certified Public Accountants
(AICPA)
1211 Avenue of the Americas
New York, NY 10036-8775
(800) 334-6961
$160.00

Excellent
Index

INCLUSIONS: Alphabetic arrangement of
authors, subjects, and titles in dictionary type
format

DESCRIPTORS: Accounting; financial
management; taxation; investments and securities

SUMMARY: This serial index is a
comprehensive guide to the collection of the AICPA
Library. Journal articles are indexed by author
and subject. All articles indexed are in the
English language. Books are indexed by author,
title, and subject. The fields of accounting,
auditing, data processing, financial reporting and
management, taxation and investments are included.
Full citations are given for each entry in this
dictionary formatted index.

RELEVANCE: This index can be used to
identify English language articles in journals as
well as books written by and from an accountant's
perspective. The business owner may use it to
locate any material desired on any aspect of
accounting. This index is available on database.

<<<<<<>>>>>>

ACCOUNTING HANDBOOK FOR NONACCOUNTANTS
1986

Third
Nickerson, Clarence
720
0-442-26754-1
Van Nostrand Reinhold Company, Inc.
115 Fifth Avenue
New York, NY 10003
(212) 254-3232
Order: 7625 Empire Dr
Florence, KY 41041
(606)525-6600

Very good
Handbook

INCLUSIONS: Index; appendices: accounting
cycle; table for the analysis of capital
expenditures; tables; charts; diagrams

DESCRIPTORS: Accounting; cost accounting;
financial statements; taxation; budgeting

SUMMARY: This work explains and
demonstrates the accounting principles used in
preparing annual reports, balance sheets, income
statements, and many other financial documents
used in business. Special attention is paid to:
transaction analysis, depreciation, budgeting,
cost accounting, and inventory valuation. Other
subjects covered are: percentage returns on
investments, capitalization of interest cost,
foreign currency translation, setting goals and
measuring performance, and adjustments for price-
level changes.

RELEVANCE: This work is specifically
written for the manager who does not have an
accounting background. It is detailed, yet
written in plain English for nonaccountants.

                        <<<<<<>>>>>>

ANALYSIS OF FINANCIAL STATEMENTS
1984
First, revised
Bernstein, Leopold

381
0-87094494-0
Dow Jones-Irwin
1818 Ridge Road
Homewood, IL 60430
(800) 323-4560
$29.00

Good
Textbook

INCLUSIONS: Index; appendix; charts;
tables; samples of financial statements;
questions; footnotes

DESCRIPTORS: Auditing; financial statements;
accounting

SUMMARY: This textbook focuses on
understanding how the data is selected and derived
for various types of financial statements. The
statement of changes in financial position, the
balance sheet, income statement, and interim
financial statements are all subjected to thorough
analysis by the use of various methods and tools.
Ratio analysis, comparative financial statements,
break-even analysis, and index-number trend series
are some of the tools explained and utilized.
Ways in which a computer can be useful to a
financial analysis are also discussed.

RELEVANCE: This work is written for the
professional financial consultant. Those who make
investing or lending decisions for the lay person
will find it most helpful.

<<<<<<>>>>>

THE COST REDUCTION AND PROFIT IMPROVEMENT
HANDBOOK
1985 (The 1983 edition was abstracted.)
Second
Figgie, Harry
231
0-442-22584-9
Van Nostrand Reinhold Co., Inc.

115 Fifth Avenue
New York, NY 10003
(212) 254-3232
Order: 7625 Empire Dr
Florence, KY 41042
(606) 525-6600
$25.95

Excellent
Handbook

INCLUSIONS: Index by subject; appendices:
work sampling techniques and sample forms; sample
wording for a company's team system booklet and
cost reduction guidelines

DESCRIPTORS: Cost control; managerial
accounting

SUMMARY: This book details the six cost
reduction techniques of: 1) ratio analysis; 2)
methods improvement; 3) value analysis; 4)
redesign for cost reduction; 5) work sampling; and
6) time and motion study. In addition it examines
the business functions most likely to need the
application of these techniques, namely:
purchasing, inventory control, product selection,
sales forecasting, product pricing, and personnel.
A constant thread throughout the text is why the
application of these techniques result in cost
savings and how cost savings affect the bottom
line.

RELEVANCE: The author was a consultant for
many years and this work is a reflection of his
experience, which should be of interest to any CEO
of a company with annual sales from $5 million to
$50 million. This work applies mainly to
manufacturing and sales businesses.

                    <<<<<<>>>>>>

FINANCIAL AND ACCOUNTING GUIDE FOR NONPROFIT
ORGANIZATIONS
1983
Third

Gross, Malvern   -   Warshauer, William
564
0-471-87113-3
John Wiley and Sons, Inc.
605 Third Avenue
New York, NY 10158
(212) 850-6418
$55.00

Excellent
Textbook

INCLUSIONS: Index; bibliography; appendix
explaining the use of rulings and underscorings
(underlinings) in financial statements; charts;
examples

DESCRIPTORS: Accounting; nonprofit
organizations; taxation

SUMMARY: This is a clearly written,
practical text covering the basics of accounting
for nonprofit organizations. Special chapters are
devoted to accounting for health and welfare
organizations, colleges and universities, and
hospitals. In addition to a section on federal
and state tax compliance, there are chapters of
procedural advice for the smaller organization.
The procedures include: setting up and keeping the
books, maintaining proper internal controls,
developing a budget, handling pooled investments,
and arranging for an external audit.

RELEVANCE: This book is especially
significant for treasurers and chief executive
officers of nonprofit organizations. It is also
useful for any small business which desires to
follow a cash basis of accounting rather than an
accrual basis.

<<<<<<>>>>>>

HOW ACCOUNTING WORKS
A Guide for the Perplexed
1983
First
Edwards, James   -   Hermanson, Roger - Salmonson, R.

Kensicki, Peter
374
0-87094-394-4
Dow Jones-Irwin
1818 Ridge Rd.
Homewood, IL 60430
(800) 323-4560
$30.00

Very good
Textbook

INCLUSIONS: Index by subject; appendix of
compound interest and annuity tables; end of
chapter exercises with answers; charts; sample
financial statements

DESCRIPTORS: Accounting; taxation;
managerial accounting; financial statements;
budgeting

SUMMARY: This textbook explains
everything from the basic accounting cycle to the
interpretation of financial statements and the
purposes of budgeting. Each chapter concludes
with questions, exercises, and their solutions as
a means to apply the concepts introduced to real-
life situations. The subject matter is presented
in three major parts consisting of twelve
chapters. The main parts are: basic concepts,
income measurement and the balance sheet, and
planning and performance analysis.

RELEVANCE: This is intended for non-
accountants who need to understand financial
accounting and managerial accounting concepts in
order to make better decisions for their
companies.

                    <<<<<<>>>>>>

HOW TO READ A FINANCIAL REPORT
Wringing Cash Flow and Other Vital Signs Out
of the Numbers
1983
Second

Tracy, John
161
0-471-88859-1
John Wiley and Sons
605 Third Avenue
New York, NY 10158
(212) 850-6418
$24.95

Excellent
Guide

INCLUSIONS: Index by subject; charts;
graphs; sample balance sheet, income statements,
and cash flow statements

DESCRIPTORS: Financial statements;
depreciation; taxation

SUMMARY: This work is a non-technical
guide to the contents and relationship between the
balance sheet, the income statement, and the cash
flow statement. An examination of depreciation
methods and explanation of the importance of
price/earnings and other ratios is also included.
The author specifically addresses managers,
indicating how they can use these statements to
assess and control their business. Creditors and
investors are also addressed as to how these
statements can reveal the financial soundness of
management decisions.

RELEVANCE: For managers, entrepreneurs,
lenders, and investors who make up the users of
financial reports, this book is a practical easy-
to-read guide to cutting through the maze to the
heart of the balance sheet, income statement, and
cash flow statement.

<<<<<<>>>>>>

INTRODUCTION TO MANAGEMENT ACCOUNTING
1987 (The 1984 edition was abstracted.)
Seventh
Horngren, Charles
696

0-13-487885-X
Prentice-Hall Inc.
Rt. 9 West
Englewood Cliffs, NJ 07632
(201) 767-5054
Order: 200 Old Tappan Road
Old Tappan, NJ 07675
(201) 767-5054

Very good
Textbook

INCLUSIONS: Index by subject; glossary;
appendix with present value of the dollar tables;
appendix of further readings; charts

DESCRIPTORS: Managerial accounting; cost
accounting; financial accounting; taxation

SUMMARY: This textbook emphasizes the
accounting concepts and techniques available for
non-profit and for-profit organizations to plan
and control their activities. Several chapters
are also devoted to a concise review of financial
accounting concepts covering: the balance sheet,
income statement, depreciation, taxes, inventory,
and accrual basis versus cash basis in determining
income. The managerial techniques covered
include: cost accounting, budgeting, job costing,
and cash flow analysis as part of capital
budgeting and taxation.

RELEVANCE: This book is intended for
students who have already studied basic
accounting, however, it is also intended for the
adult continuing education learner who may have
little by way of an accounting background.

<<<<<<>>>>>>

MANAGERIAL AND COST ACCOUNTANT'S HANDBOOK
1979
First
Black, Homer - Edwards, James
1297
0-87094-173-9

Dow Jones-Irwin, Inc.
1818 Ridge Rd.
Homewood, IL 60430
(800) 323-4560
$60.00

Very good
Handbook

INCLUSIONS: Index; tables; graphs

DESCRIPTORS: Cost accounting

SUMMARY: This work is a practical guide
to the field of cost accounting. It includes: an
historical review of cost accounting, planning,
pricing, evaluating organizational performance,
budgeting, direct and incremental costing,
standard cost systems, cost accounting for
government and nonprofit organizations, emerging
trends in cost accounting, costs in labor
negotiations, cost accounting for construction
contracts, cost accounting for land and real
estate development, and cash management.

RELEVANCE: This work provides in one
volume, information on the various aspects of cost
accounting for business and nonprofit
organizations. The material is written in non-
technical language.

                    <<<<<<>>>>>>

MANAGING THE COMPANY TAX FUNCTION
1976
First
Olenick, Arnold
321
0-13-550723-5
Prentice-Hall, Inc.
1 Gulf & Western Plaza
New York, NY 10023
(212) 373-8500
Order: 200 Old Tappan Road
Old Tappan, NJ 07675
(201) 767-5054

Very good
Handbook

INCLUSIONS: Index; sample forms; graphics;
checklists; bibliographies

DESCRIPTORS: Taxation; managerial accounting

SUMMARY: This book has practical answers
to every phase of corporate tax work: planning,
record keeping, preparing forms, filing
requirements, tax budgeting, and handling
government audits. State and local taxes are
covered as well as federal taxes. Closely held
corporations known as subchapter S are also
included. Numerous checklists and examples of
filled-in forms provide a reassuring, concrete
approach to preparing payroll, sales, property,
excise, and other tax documents.

RELEVANCE: This book is a basic tool for
all those responsible for tax planning and
compliance -- accountants, financial executives,
accounting department staff, and attorneys who
render professional tax services. Naturally,
actual tax forms may vary from year to year, so
the reader would be wise to consult other more
current sources.

                    <<<<<<>>>>>>

PORTFOLIO OF ACCOUNTING SYSTEMS FOR SMALL AND
MEDIUM-SIZED BUSINESSES
1977
Second
National Society of Public Accountants
1391
0-13-685305-6
Prentice Hall, Inc.
Rt. 9 West
Englewood Cliffs, NJ 07632
(201) 592-2000
Order: 200 Old Tappan Road
Old Tappan, NJ 07675
(201) 767-5054
$55.00

Excellent
Handbook

INCLUSIONS: Forms; diagrams; charts

DESCRIPTORS: Accounting; cost accounting

SUMMARY: Seventy types of small
businesses are included in this large volume. For
each business, information on how to design,
revise, install, and put into effect an accounting
system with sample forms is provided. The
peculiarities of the business and their effects on
the accounting system, as well as samples of
possible account names required, time and payroll
procedures, cost accounting, time-saving ideas,
and reporting to management are mentioned. Some
of the businesses included are: architects,
auction galleries, automobile dealers, bakery
shops, beauty shops, drugstores, computer service
bureaus, farmers, florists, hardware stores,
jewelry stores, motels, pet shops, printers,
restaurants, shoe stores, sporting goods stores,
taverns, travel agencies, and women's apparel
shops.

RELEVANCE: Certainly this work is a vital
resource for the public accountant who is often
contacted by a small business person who seeks
his/her services in establishing a valid
accounting system for a new enterprise. The small
business person may be able to consult this
resource directly and be able to establish an
adequate accounting system without consulting with
an accountant.

                    <<<<<<>>>>>

SIMPLIFIED ACCOUNTING FOR NON-ACCOUNTANTS
1980
First
Hayes, Rick   -   Baker, Richard
286
0-515-09099-9
Berkley Publishing Group
200 Madison Avenue

New York, NY 10016
(800) 223-0510
$3.95

Very good
Book

INCLUSIONS: Index by subject; glossary;
charts; graphs; sample business forms

DESCRIPTORS: Accounting; taxation

SUMMARY: This is written for the
owner/manager of a business who needs to acquire
an understanding of accounting. Such basic
accounting topics as original business accounting
forms, journals, ledgers, trial balances, income
statements, and balance sheets are all illustrated
and their importance explained. The important
role that accounting documentation plays in
determining the financial health of your business
is also explored. Such accounting related issues
as depreciation, operating expenses, determination
of value of various assets, investment credits,
and form of business organization, directly
related to tax consequences are explained. Tax
laws change frequently and the reader should turn
to more recent material for current tax
information. A glossary of accounting terms is
appended to this easy-to-read and understand text.

RELEVANCE: Many small business owners need
to understand the role accounting plays in the
successful operation of their enterprise. Even if
the owner hires an outside accounting service, the
need to make financial decisions which have all-
important consequences for the business remain
those of the owner. This book is written in
language the business person can understand and
will provide the reader with the financial
knowledge needed to operate the business in a
legal and financially sound manner.

CHAPTER 2

ADVERTISING AND PUBLIC RELATIONS

This chapter contains:

- advertising theory and practice

- advertising strategy

- management procedure

- planning and conducting campaigns

- building a practice

- advertising options - direct mail, mail order, radio, television, and newspaper

- buyer's guide

- advertising agencies listing

ADVERTISING MANAGER'S HANDBOOK
1982 (The 1977 edition was abstracted.)
Second
Stansfield, Richar
1503
0-85013-128-6
The Dartnell Corporation
4660 N. Ravenswood Avenue
Chicago, IL 60640
(800) 621-5463
$49.95

Very good
Handbook

INCLUSIONS: Index; advertisements;
appendices (8); case histories; checklists;
charts; data directories (mailing list brokers,
direct mail agencies); illustrations
(advertisements, graphics, photographs); tables;
samples (advertisements, forms, worksheets);
statistics; suggested readings; questionnaire

DESCRIPTORS: Advertising copy; advertising
management; industrial advertising

SUMMARY: This Handbook is a definitive
practitioner's guide describing essential
advertising management and preparation skills,
including campaign planning, selecting and working
with agencies, budgeting, selecting media,
creating and preparing copy, using direct mail
methods, exhibiting at trade shows, handling
inquiries, etc. It abounds in case histories and
practical suggestions.

RELEVANCE: This is relevant to anyone
doing advertising, whether from within a large
organization, an advertising agency, or a small
business.

                  <<<<<<>>>>>

ADVERTISING PROCEDURE
1986 (The 1979 edition was abstracted.)
Ninth

Kleppner, Otto
641
0-8240-6734-7 (1985 edition)
Garland Pub.
136 Madison Avenue
New York, NY 10016 NJ 07632
(212) 686-7492
$60.00

Excellent
Textbook; primer

INCLUSIONS: Appendices; bibliographies;
case studies; charts; checklists; cost data;
directories (associations); glossary; index;
samples (advertisements, forms, worksheets);
statistics; tables

DESCRIPTORS: Advertising; advertising
management; advertising media; advertising
textbooks

SUMMARY: This contains a thorough,
profusely illustrated discussion of the essential
media, methods and procedures practiced by today's
advertising profession. It covers planning,
targeting and marketing of advertising campaigns;
creation and production of advertisements;
selection and use of basic media and sales
promotion strategies; use of advertising agencies
and support services; and legal, regulatory,
economical, social and other aspects of
advertising.

RELEVANCE: This is an excellent
introduction to the advertising field.

                    <<<<<<>>>>>>

ADVERTISING THEORY AND PRACTICE
1985 (The 1979 edition was abstracted.)
Eleventh
This was issued in 1979, 1975, 1971, and 1967.
Sandage, Charles - Fryburger, Vernon - Rotzoll, Kim
703
0-256-02851-6

Richard D. Irwin, Inc.
1818 Ridge Road
Homewood, Ill 60430
(800) 323-4560
$33.95

Very good
Textbook; primer

INCLUSIONS: Index; advertisements; charts;
checklists; financial data; forecast;
illustrations; reference citations; samples
(advertisements, forms, questionnaires); self
study aids; statistics; tables (data, information
summaries)

DESCRIPTORS: Advertising; advertising media;
advertising methods; advertising textbooks

SUMMARY: This text explores current
advertising goals, functions, methods and
practices, and the research and knowledge
base upon which they are founded. It covers
advertising media, channels and marketplace
sectors; creation of messages and appeals;
planning, budgeting and use of media alternatives;
selection and use of agencies and services;
effectiveness testing measures; and other topics.
It is well-illustrated.

RELEVANCE: This is essentially a textbook
on advertising theory as well as practice for the
professional who wants a conceptual understanding
of the field.

<<<<<<>>>>>>

BUILDING A SUCCESSFUL PROFESSIONAL PRACTICE
WITH ADVERTISING
1981
First
Braun, Irwin
289
0-317-26844-9
Books in Demand
UMI
Division of University Microfilms, International

300 N Zeeb Road
Ann Arbor, MI 48106
(800) 521-0600
$75.30

Very good
Handbook; primer

INCLUSIONS: Index; advertisements;
appendices; case histories; checklists;
directories (federal offices, associations);
financial data (costs); glossary; illustrations
(advertisements, figures, photographs); samples
(scripts, advertisements, questionnaires);
statistics; tables

DESCRIPTORS: Advertising management;
advertising media; advertising methods;
professional advertising

SUMMARY: This is an exploration of
advertising media, practices and strategies being
used by professional organizations and firms. It
is designed to help professionals to work with
communications and media experts, to develop
effective advertising programs and materials in
print, radio, television and other forms. It
describes advertising appeals used by accountants,
lawyers and medical/dental groups.

RELEVANCE: This is intended to help the
professional make use of advertising.

<<<<<<>>>>>>

THE DARTNELL ADVERTISING MANAGER'S HANDBOOK
1982
Third (The 1977, second edition was abstracted.)
Irregular (first edition, 1969)
Stansfield, Richard
150350
0-85013-116-2
The Dartnell Corporation
4660 Ravenswood Avenue
Chicago, IL 60640
(800) 621-5463
$49.95

Very Good
Handbook

INCLUSIONS: Advertisements; appendices (8);
case histories; checklists; charts; data
(advertisement ranking, costs and rates, market
research, other); tables; directories (maillist
brokers, direct mail agencies); guidelines (many
miscellaneous), illustrations (advertisements,
graphics, photographs); index (general); reports
(market research); samples (advertisements, forms,
worksheets); statistics; suggested readings;
questionnaire

DESCRIPTORS: Advertising copy; advertising
management; industrial advertising

SUMMARY: This is a definitive
practitioner's guide describing essential
advertising management and preparation skills
(campaign planning, selecting and working with
agencies, budgeting, selecting media, creating and
preparing copy, using direct mail methods,
exhibiting at trade shows, handling inquiries,
etc.) It abounds in case histories and practical
suggestions.

RELEVANCE: This is very usable and
worthwhile for anyone concerned with improving
his/her advertising skills.

                    <<<<<<>>>>>>

DIRECT MAIL AND MAIL ORDER HANDBOOK
1980 (The 1977 edition was abstracted.)
Third
Irregular
Hodgson, Richard
1555 (1980)
0-85013-116-2
Dartnell Corporation
4660 Ravenswood Avenue
Chicago, IL 60640
(800) 621-5463
$49.95

Very good
Handbook

INCLUSIONS: Appendix; indexes by subject,
name, publication, company

DESCRIPTORS: Direct mail; direct marketing

SUMMARY: This is the "bible" about how
to do direct mail and mail order successfully. It
details techniques and procedures and gives
examples and illustrations. It explains what
direct mail is, public attitudes toward it, basic
elements - the list, offer, package; applications;
guidelines for effectiveness; campaigns;
industrial and retail mail; business and
professional mail; fund raising; computer uses;
merchandising; etc. Coverage includes discussion
of: sampling and couponing, syndicated mailings;
mailing list and controls; U.S. postal service;
copy; letter formats; computer formats;
enclosures; catalogs and price lists; self-mailers
and post cards, showmanship formats; spectaculars;
house organs, newsletters and bulletins, annual
and special reports; statement and letter
stuffers; surveys and questionnaires; order forms
and reply cards; envelopes; printing production
and finishing processes; addressing methods;
special equipment and services; paper and envelope
guide; cost cutting tips; testing and projecting;
and inquiry handling.

RELEVANCE: This book contains what one
needs to know to do effective direct mailing.

                    <<<<<<>>>>>>

HANDBOOK OF RADIO ADVERTISING
1980
First
Murphy, Jonne
240
Books on Demand
University of Michigan
Division of Microfilms International
300 N. Zeeb Rd.

Ann Arbor, MI 48106-1346
(800) 521-0600
$63.00

Excellent
Handbook

INCLUSIONS: Bibliography; case histories;
checklists; data (budgetary, demographic, market,
statistical, costs, rates and ratings); glossary;
illustrations (charts, histograms); index; tables

DESCRIPTORS: Advertising; advertising media;
advertising methods; radio advertising

SUMMARY: This reference book describes
benefits and advantages of using the radio medium.
It shows how to plan, schedule, execute and
evaluate radio advertising campaigns; select and
work with the right radio stations and advertising
personnel; prepare and test radio commercials; and
deal with radio and other media salespeople. It
contains a wealth of practical suggestions and
information.

RELEVANCE: This is useful for persons
interested in using, buying or selling radio
advertising aimed at local through national
markets and is especially useful to retail-
oriented advertisers.

<<<<<<>>>>>>

NEWSPAPER ADVERTISING HANDBOOK
1980
First
Watkins, Don
112
0-936294-00-0
Dynamo Inc.
PO Box 173
Wheaton, IL 60189
(312) 665-0060
$8.95

Excellent
Handbook

INCLUSIONS: Glossary; illustrations
(advertisements, drawings and sketches, halftones,
photographs, type styles); index (illustration
credits); samples (advertisements, logos, popular
type styles); training aids (step-by-step
photographs)

DESCRIPTORS: Advertising handbooks; graphics
production; newspaper advertising; newspaper
advertisements

SUMMARY: This is a superbly-illustrated
reference for anyone involved in the creation,
design, production or sale of newspaper
advertising. It shows how to: create, design and
layout high-impact advertisements; select and
write good copy; use various type styles; combine
type with visuals; create special effects with
simple-to-use tools and aids. It is saturated
with outstanding graphic illustrations.

RELEVANCE: Not only is this an excellent
reference for newspaper advertising professionals,
it is also useful for consultants in need of
knowledge of how to do it.

                    <<<<<<>>>>>

PROFESSIONAL'S GUIDE TO PUBLICITY
1982 (The 1978 edition was abstracted.)
Third
Irregular
Weiner, Richard
176
0-913046-07-8
Public Relations
888 Seventh Avenue
New York, NY 10106
(212) 315-8250
$9.50

Very good
Handbook; primer

INCLUSIONS: Appendices; annotated
bibliographies; glossaries; illustrations; index

by subject; reviews; samples (letters, news
releases, tip sheets)

DESCRIPTORS: News media; news releases;
publicity; public relations

SUMMARY: This is a practitioner's guide
to planning and executing public relations and
publicity efforts. It show how to: prepare and
distribute public service announcements, news
features and "exclusives", and different types of
news releases and contact letters; work with news
bureaus/syndicates, newspapers, magazines and
trade publications, press kits and photographs;
and publicize products, personnel and special
events. It is loaded with practical "how to"
suggestions and advice.

RELEVANCE: This could be useful to any
consultant interested in knowing how to do
publicity and public relations.

                    <<<<<<>>>>>

PUBLIC RELATIONS HANDBOOK
1987 (The 1979 edition was abstracted.)
Not established
Dilenschneider, Robert   -   Forrestal, Dan
920
0-85013-159-6
The Dartnell Corporation
4660 N. Ravenswood Avenue
Chicago, IL 60640
(800) 621-5463
$49.00

Very good
Handbook

INCLUSIONS: Case studies (29); index;
photographs; state of the art reports

DESCRIPTORS: Business communications;
external communications; internal communications;
public relations

SUMMARY: This is a thorough, definitive
examination of the public relations field and
current PR practices. It covers relations with
external groups (customers marketing personnel,
community organizations, etc.); internal/
"in-house" relations (28 chapters);
communications/media strategies; common problems,
pitfalls and issues; and many other topics. It
gives case histories of award-winning external
programs.

RELEVANCE: This source is useful for both
the novice and veteran practitioner and business
or organization of any size.

<<<<<<>>>>>>

STANDARD DIRECTORY OF ADVERTISING AGENCIES
1983 (The 1982 edition was abstracted.)
Published in February, June and October of
each year, with monthly updates.
0-87217-003-9
Varies, loose-leaf monthly supplement
National Register Publishing Co., Inc.
3004 Glenview Road
Wilmette, IL 60091
(800) 323-6772
$292.00 Set

Very good
Directory/catalog

INCLSUSIONS: Business profiles (agencies);
classified listings; directories (headquarters and
branch offices); financial data (annual billings);
geographic listings; illustrations
(advertisements, logos, photographs); indexes by
advertisers and new agencies, geographic, market
specialty; ranking of largest agencies; statistics
(billings for specific media)

DESCRIPTORS: Advertising; advertising
agencies; agencies; media services; sales
promotion

SUMMARY: This is a directory of advertising and sales promotion agencies and related media services. It lists approximately 4400 U.S. and foreign agencies and 30,000 key personnel (executives, managers and creative marketing contacts). Listings give year of founding, address and phone number of headquarters and branch offices, and major accounts. It is indexed by country, state and city.

RELEVANCE: This is useful for anyone wishing to locate and compare advertising agencies and related media services.

<<<<<<>>>>>>

STANDARD RATE AND DATA SERVICE CATALOGS
1982
Varies
Weekly to semiannually
Varies
U.S. 0038-948X
Standard Rate and Data Service, Inc.
5201 Old Orchard Road
Skokie, IL 60077
(312) 966-8500
$1,085.00 Set

Good - very good
Directory/catalog

INCLUSIONS: Advertisements; advertising information (costs, rates and data); business profiles; calendars; classified listings; consultant listings; geographic listings; glossaries; illustrations (advertisements; graphics; photographs); market information (analyses, area and penetration data, ranking, statistics); reader service cards; regulatory information; tables

DESCRIPTORS: Advertising; advertising media; advertising rates; advertising services

SUMMARY: This is a comprehensive set of buyer's guides designed to aid the selection and

use of conventional advertising media. Separate
titles cover: Canadian media, community
publications, consumer magazines and farm
publications, direct mail lists, direct response
media (post cards) and networks; spot radio, and
spot television. Another title gives print media
production rates and data.

RELEVANCE: This could be a relevant guide
for anyone interested in comparing advertising
media prices.

CHAPTER 3

ASSOCIATIONS AND NONPROFIT ORGANIZATIONS

This chapter contains:

- lists of associations

- marketing to/for nonprofit organizations

- how to start/manage a non-profit organization.

A COMMUNICATIONS MANUAL FOR NONPROFIT
ORGANIZATIONS
1981
First
Maddalena, Lucille
222
0-318-17153-8
The National Volunteer Center
1111 N. 19th st. Suite 500
Arlington, VA 22209
(703) 276-0542
$18.50

Good
Guide

INCLUSIONS: Index by subject; glossary;
bibliography; figures; samples

DESCRIPTORS: Nonprofit organizations;
communication; publicity

SUMMARY: This book focuses on
organizational communication, internal and
external, in nonprofit organizations, especially
volunteer-supported agencies. The author
discusses: the roles of board members, executive
director, professionals, and volunteers; training;
the speaker's bureau; program planning and
management. Special subjects include: media
relations, advertising, and publications with
emphasis on the multiple ways of reaching and
making a positive impression on the public.
Specific techniques discussed include: the news
release, photographs, display and drop-in
advertising, public service announcements,
billboards, audio-visual presentations, exhibits
and displays, newsletter, annual report,
fundraising brochure, special events and meetings,
and award presentations. The author also
discusses receiving information from the public
through listening, feedback, and evaluation, and
resolving problems, conflicts and crises.

RELEVANCE: This is recommended for persons
working in and working at running a nonprofit
organization of agency. It is introductory and
easy to read.

ENCYCLOPEDIA OF ASSOCIATIONS
1986
21st
Annual
Gruber, Katherine
2500, Vol. 1: National Organizations of the U.S.
1170, Vol. 2: Geographic and Executive Index
628, Vol. 4: International Organizations
(Vol. 3 is a periodic supplement to Vol. 1 and
lists new associations and projects.)
Vol. 1: 0-8103-2690-6
Vol. 2: 0-8103-2691-4
Gale Research Company
Book Tower
Detroit, MI 48226
(800) 223-4253
$220.00 per set

Excellent
Encyclopedia

INCLUSIONS: Indexes: Volume 1 by
organization name and keyword combined; volume 2
by executive and geographic (country and
state/province). Each index provides the
organization name, address, phone number, and
chief executive's name and title/position.

DESCRIPTORS: Associations; organizations;
labor unions; federations; chambers of commerce;
Greek letter and related organizations

SUMMARY: This reference is an annotated
guide to approximately 20,000 national and
international nonprofit organizations. It
includes professional, trade, and other
organizations and groups engaged in special
interest activities, which serve as sources and
distributors of information on subjects of
interest to the general community. It lists
professional consulting/consultant associations.
It includes the following organizational
classifications: trade, business and commercial;
agricultural and commodity; legal, governmental,
public administration, and military; scientific,
engineering, and technical; educational; cultural;
social welfare; health and medical; public
affairs; fraternal, foreign interest, nationality

and ethnic; religious; veteran, hereditary, and patriotic; hobby and avocational; athletic and sports; labor unions, associations and federations; chambers of commerce; and Greek letter and related organizations. It also includes non-membership groups; selected local, regional, foreign and citizen action groups; and selected groups involved in special projects, studies and programs. It lists inactive and defunct organizations as well. It is arranged alphabetically, by keyword (subtopics) within the subject classifications above. Many entries note the dates, locations and frequency of the organization's next national conventions/meetings.

RELEVANCE: This is the best reference to associations. It enables one to identify new consulting associations, professional organizations, and other useful special-interest groups. It can be computer accessed through Dialog   Information Systems.

<<<<<<>>>>>>

HOW TO FORM YOUR OWN NON-PROFIT CORPORATION (IN ONE DAY)
1978
First
Whitaker, Fred
250 (approximately)
Minority Management Institute
872 69th Avenue
San Francisco, CA
(415) 569-1343
$11.60

Good
Guide; handbook

INCLUSIONS: Appendices (IRS materials); directory (offices, Secretaries of State); forms (incorporation, federal tax exemption application); guidelines (incorporation); samples (articles of incorporation, bylaws)

DESCRIPTORS: Corporations; corporate planning; incorporation; nonprofit corporations

SUMMARY: This planning guide covers
steps to be taken in forming a nonprofit
corporation in any state, and California in
particular. It includes samples of completed and
blank incorporation forms, and useful IRS
materials. It discusses advantages and
disadvantages of forming a nonprofit corporation;
and shows how to use cost-saving, special permits.

RELEVANCE: Although the technical quality
of this document is poor, it provides useful
information not covered in other publications.

<<<<<<>>>>>>

HOW TO MANAGE A NONPROFIT ORGANIZATION
1978
First
Fisher, John
214
0-92043-202-6
Management and Fund Raising Center
287 MacPherson Avenue
Toronto, Ontario
(416) 961-0381
$16.50

Very good
Manual

INCLUSION: Bibliography

DESCRIPTOR: Nonprofit organization

SUMMARY: This is a practical manual of
knowledge and advice on the startup and management
of nonprofit organizations. It is applicable to
all types of nonprofit organizations --
governmental, corporate, public, private,
fraternal, foundations, human service agencies,
etc. Work groups are recommended for the
organization of any program or project in the
areas of planning and evaluation, resource
development, management, volunteers, personnel,
communications, and government relations. It discusses needs assessment technique, community

organizing, management by objectives, publicity
and media tips, fund raising, board of directors
function, program development and evaluation.

RELEVANCE: This is a simple, practical
manual on the ins, outs and details of running
nonprofit organizations relevant for
administrators, program managers, specialists,
consultants, support staff and volunteers. It
gives some tips about how nonprofits can use
consultants.

                <<<<<<>>>>>>

MARKETING FOR NONPROFIT ORGANIZATIONS
1982 (The 1975 edition was abstracted.)
Second
Kotler, Philip
592
0-318-17152-X
Prentice-Hall Inc.
Rt. 9 West
Englewood Cliffs, NJ 07632
(201) 592-2000
Order: 200 Old Tappan Road
Old Tappan, NJ 07675
(201) 767-5049
$36.95

Excellent
Textbook

INCLUSIONS: Index, cross-referenced,
figures; study questions; case studies

DESCRIPTORS: Marketing; nonprofit
organizations; promotion; advertising; publicity

SUMMARY: This book develops and applies
marketing concepts, principles and tactics to nonprofit organizations and the social sphere -- to
health, education, public services administration,
and political candidate campaigns. It clearly
presents marketing concepts and tools and
demonstrates them with case studies. The case
studies cover a variety of organizational and

situational types. The sections focus on
conceptualizing marketing, analyzing the market,
determining and administering the marketing
program. The following concepts are discussed:
publics; markets; exchange; marketing audit;
market analysis; consumer analysis; actual and
potential market; market segmentation; market
structure; undifferentiated, differentiated and
concentrated marketing; market orchestration;
marketing mix with product, price, place, and
promotion; and five tools of promotion --
advertising, publicity, personal contact
incentives and atmosphere.

RELEVANCE: This is an excellent
introductory text. It helps one to easily learn
and comprehend basic marketing concepts, and it is
well organized and written. It is a valuable "how
to" tool for marketing in the non-profit sector.
It enables one to put marketing into practice
based on a wide range and variety of examples and
commonly encountered problems.

                    <<<<<<>>>>>>

NATIONAL TRADE AND PROFESSIONAL ASSOCIATIONS
OF THE UNITED STATES AND CANADA AND LABOR UNIONS
Annual
1988 (The 1986 edition was abstracted.)
23rd
Colgate, Craig
0-910416-70-2
Columbia Books
1350 New York Avenue N.W., Suite 207
Washington, DC 20005
(202) 737-3777
$60.00

Very good
Directory

INCLUSIONS: Indexes by association, budget,
geography, executive, subject

DESCRIPTORS: Associations; labor unions;
professional societies; scientific societies

SUMMARY: This lists trade and
professional associations and labor unions with
national memberships. It is arranged by
association, subject, geographic location, budget
and executive. It excludes fraternal, sporting,
patriotic, hobby, and political action
organizations. It contains an introduction which
defines and discusses trade associations,
professional societies, scientific or learned
societies, and labor unions. It distinguishes
"horizontal" and "vertical" associations.

RELEVANCE: This provides basic information
on professional associations and labor unions, and
aids in procuring further information from them.
It is useful for marketing purposes. Multiple
indexes aid in finding items with incomplete
information. It accepts listings, and the
information is available in mailing list form. It
also has order forms for association annual budget
mailing list by budget amount category, and
association "selected subject" mailing list (e.g.
banking/finance, communications/radio/tv,
consumer affairs, foreign trade, medicine/health,
labor unions, etc.)

                    <<<<<<>>>>>>

NONPROFIT ORGANIZATION HANDBOOK
1980
Second
Not established
Connors, Tracy
0-318-17168-6
VTNC
1111 North 19th Street, Suite 500
Arlington, VA 22209
(212) 997-1221
$36.75

Very good
Compendium; how to guide

INCLUSIONS: Indexes by subject, name,
cross-referenced; appendices

DESCRIPTORS: Nonprofit organizations;
grantsmanship; marketing for nonprofit
organizations

SUMMARY: This is a comprehensive
compilation of articles composed by a wide range
of knowledgeable contributors treating the
operation and management of nonprofit
organizations (NPOs). It covers six major areas
of NPO management: organizational and corporate
principles; leadership, management, and control of
human resources management; revenue sources;
public relations; and fiscal management and
administration. It treats: 1) management-by-
objectives approach, as well as paid personnel; 2)
staffing and handling of volunteers; and 3) roles
of officers and boards of directors. It also
treats financial management, tax exemption,
grantsmanship and fund raising, public relations,
and media usage considerations. It includes
examples of solutions to problems in planning,
policy setting and decision making. Some segments
discuss these items: market conditions,
advertising programs, markets for NPO services,
fair market pricing considerations and marketing
research efforts directed toward membership needs.

RELEVANCE: This is an overall how-to guide
for persons involved with nonprofit organizations,
including administrators, management, personnel,
board members, and consultants.

CHAPTER 4

AUDIO-VISUAL COMMUNICATIONS MEDIA

This chapter contains:

- planning and evaluation

- purchase of audio-visual media

- selection and use of equipment and
  software -- films and motion
  picture; photography, prints slides;
  audio; nonprint resources; -
  projected media image

- transparencies and overheads

- training and educational media,
  materials, and aids

- media producers

- productization

- radio and TV stations

- networks and cable

ASPEN HANDBOOK ON THE MEDIA
1979 (The 1977 edition was abstracted.)
Third
Irregular
Rivers, William - Thompson, W. - Nyhan, M.J.
440
0-915436-67-1
Aspen Institute for Humanistic Studies
P.O. Box 150
Queenstown, MD 21658
(301) 827-7168
$6.95

Very good
Handbook; catalog; resources guide; directory

INCLUSIONS: Index; annotated
bibliographies; listings; directories (10);
filmography

DESCRIPTORS: Communications media; mass
media; media research

SUMMARY: This is a selective, annotated
guide to development programs, organizations,
and publications in communications. It covers
university and nonacademic research programs;
governmental/regulatory agencies; graduate
education programs; grant funding sources; new
technologies; national policy-making bodies (U.S.
and Canada); media action groups; libraries,
archives and information centers; and
international overseas and other organizations.
It lists books, bibliographies, films,
periodicals, reference materials and publishers.

RELEVANCE: Anyone involved with the fields
of communication, film, photography,
telecommunications, information storage and
retrieval, and media engineering, can benefit from
this book. It will help you identify printed as
well as people and organizational resources
related to your particular interest in
communications.

AUDIO VIDEO MARKETPLACE
A Multimedia Guide
1988
Sixteenth
Annual
Torpie, Stephen   -   Furman, Amy
693
0-8352-2270-5
R.R. Bowker Company
245 West 17th Street
New York, NY 10011
(800) 521-8110
$65.00

Excellent
Directory

INCLUSIONS: Indexes by company name,
products and services, classified

DESCRIPTORS: Audio-video marketplace; audio-
video products; audio-visual services

SUMMARY: This work is a comprehensive
directory to over 1200 products or services, and
contact information is provided for over 5000
companies which supply them. The classified
products and service index covers six major AV
categories: audio, audio-visual, film, video,
programming, and miscellaneous. In addition to
the three major indexes there are separate
sections for AV trade and related associations,
film and TV commissions in the U.S., AV awards and
festival sponsors, calendar of AV related meetings
and conventions, AV related periodicals, recent AV
book titles, and an abbreviated entry for each
company providing contact person, address and
telephone number.

RELEVANCE: Anyone looking for information
about AV products, services, companies and
associations will find this work an excellent
source.

BROADCASTING/CABLECASTING YEARBOOK
1987
47th
Annual
Taishoff, Sol
Varies
0732-7196
Broadcasting Publications, Inc.
1705 DeSales Street N.W.
Washington, D.C. 20036
(202) 659-2340
$85.00

Good
Catalog; resources guide; directory

INCLUSIONS: Indexes; advertisements;
advertising information; bibliographies
(annotated: reference); buyers guides; classified
listings; consultant listings; directories; filmography; financial information; geographic
listings; illustrations; market atlases; market
data; profiles (stations, firms, organizations);
regulatory information; reports; tables

DESCRIPTORS: Advertising; broadcasting
marketplace; cable television; radio marketplace;
television marketplace

IDENTIFIERS: Former titles: Broadcasting
Cable Yearbook, Broadcasting Cable
Sourcebook, Broadcasting Yearbook, Broadcasting
and Broadcast Advertising Yearbook

SUMMARY: This is a complete guide to all
radio and television stations, networks, cable
systems, and AM/FM stations in the United States,
U.S. Territories, Canada, Mexico, and Caribbean.
It includes advertising agencies, associations,
professional services, market summaries, NAB codes
and FCC rules. It lists thousands of key
contacts: producers, directors, managers, agents,
representatives, etc.

RELEVANCE: This resource is an invaluable
tool for those involved with radio, television,
cable television, and satellite communications.

EDUCATIONAL MEDIA AND TECHNOLOGY YEARBOOK
1987 (The 1981 edition was abstracted.)
Eleventh
Annual
Miller, Elwood - Mosley, Mary
350
0-87287-571-7
Libraries Unlimited Inc.
P.O. Box 263
Littleton, CO 80160
(303) 770-1220
$50.00

Excellent
Resources guide; yearbook

INCLUSIONS: Indexes (general, classified);
bibliographies (annotated, media, reference
materials, periodicals); classified listings;
directories (associations, organizations, grant
sources, publishers); grants information;   reports
(descriptive, market, survey, state-of-the-art)

DESCRIPTORS: Educational media;
communications media; instructional materials;
library materials; training materials

IDENTIFIER: Co-sponsor: Association for
Educational Communications and Technology (AECT)

SUMMARY: This is a guide to reference
publications, periodicals, communications media,
organizations, and current trends and
developments. It is a current awareness tool for
persons who select, evaluate, purchase and/or
produce software and hardware products used for
educational, training, and communication purposes.
It covers all types and forms of media: audio-
visual, computer, electronic, print, photography,
microform, radio, television, and
telecommunications.

RELEVANCE: This is useful to educational
media professionals and consumers.

THE EQUIPMENT DIRECTORY, 1987-88 OF AUDIO-
VISUAL, COMPUTER AND VIDEO PRODUCTS
1987
Annual
33rd
Stevens, Mary
535
International Communications Industries
Association
3150 Spring Street
Fairfax, VA 22031
(703) 273-7200
$35.00

Excellent
Directory; catalog

DESCRIPTORS: Audio-visual equipment; video
products; computer products

SUMMARY: This directory gives complete
information, including specifications,
photographs, and prices for over 2000 equipment
items. Some of the many products are: compact
disc players, microphones, mixers, record players,
tape recorders, AV production equipment, computer
graphic systems, furniture, headphones, multi-
image devices, remote control systems, projectors,
slide viewing and editing equipment, projection
screens, video equipment, and special AV charts.

RELEVANCE: While not comprehensive, this
work is very useful for anyone seeking information
on communications products.

<<<<<<>>>>>>

ESSENTIALS OF MEDIA PLANNING
A Marketing Viewpoint
1987 (The 1976 edition was abstracted.)
Second
Barban, Arnold
160
0-8442-3018-9
Crain Books
740 Rush Street

Chicago, IL 60611
(800) 621-6877
$12.95

Very good
Guide

INCLUSION: Index

DESCRIPTORS: Media; media planning;
marketing

SUMMARY: This book focuses on media
planning by examining the media process as it
relates to marketing a product. It does the
following: 1) introduces terminology of media
marketing; 2) defines media planning and shows how
marketing plans influence media plans by product
characteristics, distribution channels, pricing
policy and strategy, and promotion; 3) discusses
marketing mix as a system, uncontrollable
variables affecting the environment for media
decisions, and matching target markets and media;
and 4) explains such concepts as frequency, reach,
timing and geography, essential to setting media
objectives.

RELEVANCE: This book stimulates the reader
to raise important questions when conceiving a
media marketing plan. It is an excellent tool for
anyone responsible for setting marketing
objectives, strategy, and tactics for products.
It emphasizes the planning process rather than any
one form of media. The freelance marketing
consultant as well as the small manufacturer or
retail manager can benefit from this book.

<<<<<<>>>>>>

GRAPHIC COMMUNICATION EIGHTIES
1981
First
Gottschall, Edward
200
0-18-363382-9
Prentice Hall, Inc.

Rt. 9 West
Englewood Cliffs, NJ 07632
(201) 592-2000
Order: 200 Old Tappan Road
Old Tappan, NJ 07675
(201) 767-5049
$34.95

Excellent
Book; state of the art review

INCLUSIONS: Evaluation-selection aids
(checklist, guidelines); forecasts (new
technologies); glossary; illustrations (drawings,
photographs); reports

DESCRIPTORS: Computer graphics; graphic
communications; media production equipment; print
media; typography

SUMMARY: This is a thorough, state-of-
the-art review of current and emerging typographic
communications capabilities and technology. It
reviews methods, equipment and systems available
for creating and distributing textual, graphic and
printed images via the assistance of computer
technology. It treats these and other topics:
electronic and photo image production, filing and
retrieval systems, data communications, word
processing and electronic mail/distribution
technology, and future offices. It tells how to
best select and use available equipment, systems
and services.

RELEVANCE: This is an excellent source but
it could benefit from an updated edition.

<<<<<<>>>>>

MANAGEMENT MEDIA DIRECTORY
An Annotated Guide of Commercially Available
Audio-visual Programs for Business and Management
Schools, In-House Training and Development
Programs, Management Consultants, and Human
Resource Managers
1982

First
Provan, Jill - Phelps, Maryruth
506
0-8103-0170-9
Neal-Schuman Publishers, Inc. in association with
Gale Research Company
Book Tower
Detroit, MI 48226
(800) 223-4253
$185.00

Excellent
Annotated directory

INCLUSION: User's guide

DESCRIPTORS: Audio-visuals; media;
non-print media; audiocassettes;
films; slide-tape programs; video

SUMMARY: This is an annotated guide to
commercial, non-print media including over 3500
programs for sale by 232 U.S. distributors. It
excludes videodisc and microcomputer software,
free loan or rental, and feature-length film.
Subject area is broad, including such areas as
accounting, computers, interviewing techniques,
motivation, minorities in business, performance
appraisal, personal development, small business,
technology, women in work, and written
communication. Sections are subject listing,
titles by subjects, series titles, title listing,
distributors, and multidistributors (distribute
for several producers). Each entry under title
listing is referenced by a title number from the
title by subjects section, is described by title,
date, format(s), hue, length, supplementary
material distributor, and synopsis.

RELEVANCE: This is a well organized guide
to nonprint media useful for anyone seeking
material for training and education.

PHOTOGRAPHER'S MARKET
Where to Sell Your Photographs
1987
Annual
Eidenier, Connie
611
Writer's Digest
1507 Dana Avenue
Cincinnati, OH 45207
(800) 543-4644
$18.95

Very good
Directory; marketplace resource

INCLUSIONS: Index; glossary; appendix on
how to set up a free-lance business; photographs;
special chapters on stock photo agencies

DESCRIPTOR: Photography market

SUMMARY: This annual has 2500 listings
including: advertising and public relations firms;
audio-visual, film, and video firms; book
publishers; businesses and organizations;
galleries; newspapers and newsletters; paper
products; magazines; record companies; stock photo
agencies; and contests and workshops. Listings
provide: names and addresses, kind of photos the
listee needs, how the listee uses photographers,
and payment method and rates. Sound advice on
setting up a free-lance business is covered in an
appendix, which touches on the topics of financial
record keeping, taxes, insurance, filing prints
and transparencies, cover letters and resumes,
mailing photograph submissions, copyright, and
model releases.

RELEVANCE: Undoubtedly this is the
resource for photographers who are starting out,
and as free-lancers, desire to sell their work.
It provides information on how to contact a ready
market.

VIDEO INDUSTRY DIRECTORY
1980
First
Staffieri, Tony
250
SAVVY Management, Inc.
Video Magazine
Publishing Company Inc.
235 Park Avenue, Suite 800
New York, NY 10003
(212) 477-1717
$25.00

Very good
Directory/catalog; resources guide

INCLUSIONS: Indexes by agencies, brand
names, companies, executives, products;
advertising information (agencies; budget data);
bibliographies; business profiles; calendar (trade
shows); directories (companies, trade
associations); marketing information; statistics
(sales)

DESCRIPTORS: Video equipment; video
industry; video manufacturers; video producers;
video suppliers; home video

IDENTIFIER: Source: SAVVY Management, Inc.
Video Magazine

SUMMARY: This is an annotated guide to
major companies, equipment manufacturers, software
producers, suppliers, executives, libraries and
other resources within the home video industry.
It covers manufacturers/suppliers of video
cameras, recorders/players, cassettes and tapes,
videodiscs, television sets and related
accessories. It contains a brief report and
forecast of the home video market; and
bibliographies of pertinent directories, indexes,
magazines, market studies and news media. It is
produced in conjunction with Video Magazine.

RELEVANCE: This is a good overall source
on the video industry. This can be useful to
those who might use the video market.

CHAPTER 5

BUSINESS, SMALL BUSINESS, AND BUSINESS MANAGEMENT

This chapter contains:

- small business

- business planning

- executives

- management

- conduct of essential business functions

- maintenance of business records

AMA MANAGEMENT HANDBOOK
1983
Second
Fallon, William
1568
0-8144-0100-7
AMACOM
135 West 50th Street
New York, NY 10020
(212) 903-8087
$79.95

Very good
Handbook; compendium

INCLUSIONS: Index; diagrams; charts; list
of contributors

DESCRIPTORS: Management; business management

SUMMARY: This is a compendium of
contributions to management science and practice.
It is organized into fourteen sections, each
beginning with a detailed table of contents.   The
sections are: 1) general management; 2) finance;
3) management of research and technology; 4)
manufacturing; 5) purchasing, transportation, and
physical distribution; 6) marketing; 7) human
resources management; 8) information systems and
technology; 9) international; 10) general and
administrative services; 11) risk and insurance
management; 12) employee benefits; 13) packaging;
and 14) public relations.

RELEVANCE: This is a good handbook on
management, which might be included on the company
reference shelf.

<<<<<<>>>>>>

THE BASIC BOOK OF BUSINESS
1977
First
Klug, John
333
0-84360-751-3

CBI Publishing Company, Inc.
135 W. 50th Street
New York, NY 10022-7504

Very good
Book

INCLUSIONS: Index; case studies

DESCRIPTORS: Small business; business
management; financing; taxes; business law;
marketing

SUMMARY: This is an introduction to
business aimed at helping save money. It
discusses when you know enough and when to go for
professional help or other sources. It uses a
"life cycle" approach: how to organize a
business, operate it, sell out, and plan for
retirement and estate. It uses case studies and
management techniques taught at Harvard Business
School. It contains 22 chapters, including ones
on: organizational options; corporations;
management; financial analysis and control;
accounting techniques; sources of financing;
inventory control; legal fundamentals; tax
techniques; buying and selling; retirement;
insurance; and estate planning. Each chapter is
subdivided into topics, such as: how to form a
family partnership, how to formulate a business
strategy, critical path analysis, cash flow,
depreciation methods, basic securities laws,
basics of bankruptcy, personal dividend deduction,
grandfather trust. It also discusses marketing
myths, prevention of marketing disasters, product
life cycles, market research, and marketing mix --
product, price, promotion, and place (channels of
distribution).

RELEVANCE: This is written for owners and
managers of businesses with fewer than 500
employees. This can be used as a beginner's
reference book.

BASICS OF SUCCESSFUL BUSINESS PLANNING
1982 (The 1980 edition was abstracted.)
Osgood, William
0-81445-641-3
AMACOM
135 West 50th Street
New York, NY 10020
(212) 903-8683
$8.95

Very good
Handbook

INCLUSIONS: Index by subject; appendices;
illustrations (charts, figures); samples (business
plan, financial statements, budgets); tables

DESCRIPTORS: Business planning; business
plans; proposals

SUMMARY: This Handbook is designed to
acquaint the reader with the theory and practice
of business planning, and to enable him/her to
prepare an effective business plan. It provides a
rationale and conceptual framework for planning
and discusses basic types of planning -- market,
financial, contingency, long range, and strategic.
It illustrates and shows step-by-step, how to
prepare essential components of a good plan. It
contains a sample business plan and a summary
discussion of sources of financing for a new
business.

RELEVANCE: A business plan is an important
ingredient for a successful business. This book
shows how to do it.

<<<<<<>>>>>>

BEYOND THE BOTTOM LINE
How Business Leaders Are Turning Principles
Into Profits
1985
First
Tuleja, Tad
228

0-8160-1047-1
Facts on File Publications
460 Park Avenue South
New York, NY 10016
(800) 322-8755
$16.95

Very good
Book

INCLUSIONS: Index; appendix of corporate
ethical statements; chapter notes

DESCRIPTORS: Business ethics; big business;
corporate ethics; ethical theories; corporate
responsibility

SUMMARY: This book discusses questions
and approaches of business ethics. The author
does not indict corporate capitalism but asks
whether people in the "system" can behave morally
and whether in fact they do. In examining his
sample of ten, large, multinational corporations,
he shows that not only are ethics and social
responsibility the right thing to do but that they
pay off. He argues against the laissez-faire
approach and Milton Friedman's view that
corporations need have little concern for social
responsibility. He examines and critiques the
theoretical approaches of fundamentalism,
relativism, and utilitarianism, endorsing the
latter. He examines the corporate role as
"stakeholder" and corporate responsibility to
stockholders, employees, consumers, and larger
arenas of national and international concerns. He
discusses the ethics of competition and
multinational ethics, including the case of South
Africa. He asserts that divided loyalties in
personnel become less a problem when they are
dedicated to the ethical beliefs and practices of
the organization.

RELEVANCE: This book is written for
professional business people and managers. It
does not purport to cover all questions and
aspects of business ethics. Its perspective is
one that most business people will find acceptable
to live with as well as sensible.

BUSINESS AND ECONOMICS BOOKS AND SERIALS IN PRINT
1981
Third
1836
R. R. Bowker Company
205 E. 42nd Street
New York, NY 10017
(800) 521-8110 (U.S.), (800) 537-8416 (Canada)
$62.50

Excellent
Bibliography

INCLUSIONS: Indexes to books by subject,
title; serials subject, serials title,
bibliographies; classified listings; directory of
publishers; keys to abbreviations

DESCRIPTORS: Books; business books; business
periodicals; business; serials; economics

IDENTIFIERS: This continues Business Books
and Serials in Print.   There is a Supplement
entitled Business Books and Serials in Print
Supplement.

SUMMARY: This is an international
subject and buyers guide to 47,996 English-
language publications.   Emphasis is given to
administrative and commercial rather than
industrial aspects of business operations.
Managerial functions are fully covered.   It gives
full bibliographic and ordering information and
descriptions, including author, editor, title,
publisher, and bibliographic notes.

RELEVANCE: The publications listed are
useful for managing commercial aspects of business
and economics.

<<<<<<>>>>>>

A BUSINESS INFORMATION GUIDEBOOK
1980
First
Figueroa, Oscar - Winkler, Charles

256
0-8144-7006-X
AMACOM
135 West 50th Street
New York, NY 10020
(212) 903-8087
$9.95

Very good
Annotated bibliography

INCLUSIONS: Index by subject;
bibliographies; classified listings (publications
and sources by subject)

DESCRIPTORS: Business information; business
publications; business reference materials;
personal finance

SUMMARY: This describes about 200
commonly used business-oriented reference works,
classified under about 75 subjects. It notes the
subject emphasis, practical features, publication
frequency and source, name and address of each.
Personal finance topics treated include:
securities, mutual funds, security dealers, stock
exchanges, investment companies, and securities
research. It also provides useful suggestions for
finding needed business data and information.

RELEVANCE: This is a useful reference for
finding business information by subject.

<<<<<<>>>>>>

BUSINESS INFORMATION SOURCES
1985
Second
Irregular
Daniells, Lorna
673
0-520-05335-4
University of California Press
2120 Berkeley Way
Berkeley, CA 94720
(800) 822-6657

$40.00

Excellent
Handbook

INCLUSION: Index

DESCRIPTORS: Business bibliography;
management-bibliography

SUMMARY: This guide to business
information sources contains an introductory
chapter, Methods of Locating Facts, including
types of libraries and encyclopedic sources of
information. It is followed by eight chapters on
basic kinds of business reference sources, such as
bibliographies, indexes and abstracts, government
publications, computerized information services,
microforms and cassettes, handbooks, and loose-
leaf services. Chapters 9 through 20 contain
annotated bibliographies in areas of management.
Chapter 21 is A Basic Bookshelf with suggested
reference works for a personal business or small
public library.

RELEVANCE: This is the best source of its
kind and an easy to use guide to sources of
business information written to help the business
student, practitioner or librarian find the better
business sources.

                    <<<<<<>>>>>>

BUSINESS ORGANIZATIONS AND AGENCIES DIRECTORY
1984   (The 1980 edition was abstracted)
Second
Kruzas, Anthony   -   Thomas, Robert
894
0-8103-1199-2
Gale Research Company
Book Tower
Detroit, MI 48226
(800) 223-4253
$230.00, Supplement: $85.00

Excellent
Directory

INCLUSIONS: Indexes (9); business listings;
directories (classified listings (32), geographic
listings); grants information (federal programs);
profiles (agencies, businesses, consulting firms
(information brokers); organizations)

DESCRIPTORS: Agencies; business information;
business organizations; organizations

SUMMARY: This is an annotated,
classified guide to thousands of organizations and
groups, which promote, coordinate, support or
regulate commercial activity. It lists: better
business bureaus; business publishers; chambers of
commerce; conference and convention
centers/bureaus; data banks; libraries and
information centers/services; federal, state and
regional planning agencies; franchise companies;
graduate and independent business schools; labor
groups; metropolitan newspapers and news
syndicates; research groups; trade centers and
fairs; U.S. and foreign diplomatic offices; and
other groups.

RELEVANCE: This directory is most
significant for supplying in one volume, a
comprehensive and convenient resource book for
persons specifically interested in obtaining
information on businesses and identifying and
contacting business organizations.

<<<<<<>>>>>>

ENCYCLOPEDIA OF BUSINESS INFORMATION SOURCES
A Bibliographic Guide to Approximately 22,000
Citations Covering More Than 1100 Primary
Subjects of Interest to Business Personnel
1986, Supplement 1987
Sixth
Woy, James
878, Supplement 133
0-8103-0364-7

Gale Research Company
Book Tower
Detroit, MI 48226
(800) 223-4253
$210.00, Supplement $80.00

Excellent
Sourcebook

INCLUSION: Subject contents, cross-
referenced

DESCRIPTORS: Business sources; information
sources

SUMMARY: This source provides
information on sources for over 1100 business-
related topics. It is organized by 6 types of
source (e.g. general works, bibliographies,
directories) within subject areas. Examples of
subject classification are: accounting,
administration, acid rain, adult education,
adhesions, air freight, alcoholism, aluminum
industry, arbitration, associations, and
automobiles. Entries include: publisher's name,
address, telephone number, frequency of
publication or publication date, and price.
Entries for agencies and organizations include:
name, address, and telephone number.

RELEVANCE: This source is intended for
executives, librarians, researchers, analysts,
planners and others. It provides a quick
reference to subject area resources. It is quite
complete though not comprehensive. It does not
have abstracts of works or indices of any kind,
but the table of contents is quite detailed.

<<<<<<>>>>>>

THE ENTREPRENEUR'S GUIDE
Planning Guide for Management
1986
First
Gruber, Frank - Keenan, William
494

The Research Institute of America
90 Fifth Avenue
New York, NY 10011
(212) 645-4800

Good
Guide

DESCRIPTORS: Business management; financial
management; marketing; human resource development;
computer-aided management

SUMMARY: This combines four previously
separately published pieces: human resource
management, marketing management, computer-aided
management, and financial management. Together
these are meant to aid the executive in managing a
business. Each section begins with a table of
contents and simple overview of the field
explaining the rationale for and importance of the
area followed by key concepts, considerations and
information. Topics covered include: 1) human
resource management -- forecasting needs,
strategic planning, plan implementation,
recruitment and building; 2) marketing management
-- market research, marketing plan, market
segmentation and mix, the marketing unit, and
legal restraints; 3) computer-aided management --
management support system choice and
implementation; 4) financial management --
financial resources, ratios, emerging and
established company financial issues, special
problems of growth, financial emergency, business
slowdown, and new capital.

RELEVANCE: This can serve as an overview
of management considerations in human resource
development, marketing, computers and finance.

                    <<<<<<>>>>>>

ETHICAL THEORY AND BUSINESS
1988 (The 1983 edition was abstracted.)
Third
Beauchamp, Tom   - Bowie, Norman
512

0-13-290503-5
Prentice-Hall, Inc.
Rt. 9 West
Englewood Cliffs, NJ 07632
(201) 592-2000
Order: 200 Old Tappan Road
Old Tappan, NJ 07675
(201) 767-5049

Very good
Textbook; anthology

INCLUSIONS: Chapter supplementary readings;
chapter notes; cases

DESCRIPTORS: Business ethics; government
regulation; cost-benefit analysis; ethical
theories; disclosure; preferential hiring; reverse
discrimination; affirmative action; employee
rights; trade secrets; free speech; worker safety;
conflicts of interest; corporate responsibility

SUMMARY: This is a basic text on
business ethics. It begins with an examination of
ethical theory and its application to business.
The following eight chapters are comprised of
contributor essays within these subject areas:
corporate social responsibility, employee rights;
conflicts of interest and roles; advertising and
information disclosure; the environment;
preferential hiring and reverse discrimination;
self and government regulation; and theories of
economic justice. Each of these chapters includes
sections on legal perspectives and cases with
questions.

RELEVANCE: This is a good introduction to
the field of business ethics. It represents a
marriage between business and philosophy. While
it takes an academic, student oriented approach,
it can be used by business persons as well.

<<<<<<>>>>>

HANDBOOK FOR PROFESSIONAL MANAGERS
1985

Second
Bittel, Lester   -   Ramsey, Jackson
1000
0-07-005469-X
McGraw-Hill, Inc.
1221 Avenue of the Americas
New York, NY 10020
(800) 262-4729
$59.95

Excellent
Handbook; manual

INCLUSIONS: Index, cross-referenced; table
of contents with subject locator guide of major
and sub-headings

DESCRIPTORS: Management handbook; business
handbook

IDENTIFIER: Formerly titled Encyclopedia of
Professional Management

SUMMARY: This handbook provides
explanations of concepts, techniques and their
applications in management. It contains in 239
entries arranged alphabetically and contains over
3000 definitions. Contributors are 229 business
leaders and academic authorities writing on 50
major areas of business and management. Topics
include accounting, behavior, budget,
compensation, computers, government regulations,
health, human resources, labor-management
relations, marketing and sales, markets,
personnel, and productivity.

RELEVANCE: This Handbook was written for
managers and is a useful deskbook to obtain quick
and authoritative information on a variety of
subjects. The editors have done a responsible job
of acknowledging terminological problems and
contributor disparities.

MANAGING THE SMALL BUSINESS
1982
Third
Irregular
Kline, John - Stegall, Donald - Steinmetz,
Lawrence
466
0-256-02508-8
Richard D. Irwin, Inc.
1818 Ridge Road
Homewood, Ill 60430
(800) 323-4560
$29.95

Very good
Textbook

INCLUSIONS: Index by subject; case studies;
appendices on U.S. and Canadian resource materials

DESCRIPTORS: Small business management;
business planning; entrepreneurship; management
skills; small business; business management

SUMMARY: This textbook treats basic
small business planning and management
considerations, from startup through sale of the
business enterprise. It covers these topics:
buying/selling a business; preparing and using a
prospectus; organizing, assembling and controlling
resources: controlling inventories and finances;
image-building; marketing and advertising; credit
sales; and pricing of products and services. It
also treats why businesses succeed or fail;
personnel and employee relations; sources of help
and training resources; forms of ownership laws,
regulations and taxes; capital needs and sources;
business locations and facilities; franchises;
insurance; and other topics. Case studies are
included in each chapter.

RELEVANCE: This book is an aid to new
entrepreneurs. It includes a paragraph on the
role of consulting firms as a resource for small
business.

PROJECT MANAGEMENT
A Systems Approach to Planning, Scheduling and
Controlling
1984 (The 1979 edition was abstracted.)
Kerzner, Harol
672
0-442-24879-2
Van Nostrand Reinhold Co.
115 Fifth Avenue
New York, NY 10003
$38.95

Very good
Textbook; handbook

INCLUSIONS: Indexes by author, subject;
figures; tables; bibliographies (3); appendix on
contracts; end of chapter problems; case studies

DESCRIPTORS: Project management; business
management

SUMMARY: This book covers the
development, rationale, and technical aspects of
project management. It compares project
management to traditional management issues and
traces project management to a marriage between
systems theory and business resulting in system
management. The book contains 12 chapters and 88
sections with 30 case studies and 185 problems.
It deals with: types of organizational structures
-- line-staff, pure product, matrix, modified
matrix; the project office and team; management
functions; strategic planning, network analysis;
and human factors of leadership, motivation,
communication, conflict resolution, time
management, selection and training of project
managers, levels of managers and subordinates. It
devotes two chapters to problems and conflicts and
four to basic tools for scheduling and control.
The latter include: work breakdown structure, bar
(GANTT) chart, PERT (program evaluation and review
technique), PERT/CPM (critical path method)
models, and cost control.

RELEVANCE: This is written for students,
managers, and executives. It applies to any size
or type of organization. The project management

approach provides a means of organizational
responsiveness to a complex, changing marketplace.

<<<<<<>>>>>>

SMALL BUSINESS
Look Before You Leap: A Catalog of Sources of
Information To Help Start and Manage Your Own
Small Business
1981 (The 1978 edition was abstracted.)
First
Mucciolo, Louis
304
Arco
1 Gulf & Western Building
New York, NY 10023
(212) 333-5800
$8.95

Good
Guide

INCLUSIONS: Bibliographies (annotated; many);
book reviews; directories (government offices,
franchise sources, SBICs, marketing); forms (SBA);
glossary; guidelines (information seeking);
indexes by subject, USGPO bibliographies

DESCRIPTORS: Business information; business
publications; new ventures; small business
management

SUMMARY: This work describes services of
government agencies and other organizations and
groups. It lists hundreds of publications and
reviews some popular handbooks, guides and
textbooks. It lists materials available from
government sources (IRS, Department of Commerce,
Post Office, SBA, USGPO).

RELEVANCE: This treats items of interest to
business managers and opportunity entrepreneurs,
franchise and mail order advocates, minorities,
women, and others.

SMALL BUSINESS INFORMATION SOURCES
1976
First
Schabacker, Joseph
318
National Council for Small Business Management
Development
University of Wisconsin Extension
929 North 6th Street
Milwaukee, WI 53202

Good
Catalog; resources guide

INCLUSIONS: Indexes by author, subject;
bibliographies; bibliography of bibliographies;
classified listings

DESCRIPTORS: Business information; business
publications; small business; small business
management

SUMMARY: This is an annotated guide to
over 110 publications pertinent to the study and
practice of small business, published from 1953 to
1976. It treats these items and subjects: 1)
books; 2) textbooks; 3) pamphlets, booklets and
periodicals; 4) research studies; 5) SBA
materials; 6) government publications; 7) Journal
of Small Business Management; 8) Conference
Proceedings; 9) the Bank of America's Small
Business Reporter; 10) minority enterprise; and
11) international business. It lists the table of
contents of each publication described.

RELEVANCE: This provides information
sources to small business but it is somewhat out
of date.

                    <<<<<<>>>>>>

STAY HOME AND MIND YOUR OWN BUSINESS
How to Manage Your Time, Space, Personal
Obligations, Money, Business, and Yourself While
Working at Home
1987
First

Forhbieter-Mueller, Jo
280
0-932620-83-3
Betterway Publications, Inc.
Box 83
White Hall, VA 22987
(804) 823-5661

Excellent
Guide

INCLUSIONS: Index; references and
resources; appendix; case examples

DESCRIPTORS: Home business; cottage
industry; small business; entrepreneurship

SUMMARY: This book is divided into two
parts: Managing Your Time, Space, Home, and Self
While Working at Home, and Managing Your Home
Business. The first part covers goal-setting,
types of businesses (manufacturing, creative,
service), case examples, time and space
management, family and self. The second part
covers business plans, legal form of business,
image, financial management, record keeping, and
collections, taxes, insurance, inventory,
employees, pricing, marketing, packaging and
shipping, and evaluation.

RELEVANCE: This book is full of details
and practical advice. It is recommended for
anyone interested or involved in setting up a
home-based business. It covers the kinds of
details those involved in home business really
deal with, such as self-discipline, scheduling,
procedures, priorities, balancing time and space
for the business, family, friends, community, and
oneself. Its emphasis or strong point is on non-
business concerns, which surround any home
business.

<<<<<<>>>>>>

WHERE TO FIND BUSINESS INFORMATION
QUESTIONS

A Worldwide Guide for Everyone Who Needs the
Answers to Business Questions
1982 (The 1979 edition was abstracted.)
Second
Brownstone, David   -   Carruth , Gorton
632
0-471-08736-X
John Wiley and Sons, Inc.
605 Third Avenue
New York, NY 10158
(212) 850-6418
$75.00

Very good
Annotated bibliography; directory/catalog;
resources guide

INCLUSIONS: Indexes of titles by subject,
source; bibliographies current awareness
materials, geographic materials, references
materials and sources); classified listings;
geographic listings; directories (publication
sources)

DESCRIPTORS: Business sources; business
publications

SUMMARY: This is a subject, geographic,
and source (publisher) guide to English-language
business publications internationally. It covers
frequently revised/ updated items: database and
information service materials; directories; loose-
leaf and microform materials; magazines and
newsletters; printouts and reports; serials;
yearbooks; and others. It lists American,
Canadian, and foreign publications.

RELEVANCE: This provides a key to business
information sources, with helpful user
information. It can be useful for marketing
purposes. It has an international perspective and
covers a variety of materials. However, this
source purports to be "current," which it is not.

CHAPTER 6

CAREER AND LIFEWORK PLANNING AND DEVELOPMENT

This chapter contains:

- career planning and strategies

- career development

- executive placement and compensation

- occupations directories

- employee counseling

THE 1988 WHAT COLOR IS YOUR PARACHUTE
A Practical Manual for Job-Hunters and Career
Changers
1988
Annual
Sixteenth
Bolles, Richard
352
0-89815-228-3
Ten Speed Press
P.O. Box 7123
Berkeley, CA 94707
(415) 845-8414
$8.95

Excellent
Guide

INCLUSIONS: Index; author index; appendices
(5); bibliography; resources; tips; cartoons;
quotes; asides; tables; samples; forms;
checklists; self-evaluation aids

DESCRIPTORS: Career; lifework planning; job-
hunting; career change

SUMMARY: This running commentary on job-
seeking includes the following contents: 1) a
poem on job-hunting; 2) the usual ways personnel
experts say to look for a job and why they and the
"numbers game" approach don't work; 3) what
skills, where to locate, and how to find the hirer
issues through research and contacts; and 4) the
resumé, interview, and thank-you note. The five
appendices contain a collection of comments and
miscellania including: 1) problems of women,
minorities, handicapped, and others, and other
special concerns, for examples, creativity, making
a living as a writer, overseas work, part-time and
work at home; summer jobs, etc.; 2) utilizing
career counselors and other "live resources;" 3)
understanding your brain; and 4) finding "your
mission in life" as a religious and personal
issue.

RELEVANCE: This book is a unique, upbeat,
contribution to the career literature in approach,
style, and topical coverage. It is probably the

most popular book for job-hunters ever published.
It has varied slightly from year to year, and
always having its cartoons and folksy style.
Authors can look at this book as an example of how
to make a career and tremendous financial success
out of one publication.

<<<<<<>>>>>>

THE 40+ JOB-HUNTING GUIDE
Official Handbook of the 40+ Club
1987
Revised
Birsner, Patricia
272
0-13-329152-9
ARCO
One Gulf and Western Bldg.
New York, NY 10023
(212) 373-8931
$8.95

Very good
Guide

INCLUSIONS: Index; appendix on 40+ clubs;
self-evaluation tools; charts; sample resumés;
sample letters

DESCRIPTORS: Career; job hunting; executives

IDENTIFIER: Former title: Job Hunting for the 40+
Executive

SUMMARY: This book deals with questions
related to how the older job-seeker finds suitable
work. Part one discusses the emotional issues
involved in being out-of-work and looking, getting
motivated, organized, and looking appropriately
for the job search. Part two discusses self-
evaluation, making contacts, and matching personal
and job characteristics. Four communication
styles are defined and matched with suggested
occupations. Part three covers job research and
resources, prospecting for jobs, writing winning
resumes and letters, and the interview. Part four

is about what it's called: "Evaluating the Job
Offer, Making the Decision, and Beginning Work."

RELEVANCE: This book is a good job-
searching guide and is especially relevant to the
over forty job-seeker, offering helpful
troubleshooting and support. Many of the
interviews and information for the book came from
members of the Forty Plus Club and Forty Plus
Educational Center in New York.

                    <<<<<<>>>>>>

AMERICAN ALMANAC OF JOBS AND SALARIES, 1987-1988
1987
Third
Wright, John
848
Avon Books
105 Madison Avenue
New York, NY 10016
(800) 367-2494
$12.95

Very good
Sourcebook

INCLUSIONS: Index; tables

DESCRIPTORS: Career; wages; salaries

SUMMARY: This book presents an overview
of jobs and salaries in the American workforce.
Numerous tables containing statistical data have
been included and analyzed by the author to give
the reader meaningful insights into the past
nature, present status, and future directions, of
hundreds of careers. The reader will find
complete job descriptions and an evaluation of
future job opportunities in addition to salary and
wage information. The book includes chapters on:
1) working in governmental public service; 2)
working in the limelight of film, modeling,
television, etc.; 3) working in the professions;
4) working in the sciences and technology; 5)
working in health care; 6) working in sales,

brokering, insurance; and 7) working in the
trades, agriculture, sports, etc.

RELEVANCE: This is a work for career
changers, women seeking equal pay for equal work,
and for anyone considering or beginning life in
the world of work.

<<<<<<<>>>>>>

CAREER CHOICE AND DEVELOPMENT
Applying Contemporary Theories to Practice
1984
First
Brown, Duane - Brooks, Linda - Associates
505
0-87589-593-X
Jossey-Bass Inc., Publishers
433 California Street
San Francisco, CA 94104
(415) 433-1740
$25.95

Very Good
Reference; textbook

INCLUSIONS: Indexes by subject, cross-
referenced, and main; bibliography

DESCRIPTORS: Career; vocational guidance

IDENTIFIER: A joint publication in the
Jossey-Bass Management Series and Social and
Behavioral Science Series

SUMMARY: This source covers career
development theories and research findings and the
use of theories in career counseling. The first
chapter introduces the others and discusses the
history of career development. Theories discussed
in the volume are trait and factor, need, John
Holland's typology, psychological factors,
Ginzberg's and Super's development theories, and
Krumlaltz's social learning theory. Four chapters
are devoted to career counseling, including its
provision to women, minorities, mid-life career
changers, and adults in the workplace.

RELEVANCE: This work is written for
practitioners and researchers and is academically
oriented.

<<<<<<>>>>>>

CAREER STRATEGIES
Planning for Personal Achievement
1978
Souerwine, Andrew
First
292
AMACOM
135 West 50th Street
New York, NY 10020
(212) 903-8087
$8.95

Very good
Guide

INCLUSIONS: Index; bibliography;
worksheets; case history; examples

DESCRIPTORS: Career planning; work life;
career strategy; job

SUMMARY: This covers the individual,
social, economic, cultural, political,
organizational considerations that go into career
planning and execution. It discusses: the ways in
which our views of careers and organizational
concerns have changed; the need for planning;
important elements of successful career strategy;
assessing resources and opportunities; values; the
significance of assessing resources and
opportunities; values; the significance of family,
peers, subordinates, bosses, job and organization;
issues in getting started; motivation; learning
styles and issues; etc. A summary chapter
includes 34 statements of basic principles of
career strategy.

RELEVANCE: This is an easy-to-read book,
and it can be useful for someone beginning or
reviewing their career.

DESIGNING CAREER DEVELOPMENT SYSTEMS
1986
First
Leibowitz, Zandy - Farren, Caela - Kaye,
Beverly
323
Jossey-Bass Inc., Publications
433 California Street
San Francisco, CA 94104
(415) 433-1740
$25.95

Excellent
Guide

INCLUSIONS: Index; bibliography, tables;
tools; appendices (3)

DESCRIPTORS: Career development systems;
employee development; human resource development;
organization development

IDENTIFIER: Jossey-Bass Management Series
and Social and Behavioral Science Series

SUMMARY: The authors have combined
career development and organization development.
They go beyond an individual approach to career
change and look at designing systems or programs
for employee development in an organization. The
text is organized into four steps and parts: 1)
assessing needs and current systems; 2) creating a
vision and plan; 3) implementing action plans; and
4) ensuring results and maintaining change. Three
appendices contain: 1) needs assessment examples;
2) program models; and 3) resources for career
development professionals, including professional
organizations, journals and newsletters, and
assessment instruments.

RELEVANCE: This book is designed for
professional career consultants, human resource
personnel and consultants, trainers, and
organization development consultants. This is a
creative, integrative, useful guide, and it is
well presented.

DICTIONARY OF HOLLAND OCCUPATIONAL CODES
A Comprehensive Cross-Index of Holland's
RIASEC Codes with 12,000 DOT Occupations
1982
First
Gottfredson, Gary - Holland, John - Ogawa,
Deborah
520
0-89106-020-0
Consulting Psychologists Press, Inc.
577 College Avenue
Palo Alto, CA 94306
(415) 857-1444
$18.75

Very good
Handbook

INCLUSIONS: Bibliography; classified index
of job titles; alphabetic index of job titles;
user's self-test; tables

DESCRIPTORS: Occupations; career; job titles

SUMMARY: The Dictionary of Occupational
Titles classifies jobs by the level of their
involvement with people, data, and things. This
work uses the six Holland codes (classifications)
which are: 1) R, involves practical use of
machines, tools, or materials; 2) I, involves
intellectual problem solving abilities; 3) A,
involves creative work in the arts; 4) S, involves
helping other people; 5) E, involves supervision
of others; and 6) C, involves record keeping and
clerical type organizing. Holland's
classification is used as the test results in
taking vocational interest survey tests and this
work takes the Holland codes and converts them for
you into the Dictionary of Occupational Titles
classifications.

RELEVANCE: This book is designed for
anyone who has taken vocational interests tests
and now wishes to apply their test results to
identifying specific job title and description of
relevance in the Dictionary of Occupational Titles
(see abstract).

DICTIONARY OF OCCUPATIONAL TITLES
1977, Supplement 1982, 1984 Reprint
Fourth
1371 (plus 36 in Supplement)
0-318-04550-8
U.S. Government Printing Office
Superintendent of Documents
Washington, DC 20402-9325
(202) 783-3238
$23.00

Excellent
Job Descriptions

INCLUSIONS: Introduction and user
information; summary listing of occupational
categories, divisions and groups; master titles
and definitions; term titles and definitions;
index of occupational titles; occupational titles
arranged by industry designation,; industry index;
appendix (explanation of data, people and things);
glossary

DESCRIPTORS: Job descriptions; occupations

SUMMARY: The bulk of the DOT consists of
standardized classification and description of
20,000 jobs. The entries are arranged
alphabetically by categories, divisions, and
groups. Each digit of the nine-digit code
contains meaningful job analysis information: the
occupational code number and title, the industry
designation, alternate titles, and the body of the
definition (lead and task element statements,
"May" items, and undefined related titles). Many
jobs have a three-digit occupational code, which
contains worker function ratings.

RELEVANCE: This is self-described as "the
most comprehensive, up-to-date [1977 with 1984
reprint is the latest] occupational information on
job duties and requirements in the United States
ever assembled in a single volume." It is the
reference book of occupations which job seekers
and counselors can draw on for vocational ideas
and job descriptions and personnel specialists can
refer to in preparing and comparing systematic job
definitions and matching the job with the worker.

It was originally prepared for purposes of
systematizing job descriptions in public service.

<<<<<<>>>>>>

EMPLOYEE COUNSELING IN INDUSTRY AND GOVERNMENT
A Guide to Information Sources
1979
First
Peck, Theodore
121
Gale Research Company
Book Tower
Detroit MI 48226
(800) 223-4253
$65.00

Very good
Directory; sourcebook

INCLUSION: Index by subject, cross-
referenced

DESCRIPTORS: Employee assistance; employee
counseling; career advancement; women in the work
force; pre-retirement counseling; personnel

SUMMARY: This is a directory of private
and government information sources on employee
counseling. Five topical areas are covered: 1)
alcohol and drug abuse; 2) emotional and mental
health problems; 3) pre-retirement counseling; 4)
career advancement, testing and training; and 5)
women in the work force. Information sources
include: organizations, institutes, and
associations; literature dealing with specific
problems, corrective measures, counseling, and
counseling related techniques; journals;
abstracting and indexing services; directories;
and data bases.

RELEVANCE: This is a well-organized guide,
relevant for professional and personal use.
Although it is in need of an update, it provides
useful information and leads for further research
and follow-up.

EXECUTIVE COMPENSATION - A TOTAL PAY
PERSPECTIVE
1981
First
Ellig, Bruce
343
McGraw-Hill, Inc.
1221 Avenue of the Americas
New York, NY 10020
(800) 262-4729
$35.95

Very good
Handbook

INCLUSIONS: Index by subject, cross-
referenced; tables; charts; examples

DESCRIPTORS: Executive compensation; salary;
employee benefits; perquisites (perks); incentives

SUMMARY: This is a comprehensive work on
executive compensation. It discusses these
elements of executive pay in detail: salary;
employee benefits; perquisites; short-term
incentives; and long-term incentives. It analyzes
tax, accounting, and SEC (Securities Exchange
Commission) considerations for each element of
pay. The elements of pay are also discussed in
relation to executive needs and company
executives. The author discusses the executive's
perception of pay, deferred compensation, the
compensation committee, and plan objectives.

RELEVANCE: This is relevant for persons
involved in negotiating their own compensation, or
deciding, implementing or consulting on
compensation plans.

<<<<<<>>>>>

HOW TO ANSWER A HEADHUNTER'S CALL
A Complete Guide to Executive Search
1985 (The 1984 edition was abstracted.)
First
Perry, Robert

249
0-317-31391-6
AMACOM
135 West 50th Street
New York, NY 10020
(212)903-8087
$16.95

Very good
Book

INCLUSION: Index

DESCRIPTORS: Executive search; headhunting;
career options; executive; entrepreneur;
outplacement; women employment; minority
employment

SUMMARY: This book provides an overview
of headhunting from both the points of view of the
executive in search of a job and the headhunter.
Executive search is said to be over thirty years
old with about 1000 firms, which make 3.3 percent
of placements. Topics discussed include why
executives search elsewhere for jobs; women and
minorities considerations; the role of the
headhunter and the client relationship; unsavory
practices of headhunters;the resume, interview,
psychological testing, compensation and reference
checking; negotiations; and career options of
outplacement, the federal bureaucracy, academia,
and entrepreneurship. The author looks at the
future of executive search and offers
recommendations for search firms.

RELEVANCE: This is in an easy-to-read
style and would prove interesting to either
executives or headhunters.

                    <<<<<<>>>>>>

HOW TO CHOOSE, CHANGE, ADVANCE YOUR CAREER
1983
First
Lewis, Adele - Lewis, Bill - Radlaner, Steven
178

0-8126-2245-9
Barron's Educational Series, Inc.
250 Wireless Blvd.
Hauppauge, NY 11788
(800) 257-5729
$6.95

Good
Guide

INCLUSIONS: Checklists; samples

DESCRIPTORS: Career; vocational guidance;
job hunting

SUMMARY: This book discusses, gives
pointers and advice, and attempts to enlighten the
job seeker or changer. Part one is about
assessing your goals, yourself, and your current
employment status in order to evaluate career
choices and strategy. Part two is about how to
present yourself and your credentials, do a job
search, succeed at the interview, negotiate the
job offer, stay or leave a job. It covers resumés
and cover letters preparation, employment agencies
and want ads. The discussion is based on what the
"insiders" of the job market say they're looking
for.

RELEVANCE: This is a simple to read, human
approach to job and career. It is neither
sophisticated nor technical.

<<<<<<<>>>>>>

JOB DESCRIPTIONS IN HUMAN RESOURCES
1985
First
Sperling, JoAnn
402
0-8144-5806
AMACOM
135 West 50th Street
New York, NY 10020
(212) 903-8087
$75.00

Very good
Job Descriptions

INCLUSIONS: Glossary; bibliography; forms

DESCRIPTORS: Human resource development;
career planning; training and development; job
descriptions; personnel management; employee
recruitment; employee development

SUMMARY: Based on information obtained
from the results of a questionnaire returned by
244 company and government employers, this source
provides: 1) a survey of company practices; and 2)
selected job descriptions in human resources.
Major job areas described are: human resources top
management, general personnel administration,
recruitment, training and development,
compensation, benefits, health and safety, equal
employment opportunity, and employee
communications. Each of these areas is broken
down into specific positions. Actual examples
from a range of companies in manufacturing,
retailing, and service industries are presented.
Each is two to four pages in length and
distinctive.

RELEVANCE: This can provide helpful
examples to potential candidates for human
resource development positions of what to expect
of particular careers and jobs available in fields
which are not always obvious and well-defined.

                    <<<<<<>>>>>>

THE JOBS RATED ALMANAC 250 JOBS!
1988
First
Krantz, Leo
352
0-345-34885-0
Pharos Books
200 Park Avenue
New York, NY 10166
(212) 751-2600
$14.95

Excellent
Ranking catalog

INCLUSIONS: Graphics; tables

DESCRIPTORS: Careers; occupations; job
ranking

SUMMARY: This describes, scores, and
ranks 250 selected jobs, chosen on the bases of
commonness, visibility, desirability, and growth.
Nine criteria were used for ranking and chapters:
1) work environment; 2) income; 3) outlook; 4)
stress; 5) travel opportunities; 6) physical
demands; 7) extras; 8) security; and 9) geography.
The last chapter has an overall ranking based on
accumulated ranks on factors of environment,
income, outlook, stress, physical demands, and
security. This is followed by focused reports on
the arts, technical and repair fields, media and
communications, travel and transportation,
medicine and health, production and manufacturing,
public service, mathematics and science, and
construction. A final ranking is done when income
is the dominant criterion.

RELEVANCE: This book is an interesting
eye-opener. The job rankings results are
surprising. For example, actuary scores highest
both overall and when income is the dominant
factor. Some glamour jobs, medical professions,
and sports, may actually have poor work
environments, long hours, and high stress, along
with their high pay. Growth and technical fields
generally rank high. Traditional jobs in
production and the trades have declined in job
security. Sales and administration jobs rank
quite high, while service jobs and professions
have problem areas. Consultant is not included
among the 250 jobs. The book has insightful
discussion and is easy to read.

<<<<<<>>>>>>

MANAGING THE NEW CAREERISTS
The Diverse Career Success Orientations of
Today's Workers

1986
First
Derr, Brooklyn
288
0-87589-677-4
Jossey-Bass Inc., Publications
433 California Street
San Francisco, CA 94104
(415) 433-1740
$24.95

Excellent
Book

INCLUSIONS: Index; bibliography; case
studies and examples; tools

DESCRIPTORS: Career development;
organization development; personnel; training

IDENTIFIER: The Jossey-Bass Management
Series and Social and Behavioral Science Series

SUMMARY: This book discusses the
diversity of workers and their changing concepts
of success and motivations in the 1980s, and how
the modern manager can best deal with this reality
to maximize employee and company benefits. The
author identifies five careerist orientations:
classic getting-ahead, getting-secure, getting-
free, getting-high, and getting-balanced. The
author shows how managers can assess and work
effectively with the different career orientations
essentially by bringing together what the
individual and the company wants and "downplaying
organizational conflict and covert politics."
Other topics discussed are the situation of the
multinational manager, and application of the
multiple career orientations concept for the work
of organization development, training, personnel
and career development and counseling
professionals.

RELEVANCE: This book displays sharpness,
creativity and common sense in analyzing current
individual, organizational and national realities
and cultures and in making recommendations. The
author is able to apply his awareness to a variety

of human resource development professional
concerns and circumstances. This is highly
recommended for workers, managers, consultants and
social scientists.

<<<<<<>>>>>>

MUST SUCCESS COST SO MUCH?
1980
First
Evans, Paul - Bartolome, Fernando
250
Basic Books, Inc.
10 East 53rd Street
New York, NY 10022
(800) 242-7737
$13.95

Good
Research report

INCLUSIONS: Index, cross-referenced;
bibliography; appendices: questionnaire; survey
methodology; methodological notes

DESCRIPTORS: Professional life; private
life; success; men at work

SUMMARY: This is a study of the
professional and private lives of male managers.
The research methodology consisted of a
questionnaire, interviews, and participant
observation. Part one is entitled Life
Investments and deals with the investment and
balance in personal and professional life. Part
two, Finding Professional Identity, deals with
launching the career and what happens at home
during this period. Some men are successful and
some are not in both private and work lives. Part
three, Private Life, deals with married couple
relationships. Part four, Lifestyles, deals with
life after 40, the time of men's "mid-life
crisis". Part five presents Conclusions and
explores why some men pay a high price for their
success while others do not. A conclusion is that
the main responsibility for managing professional

and private life lies with the individual, and
that organizational policies and practices can
either contribute or detract from making life
difficult for managers.

RELEVANCE: This is interesting reading for
persons wondering out of personal or professional
concerns about stereotypes and questions regarding
male managers.

                    <<<<<<>>>>>>

NEW CAREER OPTIONS
A Woman's Guide
1977
Farmer, Helen   -   Backer, Thomas
50
Human Interaction Research Institute
10889 Wilshire Boulevard
Los Angeles, CA
Human Sciences Press
72 Fifth Avenue
New York, NY 10011
(802) 658-1238

Good
Guide

INCLUSION: Lists of information sources

DESCRIPTOR: Career-women

IDENTIFIER: National Institute of
Education funded

SUMMARY: The authors discuss the
problems and opportunities for women at work in
the U.S., provide some statistics on women in the
crafts, management, and professions, and discuss
the chances for women in these fields. They cover
issues of marriage, family and career, career
planning and where to turn for help, how to look
for a job, and where to get information, including
government and non-government publications,
publishing houses with materials on women,
Catalyst and its national network of local

resource centers, and women's units in 67
organizations.

RELEVANCE: This is a handy little pamphlet
intended for the 1970's, so it is somewhat
outdated, yet it contains some useful information.
A companion work for counselors is New Career
Options for Women: A Counselor's Sourcebook.

<<<<<<>>>>>

SUPER JOB SEARCH
The Complete Manual for Job-Seekers and
Career-Changers
1987
First
Studner, Peter
330
0-938667-00-9
Jamenair Ltd.
P.O. Box 241957
Los Angeles, CA 90024-9757
(213) 470-6688
$22.95

Very good
Handbook; manual; workbook

INCLUSIONS: Index; glossary; appendices:
sample resumes; sample letters; references and
resources; checklists; forms; samples

DESCRIPTORS: Career; lifework planning; job
hunting; career change

SUMMARY: This is intended as a step-by-
step, day-by-day manual for job-seeking and
career-changing. It consists of seven training
sessions and homework assignments in chapter
sequence: 1) assessment and goal-setting; 2)
accomplishments; 3) the resume; 4) the marketing
plan; 5) networking; 6) telemarketing; yourself;
and 7) the interview, negotiation and action plan.
The last chapter, "When Clouds Hang Overhead,"
discusses what to do after following the plan and
not getting a job: reassessing job objective,

career change, network, company target list,
joining other job-seekers, part-time work, resume,
moving elsewhere, and consulting a professional.
Sections on "After the Search" and an afterword
discuss network maintenance and tips for the job.

RELEVANCE: This is a good, working manual
that details what actions the job-seeker should
take, even providing questionnaires, when each
step should be done, and how long the work of
getting a job should entail -- it's a full-time
job!

<<<<<<>>>>>

THE WAY OF THE RONIN
A Guide to Career Strategy
1984
First
Potter, Beverly
192
0-8144-5798-3
AMACOM
135 West 50th Street
New York, NY 10020
(212) 903-8087
$17.95

Excellent
Guide

INCLUSIONS: Index, cross-referenced;
bibliography; illustrations

DESCRIPTORS: Vocational guidance; career

SUMMARY: This book describes the
characteristics and strategy of a ronin. Ronin is
a Japanese word meaning "wave-people," those who
left allotted stations in life. Potter contrasts
feudal and ronin approaches. She shows that our
changing economic, demographic and personal
realities indicate the wisdom of ronin rather than
traditional strategies of career choices. Rather
than focusing on a single career specialty and
linear movement up the ladder of success, the

ronin often moves laterally, works autonomously or
like contractors, learns many skills, becomes a
generalist with many specialties who can
creatively change by putting together combinations
of skills to adapt to changing circumstances.
Ronins are not afraid to change and prepare for
it. She shows how traditional approaches based on
financial and career ladder success can lead to
burn-out, stultification, and failure to adapt to
the unexpected. She shows how organizations can
adopt ronin characteristics to become more
innovative and encourage excellence.

RELEVANCE: This is a recommended book,
interesting and insightful reading applicable to
our career development and work lives. The text
is amply illustrated and full of quotations and
sayings drawn from the Zen masters, Alvin Toffler,
John Naisbitt, Carlos Castaneda and others. It
has thoughtful explanations of stress, burn-out,
personal and organizational characteristics.

<<<<<<>>>>>

YOUR CAREER
How to Plan It, Manage It, Change It
1977
First
Buskirk, Richard
192
0-451-62559-5
NAL
1633 Broadway
New York, NY 10019
(800) 256-0275
Order: NAL
120 Woodbine St.
Bergenfield, NJ 07621
$3.50

Good
Guide

INCLUSIONS: Bibliography; case examples

DESCRIPTOR: Career

SUMMARY: This is a guide to career
planning, management and advancement. It
elucidates the nature of pitfalls and bad
decisions through discussion and case examples,
giving warnings where deemed appropriate. Part
one covers aspects of planning a career, including
preparation in personal and educational spheres.
Part two covers the first job, what can go wrong
and right, and what to think and do about it.
Part three covers career advancement in the big
city or small town, occupational ladders, the
"grass looks greener" phenomenon, which it often
is not, your image and whether it is a winning
one. Part four is on the role of personality,
Part five is on women in business, and Part six is
on increasing your productivity.

RELEVANCE: This provides general reading
for those wanting to reflect on career management.
It takes an advice giving approach and is neither
technical nor sophisticated.

CHAPTER 7

COMPUTERS AND COMPUTERIZATION

This chapter contains:

- reader's guide

- software reviews

- office automation

- computerization of business
  functions

- how to use microcomputers to make
  money

- hardware and peripheral equipment

- evaluation, selection, and
  purchasing

ACM GUIDE TO COMPUTING LITERATURE
1987
Annual
Tenth
1063
0149-1199
Association for Computing Machinery
P.O. Box 64145
Baltimore, MD 21264
(800) 342-6626
$75.00 (members); $150 (non-members); plus
handling

Very good
Directory

INCLUSIONS: Indexes by author, keyword,
category (subject), proper noun subject, general
terms, reviewer, and source (publisher); user's
guide

DESCRIPTORS: Computer literature; computing
reviews; computer bibliography; computer authors;
computer reviewers

IDENTIFIERS: Formerly titled (1963-76)
Bibliography and Subject Index; Indexes Computing
Reviews, volume 27, 1986

SUMMARY: This covers bibliographic
listings for books (over 16,000), journals,
proceedings, doctoral theses, reports and reviews.
Numbering of citations, excluding books, is
continuous from entries in previous editions.
Indexes refer to bibliographic listings by
citation identification number. Arrangement is by
author's last name for books; alphabetically by
journal name with papers listed under that; main
entry arranged alphabetically with contents
underneath by publisher for proceedings;
alphabetically by publisher for reports; and by
university for theses. Its classification scheme
consists of a multi-leveled tree with eleven
"first level nodes": general literature,
hardware, computer system organization, software,
data, theory of computation, mathematics of
computing, information systems, computing
methodologies, computing applications, and
computing milieux.

RELEVANCE: This directory provides
information on what is available in the
professional literature. It is technically
oriented for computer professionals and subject
specialists.

                    <<<<<<>>>>>

AUTOMATING YOUR OFFICE
1984
Green, James
256
0-07-024318-2
McGraw-Hill Book Company
1221 Avenue of Americas
New York, NY 10020
(800) 262-4729
$27.50

Very good
Book

INCLUSIONS: Index; bibliography; glossary;
tables; diagrams

DESCRIPTORS: Office automation; computer;
telecommunications

SUMMARY: The first part of this book is
on the nature of office work workers and
productivity. The second part is on several kinds
of office automation systems -- text management,
telecommunications networks, and executive
support with an emphasis on telecommunications.
The third part is on applying office automation,
including conducting an officework study, setting
objectives, making a feasibility study, analyzing
life cycle data, selecting equipment, introducing
automation to the office, doing follow-up study
and future trends.

RELEVANCE: This book can be useful to
consultants for automating their own offices as
well as to providers of consulting services. It
is written for the non-technically expert reader.

THE COMPLETE MICROCOMPUTER SYSTEMS HANDBOOK
1980
Second
Safford, Edward
322
0-8306-1201-7
Tab Books, Inc.
P.O. Box 40
Blue Ridge Summit, PA 17214
(800) 233-1128
$9.95

Very good
Handbook

INCLUSION: Index by subject

DESCRIPTORS: Computers; robots; computer
systems

SUMMARY: This book discusses the
following: 1) what computers are, how they
operate, and what programs are all about. It
includes basic concepts, terminology, program
languages, multiplexing, signal transmission, data
rates, and magnetic fields; 2) Computer problems
and how to test for and fix them; 3) computerized
decision-making; 4) concepts of learning and
methods of teaching machines; 5) costs involved in
relation to computer sophistication; 6) digital
music; 7) talking computers; 8) idea displays on
home TVs; 9) moving-vehicle computers; 10) plasma
computer displays; 11) computer crime codes; 12)
magnetic bubble memories; 13) what is involved
with robots; and 14) what to look for in
considering a computer for purchase. It also
explores computer interface with other systems,
such as radio and television.

RELEVANCE: This nifty combination of basic
knowledge with imaginative exploration is written
by a skilled expert on the subject, who stimulates
reader interest in computers.

COMPUTING INFORMATION DIRECTORY
1988
Fifth
Hildebrandt, Darlene
893
0-933113-03-X
Pedaro Inc.
32606 Seventh Avenue S.W.
Federal Way, WA 98023
(206) 874-2555
$139.95

Excellent
Resources directory

INCLUSIONS: Indexes by subject, chapter
key-word-in-context; appendices(6)

DESCRIPTORS: Computer resources; computer
periodicals; software resources; hardware
resources; computer languages

SUMMARY: This Directory lists: 1)
computing journals; 2) university computer center
newsletters; 3) computer manufacturers; 4) books,
bibliographies, and special issues; 5)
dictionaries and glossaries; 6) indexing and
abstracting services (of computer-related
publications), including a table of resources by
date of coverage and detailed annotations for each
title; 7) software resources, including commercial
and public domain, arranged alphabetically; 8)
review resources; 9) hardware resources; 10)
directories, encyclopedias, and handbooks, and 11)
computer languages. The appendices include: 1)
bibliographies of curriculum development; 2)
bibliography of career and salary trends; 3)
Library of Congress classification schedule; 4)
Proceedings of the Association for Computing
Machinery Special Interest Group, 1969-86; 5)
publishers' addresses; and 6) master subject
index.

RELEVANCE: This is a wide-ranging
resources directory to the computing field. It is
a place to start to locate other resources, and
can be useful for a variety of persons and
purposes.

DATAPRO DIRECTORY OF MICROCOMPUTER HARDWARE
1988
Annual
Peck, Richard
2 volumes
0276-1866
Datapro Research
1805 Underwood Blvd.
Delran, NJ 08075
(800) 328-2776
$700.00

Excellent
Loose-leaf information service; current awareness
service

INCLUSIONS: Index; glossary; newsletter;
user's guide; vendor listing service

DESCRIPTOR: Microcomputer hardware

SUMMARY: This is a collection of
information materials on: PCs, displays,
printers, add-in cards, mass storage, LANs, and
company profiles. Included are "feature reports,"
"a broad overview of a specific subject area,"
with sections of tutorial, vendors and suppliers,
and comparison tables; product reports, with
sections of management summary and
characteristics; and new product announcements.

RELEVANCE: This resource can be useful to
users, vendors and consultants. It can be an
invaluable aid to evaluation, comparison,
decision-making, and selection of computer
hardware. It can also keep you up-to-date on the
state of the art. This is one of many Datapro
information services on the information technology
market. They are on-line and in addition to
loose-leaf, are available on diskette, magnetic
tape, and microfiche; and special services include
courier, facsimile, and special packaging.

DATAPRO MANAGEMENT OF APPLICATIONS SOFTWARE
1988; monthly report, monthly newsletter
Annual, monthly update
Peck, Richard
2 volumes
8756-6516
Datapro Research Corporation
1805 Underwood Blvd.
Delran, NJ 08075
(800) 328-2776
$525.00

Very good
Loose-leaf information service; current awareness
service; buyer's guide

INCLUSIONS: Index; glossary; user's guide;
newsletter

DESCRIPTORS: Applications software; software
management

IDENTIFIER: Solutions Series

SUMMARY: This contains approximately 200
reports and 1800 pages on particular software
management problems and solutions. New reports
are added monthly to keep up-to-date. Its tabbed
sections are: index, user's guide, software
development concepts, guide to software products,
planning and cost justification, make or buy
tradeoffs, software design, software production,
selection and acquisition, reliability and vendor
support, installation and testing, maintenance,
performance measurement, future systems, user
ratings, standards, trade directories, glossary,
and newsletter.

RELEVANCE: This is intended for
instructional, planning, operational, and current
awareness purposes. It is not recommended for
computer novices but rather for computer
professionals, managers, and consultants.

DATAPRO MANAGEMENT OF MICROCOMPUTER SYSTEMS
1985
Shelton, James
2 volumes
8750-6858
Datapro Research Corporation
1805 Underwood Blvd.
Delran, NJ 08075
(800) 257-9406
$525.00

Excellent
Loose-leaf information service; current awareness
service

INCLUSIONS: Indexes: alphabetic list of
titles; descriptor index; author index; glossary;
user's guide; inquiry service

DESCRIPTORS: Microcomputers; microcomputer
hardware; microcomputer software; computer
management

SUMMARY: This service provides
information on a variety of subjects concerning
microcomputers. It is divided into "perspective,"
reports on various subjects, and "guidelines,"
containing advice. It is organized into these
tabbed subject sections: 1) perspective --
hardware, software, communications, data
processing concepts, files, micro-mainframe
connection, data processing applications; 2)
perspective -- planning for a computer, cost
justification, system architecture vs. costs,
system selection and acquisition, acquiring
software, developing software, installation and
testing, personnel, operations, management and
administration, future systems and trends, listing
of vendors, and user ratings of products.

RELEVANCE: This contains both introductory
and technical information. It can be useful for
computer consultants, professionals, and users.
Volume 2 contains sections on the dos and don'ts
of hiring consultants and reviewing consultant
credentials.

ENCYCLOPEDIA OF COMPUTER SCIENCE AND
TECHNOLOGY
Supplement
1980
Continuation of the set
10,000 (approximately, in 15 volumes)
0-8247-2265-5
Marcel Dekker, Inc.
270 Madison Avenue
New York, NY 10016
(800) 228-1160
$115.00 per volume, $161.00 per set

Very good
Encyclopedia

INCLUSION: Bibliography

DESCRIPTORS: Computers; computer technology

IDENTIFIER: Supplement 1 is also called
volume 15 - in continuation of the monographic set
with the same title

SUMMARY: This contains scholarly,
individually written articles on specific and
generic aspects of computers and their uses, from
basics to state of the art. The scope is
topically diverse and also includes articles on
some significant individuals -- John von Neumann,
Samuel Alexander, and Norbert Wiener. There are
289 articles in 15 volumes. Sample articles
include aerospace corporation, American
Statistical Association, IBM Corporation,
electronic displays, macroprocessors, simula 67,
technology transfer, work measurement, very large
database systems, virtual machine monitors,
copyright and computers, curriculum committee on
computer science, machine translation, man-machine
communication, pattern recognition, process
control, production and inventory control,
reliability of computer systems. etc.

RELEVANCE: This can be of interest to
computer hardware specialists, programmers, system
analysts, engineers, operations researchers,
mathematicians and those who use computers in
solving problems or providing consulting services.

FAULKNER'S ELECTRONIC OFFICE (OFFICE
AUTOMATION)
1988
Martin, Randi
2 volumes
Vol. 1: 0-942155-16-5
Vol. 2: 0-942155-17-3
Faulkner Technical Reports, Inc.
6560 North Park Drive
Pennsauken, NJ 08109
(800) 843-0460
$915

Excellent
Loose-leaf information service; current awareness
service; buyer's guide

INCLUSION: Index

DESCRIPTORS: Office automation; computer
management; microcomputers; minicomputers;
telecommunications; telephone systems; local area
networks; workstations; copiers; dictation
equipment; facsimile; word processors; electronic
typewriters; integrated office systems; optical
character recognition; electronic publishing;
desktop publishing

IDENTIFIER: Formerly an Auerbach
publication

SUMMARY: This information service covers
all sorts of automated office equipment. It
contains the following content sections: 1)
management strategies - management reports; 2)
technologies - management reports; 3) applications
- management reports; 4) case studies - management
reports; 5) microcomputers - overview reports,
product reports; 6) executive and professional
workstations - product reports; 7) minicomputers -
overview reports, product reports; 8) office
copiers - overview reports, product reports; 9)
dictation equipment - overview reports; 10) word
processors - overview reports, product reports;
11) electronic typewriters - overview reports,
product reports; 12) integrated office systems -
product reports; 13) optical character recognition
- overview reports, product reports; 14) office

systems software - overview reports, product
reports; 15) electronic mail and message systems -
overview reports; 16) optical disk based systems -
overview reports; 17) electronic publishing -
overview reports, product reports; 18) desktop
publishing - overview reports, product reports;
19) facsimile equipment - overview reports,
product reports; 20) communications facilities -
overview reports; 21) local area networks -
overview reports; 22) PBX systems -overview
reports; 23) voice and data terminals - overview
reports, product reports; 24) office printers -
overview reports; and 25) plotters - overview
reports.

RELEVANCE: This source contains a wealth
of information on automated office equipment. It
includes discussion, lists of product information,
and prices.

                <<<<<<>>>>>>

HOW TO COMPUTERIZE YOUR SMALL BUSINESS
1980
First
Cohen, Jules   -   McKinney, Catherine
171
0-13403-857-6
Prentice-Hall Inc.
Rt. 9 West
Englewood Cliffs, NJ 07632
(201) 542-2015
Order: 200 Old Tappan Rd.
Old Tappan, NJ 07632
(201) 767-5059
$7.95

Very good
Guide

INCLUSIONS: Index by subject; charts;
forms; sample proposal letter

DESCRIPTORS: Computers; computer business
applications

SUMMARY: This work is about approaches
to using computers in the small business. It
describes how a compute works, and the advantages
and limitations of computer equipment. It
presents an eleven-step process essential to
making a decision to purchase your own computer or
buy computer time. It emphasizes the steps a
business executive needs to go through to make a
sound decision, including the following: defining
business objectives; deciding how the computer can
help attain these objectives; examining the
emotional component of the decision process;
assessing how the computer will affect the
structure of the business; documenting the type,
rate, and flow of information expected from the
computer; sending out requests for proposals from
vendors; evaluating proposals and selecting
equipment; negotiating the costs; justifying the
costs; making the decision; and testing the new
system. Case study includes flow charts, sample
report forms, and a sample request for proposal
letter.

RELEVANCE: Computers are and will continue
to be useful tools in creating marketable
products, in analyzing and reaching the market,
and in achieving financial records control. The
large and the small firm can profit from the
advantages computers offer. This work is designed
to help the small business make the best use of
the computer.

<<<<<<>>>>>

HOW TO PROFIT FROM YOUR PERSONAL COMPUTER
Professional, Business, and Home Applications
1978
First
Lewis, G
192
0-8845-761-X
Hayden Book Co., Inc.
10 Mulholland Drive
Hasbrouck Heights, NJ 07604
(800) 631-0856
$13.95

Very good
Book

INCLUSIONS: Index by subject; glossary

DESCRIPTORS: Computers; computer business
applications

SUMMARY: This discusses computer
hardware, software, anatomy and operations. It
does the following: 1) takes a case history
approach to problem-solving in common; 2) examines
applications for mortgage, mailing list,
accounting, and real estate; 3) focuses on use of
the BASIC language, and illustrates programs and
computations; 4) presents definition of terms,
programming techniques and structural design using
blueprints; 5) discusses the computer store,
computer characteristics and limitations, custom
and store-bought software, and the development of
personalized systems; and 6) speculates on the
future of personal computers.

RELEVANCE: This book is designed to
increase awareness of the growing market for
personal computer work and the outlook for the
future.

                    <<<<<<>>>>>>

THE INFORMATION SYSTEMS HANDBOOK
The Executive Guide to Planning and Utilizing
the System Most Effective for the Company's
Needs
1975
First
McFarlan, Warren - Nolan, Richard
887
0-87094-103-8
Dow Jones-Irwin, Inc.
1818 Ridge Road
Homewood, IL 60430
(800) 323-4560

Very good
Handbook

INCLUSION: Index by subject, cross-
referenced

DESCRIPTORS: Data processing; computers;
information systems

SUMMARY: This is intended to help
experienced data processing executives in choosing
the most appropriate data processing system for
their company. It was written by 43 business
authorities and reviewed by business persons and
academicians. Major parts, each with an
introduction, deal with the responsibilities of
the data processing executive as a member of the
top management team (2 parts), manpower
administration and development (1 part), methods
and tools for evaluating technical alternatives of
an organization (1 part), and issues relative to
development of new applications and managing
computer operations activity (2 parts). The 40
articles include the following: an overview;
corporate organization and information systems;
evaluating information systems; EDP internal
auditing; managing systems analysts; training and
recruiting programs; feasibility and replacement
study, computer options -- large centralized
computers versus minicomputers; project
management; business systems analysis; management
science model development; real-time system
design; databases; conversion; scheduling and cost
control of data center; individual privacy and the
corporate computer.

RELEVANCE: This is an authoritative
business approach written in a scholarly style.
However it is in need of an update.

                    <<<<<<>>>>>>

INTRODUCTION TO THE COMPUTER
The Tool of Business
1981 (The 1977 edition was abstracted).
Third
Fuori, William
720
0-13-480343-4

Prentice-Hall Inc.
Rt. 9 West
Old Tappen, NJ 07675
(201) 592-2000
Order: 200 Old Tappan Rd
Old Tappan, NJ 07675
(201) 767-5054
$17.95

Very good
Textbook

INCLUSIONS: Index, cross-referenced;
appendices (glossary of data processing terms;
selected bibliography; answers to selected
exercises); end of chapter exercises; figures;
illustrations

DESCRIPTORS: Computers; data processing;
computer programming; systems analysis

SUMMARY: This text covers what computers
are, do, and how they can be used in business. It
contains five units: 1) the development and impact
of computers on business; 2) components of data
processing, computers, and related equipment; 3)
software, program preparation and problem-solving;
4) business program languages - COBOL and BASIC;
and 5) systems analysis and design. It does the
following: 1) explains unit records concepts,
process and storage devices, input/output media
and devices, and computer number system; 2)
discusses flowchart and decision tables; 3) covers
systems considerations -- form design, card layout
and design, file structure, input code, system
flowchart, test, and documentation; 4) introduces
batch on-line processing, multiprogramming,
multiprocessing, and time-sharing; and 5) applies
computers to payroll, accounts payable, and
accounts receivable.

RELEVANCE: This could be used as a
teaching aid for an introductory computer course
or as a business person's self education tool.

MICROCOMPUTER MARKETPLACE
The Comprehensive Directory of the
Microcomputer Industry
1987
Fifth
Sutton-McElroy, Brenda
R. R. Bowker Company's Database Publishing Group
1115
0-8352-2267-5
R. R. Bowker Company
245 W. 17th Street
New York, NY 10011
(800) 521-8100
$110.00

Excellent
Directory

INCLUSIONS: Indexes; advertisements

DESCRIPTORS: Computer companies; computer
personnel; computer periodicals; computer
applications; software directory; consumer
software; computer wholesalers; computer
associations; computer services; computer systems;
computer distributors; computer mail-order houses;
computer manufacturers

SUMMARY: This is divided into these
sections: 1)software publishers/manufacturers; 2)
microcomputer systems index; 3) operating systems
index; 4) business/professional applications
index; 5) utility applications index; 6)
educational applications index; 7) consumer
applications index; 8) distributors, wholesalers
and mail order houses; 9) distributors,
wholesalers and mail order houses index; 10)
distributors' geographic index; 11) CD/ROM
manufacturers; 12) microcomputer
systems/manufacturers; 13) peripheral
manufacturers; 14) peripheral manufacturers'
index; 15) supplies manufacturers; 16) supplies
manufacturers index; 17) periodicals; 18)
associations; 19) CD/ROM special services by
fields of activity; 20) CD/ROM special services;
21) special services index; 22) special services;
23) calendar of meetings and exhibits; and 24)
names and numbers.

RELEVANCE: This reference can be useful to
consumers and computer companies personnel. It
can assist in marketing efforts.

                 <<<<<<>>>>>>

THE READER'S GUIDE TO MICROCOMPUTER BOOKS
1984
First
Nicita, Michal - Petrusha, Ronald
500
0-912331-003
Knowledge Industry Sciences
701 Westchester AVenue
White Plains, NY 10604
(800)248-5474
$29.95

Good
Guide

INCLUSIONS: Indexes by author, alphabet,
rating, rating within subject, title; appendix on
model inventories

DESCRIPTORS: Microcomputer books; software
books

SUMMARY: This is an evaluative guide to
books on microcomputers and software. It is
organized in the following chapters:
microcomputer introductions, microprocessors,
operating systems and hardware design, programming
(general, BASIC, FORTRAN, PASCAL, others),
software and applications (general, Visicalc, word
processing), and specific microcomputer systems
(Apple, IBM, TRS-80, Atari, Commodore,
Timex/Sinclair). It provides a half page to page
evaluation of over 400 books, rating each on a
scale from 10 (worst) to 100 (best).

RELEVANCE: This book could be helpful
either to prospective buyers of microcomputer
literature or to booksellers. The appendix on
model inventory is geared to computer stores.
While the concept of a microcomputer literary

guide is a good one, the book itself is limited in
scope and to pre-1983 books and products. An
obvious example of shortcoming is its coverage of
software applications, in which Visicalc is the
only spreadsheet covered and Wordstar the only
specific word processor covered.

<<<<<<>>>>>>

THE SOFTWARE CATALOG: MICROCOMPUTERS
Winter 1988
Biennial, with two updates per year
2614 in 2 volumes
0736-2730
Elsevier Science Publishing Co., Inc.
52 Vanderbilt Avenue
New York, NY 10017
(800) 223-2115
$170.00

Excellent
Software catalog; buyer's guide

INCLUSIONS: Indexes by systems, operating
system, programming language, microprocessor,
subject and applications, and keyword and program
name; subject category list; user's guide; subject
categories; glossary

DESCRIPTOR: Microcomputer software

SUMMARY: This contains over 25,000
microcomputer program descriptions. It is
produced from .MENU international software
database and is available on-line. It is arranged
alphabetically by vendor with the programs
arranged by ISPN (International Standard Program
Number). Each description is paragraph length.
The indexes volume contains: 1) systems index
based on named computer systems; 2) operating
system index to see programs for various operating
systems; 3) programming index for programs in a
given programming language; 4) microprocessor
index for programs that can run on a given
microprocessor; and 5) subject and application
index listing programs in one or more subject
categories with one-sentence annotations.

RELEVANCE: This is a thorough,
comprehensive, and well-indexed source.   Other
Elsevier catalogs in The Software Catalog set are:
Minicomputers, Business Software, Science and
Engineering, Health Professions, and Systems
Software: A Directory of Programs for the Computer
Professional.

<<<<<<>>>>>>

THE SOFTWARE ENCYCLOPEDIA 1986/1987
1986
Second
R. R. Bowker Company's Database Publishing Group
2050, 2 volumes
0-8352-2090-7
R. R. Bowker Company
245 W. 17th Street
New York, NY 10011
(800) 521-8100
$125.00

Excellent
Directory; index

INCLUSIONS: Indexes by title, publisher,
systems compatibility/applications; user's guide;
guides to systems; applications

DESCRIPTORS: Computer software; software
directory; computer applications; computer systems

SUMMARY: This lists over 27,000
microcomputer programs from 4000 publishers.
Volume one contains title index and publishers.
Volume two contains system
compatibility/applications and publishers.   The
3600 publishers in both volumes are identical.
Entries include: name, address, telephone, ISBN
and SAN.   Titles are arranged alphabetically.
Entries contain: title, sub-title, volume,
number, number of disks/cassettes, version,
series, author(s), grade level, release date,
compatible hardware, microprocessor types(s),
operating system(s), language(s), memory
requirement, other requirements, price, ISBN,

order number, publisher name, and descriptive
annotation. System compatibility/applications
lists programs alphabetically by application then
alphabetically by program title. The 850
applications are grouped in categories:
business/professional, consumer, educational, and
utility. The systems include: Apple II family
and compatibles, Macintosh/Lisa, IBM and
compatibles, Oasis, Radio Shack, Texas
Instruments, Timex-Sinclair, UCSDP, Unix, and
Xerox.

RELEVANCE: This is a well-organized index
of micro- computer software.

                    <<<<<<>>>>>

SOFTWARE REVIEWS
A Professional Guide from the Editors of
Infoworld
1985
First
Dunn, Robert
205
Infoworld
1060 Marsh Road, Suite C-200
Menlo Park, CA 94025
(617) 547-7423

Very good
Review

INCLUSIONS: Appendices: review updates;
user-supported software; review authors

DESCRIPTORS: Software reviews; computer
software; microcomputer programs

SUMMARY: This compendium of reviews on
popular microcomputer software includes eight
integrated packages; nineteen databases and file
managers; ten word processors; seven spreadsheets;
and six graphics programs. The reviews were
originally published in Infoworld magazine and are
written by a variety of individuals who use the
particular program reviewed. Each review has a

narrative and a standard "report card" which
covers performance, documentation, ease of use,
error handling, and support, rating each program
as excellent, good, fair, and poor. The reviews
and report cards are not standardized from the
point of view of the reviewer, and when it comes
to computer software, there are wide differences
of opinion. Infoworld reviews are considered to
be good and are influential.

RELEVANCE: This book is a consumer report
for popular programs and can help potential users
to evaluate software choices and look before
leaping to buy software.

CHAPTER 8

CONSULTANTS AND CONSULTING

This chapter contains:

- consulting entrepreneurship

- professional development resources

- consulting theory and methodology

- consulting specializations,
  especially management consulting,
  consultation in social work, real
  estate, and education.

- financial and legal issues

- directories of consulting agencies
  and individuals

THE APPLICATION OF SOCIAL SYSTEMS THINKING TO
ORGANIZATIONAL CONSULTING
1986
First
Czander, William
243
0-8191-5183-1
University Press of America, Inc.
4720 Boston Way
Lanham, MD 20706
(301) 459-3366
$24.75

Very good
Book

INCLUSIONS: Bibliography; case studies

DESCRIPTORS: Consulting; organization
development; organizational change; systems
approach

SUMMARY: The author aims to throw light
on the nature of the consulting field. He reviews
and clarifies methods of consultation:
organizational development, mental health,
consulcube, change, process, systems, technical,
feedback, organizing, and technique/management.
Chapters are devoted to each of six "critical
guidelines" for systems consultation (which is
author-defined): boundary maintenance and
regulation, task analysis, authority and power,
subsystem dependency and autonomy, inter-
organizational relations, and role definition.
The last two chapters deal with work stages of
consulting and the future of consulting.

RELEVANCE: The distinctions presented of
consulting methods, tasks, and future are helpful
orientation for new consultants.

                    <<<<<<>>>>>>

BECOME A TOP CONSULTANT
How the Experts Do It
1987

Tepper, Ron
264
0-471-85938-9
John Wiley & Sons
605 Third Avenue
New York, NY 10158
(212) 850-6418
$12.95

Very good
Guide

INCLUSIONS: Index; samples of contracts,
proposals, letters; news articles; diagrams; case
studies

DESCRIPTORS: Consultants; consulting

SUMMARY: This book demonstrates what
being a top consultant is like and entails through
examples of how issues are handled by ten
consultants in diverse fields. Their specialties
include accounting, data processing, headhunting,
engineering, law, sales, management, government,
and investment consulting. Shared characteristics
are a positive attitude, will to succeed, hard
work, sticking to it, discipline, self-esteem, and
abilities to take risk and to work with people.
The book also covers the market, starting part-
time, how to sell, fee setting, and problems and
opportunities. Five case studies of consulting
situations illustrate specifically how jobs were
successfully handled.

RELEVANCE: This is written in a down-to
earth, anecdotal style and the author encourages
anyone to try consulting as a profession.

                    <<<<<<>>>>>>

CONSULTANTS AND CONSULTING
A Corporate Guide
1981
First
McGonagle, John
210

Chilton Book Company
Chilton Way
Radnor, PA 19089
(800) 345-1214
Out of print

Excellent
Guide

INCLUSIONS: Index by subject; Appendix:
sample corporate policy; federal definitions;
Office of Management and Budget Circular A-120;
consultant retention form; sample letter
confirming retention of consultant services;
letter agreement; master consulting contract;
Department of Housing and Urban Development
professional services contracts; fund-raising
agreement; arbitration clauses; extracts from a
commercial arbitration guide for business people;
basic references (American Arbitration Regional
Offices; consultant organizations; publications;
the U.S. Government and consultants); case study

DESCRIPTORS: Consulting; corporate
consulting; consulting contracts; contracts;
consulting - legal issues; managing consultants;
consulting management; ethics

SUMMARY: This is written from the
perspective of a manager hiring and managing a
consultant. The author recommends caution and
care in contracting with "the consultant...a
nontraditional creature of the law." The author
lays out the process of entering into a consulting
relationship - definition of need and task, and
finding a consultant. Other chapters cover: 1)
management issues - budget, conflict of interest,
insurance and risk, confidentiality, recruiting
employees of corporation and consultant, and fees;
2) corporate policy; 3) legal issues; 4) the
letter agreement; 5) master consulting contract
and how to adapt it to your needs; and 6) when
things go wrong - disputes, mediation, agreement,
and arbitration. Topics included are: risk
management; insider trading; patents and
copyrights; recruiting; finder's fees;
compensation; termination; restrictive covenant;
foreign corrupt practices act; references; and
standards of ethics; among other topics.

RELEVANCE: This is a practical, useful
guide for corporate managers of consultants as
well as consultants doing business with
corporations and consultants in general. It is
particularly strong in the area of legal and
contractual considerations. Appendix samples and
forms are helpful.

<<<<<<>>>>>>

CONSULTANTS AND CONSULTING ORGANIZATIONS DIRECTORY
A Reference Guide to Concerns and Individuals
Engaged in Consultation for Business,
Industry, and Government
1988
Eighth
McLean, Janice
Volume 1 - 1118; Volume 2 - 2289
0-8103-2526-8
Gale Research Company
Book Tower
Detroit, MI 48226
(800) 223-4253
$380.00

Excellent
Directory

INCLUSIONS: Indexes by geography, subject,
industries served (thesaurus, index listings),
personal name, consulting firms

DESCRIPTORS: Consultants; consulting firms;
consulting organizations; consultant directories;
consulting services; consulting specialties

SUMMARY: This lists over 12,000
independent consultants and consulting firms in
the United States and Canada. It is divided into
two volumes. Volume one describes each firm. It
is arranged by subject: agriculture, forestry and
landscaping; architecture and interior design;
arts, entertainment and communications media;
business and finance; data processing,
telecommunications and information services;
education and personal development; engineering,

science, and technology; environment and land use;
health, medicine and safety; human resources;
management; manufacturing/industrial/transportation
operations; marketing and sales; and politics and
social issues. While entries vary, they generally
contain: firm name, address, phone, date founded,
principal executive(s), annual revenue, purpose
and activity, and sometimes branch offices, number
of staff, conferences, and recent publications.
Volume 2 contains indexes: geographic, subject -
thesaurus of fields of consulting activities and
index listings; industries served - thesaurus of
terms and index listings; personal name index; and
consulting firms index.

RELEVANCE   This is a well-organized,
indexed listing of consulting firms. It is the
most complete listing though is not comprehensive.
It's a valuable resource for persons inside and
outside of the consulting industry for a variety
of purposes.

                    <<<<<<>>>>>>

THE CONSULTANT'S EDGE
Using the Computer as a Marketing Tool
1985
First
Holtz, Herman
364
0-471-81190-4
John Wiley & Sons
605 Third Avenue
New York, NY 10158
(212) 850-6418
$24.95

Excellent
Guide

INCLUSIONS: Index; glossary; tables;
checklists; illustrations

DESCRIPTORS: Computers; consulting;
marketing

SUMMARY: This provides basic information
about the use of computers, hardware and software
selection for a consulting practice. It covers
the use of a computer as a marketing aid and
consulting tool. Consulting applications
discussed include word processing, database report
generation, and online databases. Specifics
include aid in writing proposals, doing
presentations and seminars, brochures, mailing
lists, newsletters, and management functions. The
book also includes information sources -- on-line
services, bibliography, vendor lists -- equipment
manufacturers, and software producers.

RELEVANCE: Computers are almost a modern-
day business necessity. This book is recommended
for consultants intending to computerize in
particular, and can also helpful for other
business and professional people. It is well
rounded in its chosen subject area. Each topic is
discussed in sufficient detail to provide the
computer newcomer with the rationale and knowledge
needed to proceed to the next step -- learning how
to operate computer software and hardware. This
and specific product recommendations are not found
in this book. We suggest taking some courses and
doing some actual work on a system before choosing
to buy one. Look before you leap, and remember,
although this book covers the basics, computer
technology changes.

<<<<<<>>>>>>

THE CONSULTANT'S KIT
Establishing and Operating Your Successful
Consulting Business
1981
Second Revised
Lant, Jeffrey
204
0-318-17146-5
JLA Publications
A Division of Jeffrey Lant Associates, Inc.
50 Follen Street, Suite 507
Cambridge, MA 02138
(617) 547-6372
$30.00

Excellent
Handbook

INCLUSIONS: Samples; bibliography; IRS
publications; Small Business Administration
publications; resources list - bibliographies,
listings, references; articles on consulting;
periodicals; associations listing; products and
services of Jeffrey Lant Associates; resource
directory

DESCRIPTORS: Consulting; consultants; small
business; contracts; networking; marketing; forms
of business; incorporating; proposals

SUMMARY: This is an enthusiastic
handbook on how to be a professional consultant.
It covers: defining a specialty; establishing a
contact network; marketing and promoting;
proposals, negotiations, and contracts; getting
started in business by establishing a name,
location, business supplies, and services; forms
of business, e.g. moving from a sole
proprietorship to a corporation; and bookkeeping
and accounting. Extensive samples are provided
of: potential client log sheet, contact and
marketing letters, project listing; service-line
synopsis, brochures, articles, press release,
letters of intent, contracts, by-laws, transfer of
shares of stock, and articles of incorporation.

RELEVANCE: This Kit sold over 21,000
copies as of 1981, presumably to prospective
consultants. It is an excellent guide to key
areas involved in establishing a consultant
practice. Further information on consulting by
the same author is contained in the Get Ahead
Series: The Unabashed Self-Promoter's Guide; Money
Talks: The Complete Guide to Creating a Profitable
Workshop or Seminar In Any Field; and Tricks of
the Trade: The Complete Guide to Succeeding.

<<<<<<>>>>>>

THE CONSULTANT'S LEGAL GUIDE
1980

First
Pyeatt, Nancy
146
0-930686-09-8
Bermont Books
P.O. Box 309
Glenelg, MD 21737
(301) 531-3560
$19.00

Very good
Guide

INCLUSIONS: Index; appendix of samples

DESCRIPTORS: Law; wills; contracts; forms of
business; lawyer; legal issues

SUMMARY: This legal guide covers basic
information and pointers and gives advice in the
areas of choosing a lawyer, choosing a form of
business, contracts, avoiding unauthorized
practice of law and malpractice, staying out of
court, and estate planning. The author advises
consultants to have a lawyer and discusses: how to
and not to work with one, the importance of having
a good accountant, keeping good records, the
importance of good faith on both sides of a
contract, the importance of not giving legal
advice if you're not an attorney, how to avoid
malpractice insurance by avoiding mistakes and not
promising more than you can deliver, carrying out
what you say you will, staying out of court, and
hiring a lawyer to do estate planning and wills.
The appendix includes samples of a partnership
agreement, partnership dissolution agreement,
letter of intent (consultant to client), letter of
intent (client to consultant), simple wills,
complex will with trusts, and stock-retirement
agreement (for corporations).

RELEVANCE: This is a simple to read,
direct and personable introduction to basic legal
issues. It is geared to consultants. Don't
expect a more sophisticated, detailed legal
treatise.

CONSULTATION
A Handbook for Individual and Organization
Development
1985
Second
Blake, Robert - Mouton, Jane
596
Scientific Methods, Inc.
0-201-10165-3
Addison-Wesley Publishing Company
1 Jacob Way
Reading, MA 01867
(800) 447-2226

Excellent
Handbook; textbook

INCLUSIONS: Indexes by author, subject;
chapter notes; chapter summaries; tables; case
examples

DESCRIPTORS: Consultation; consultant;
intervention

SUMMARY: This is a comprehensive,
systematic overview of the consulting field.
Approaches to consultation are analyzed through
the use of the "consulcube" containing 100 cells
organized into three dimensions: the client, kinds
of interventions, and focal issues. The client
breaks down into the categories of individual,
group, inter-group, organization, and larger
social system. The kinds of interventions breaks
down into theory principles, prescriptive,
confrontation, catalytic, and acceptant. The
focal issues breaks down into power/authority,
morale/cohesion, norms/standards, and
goals/objectives. The book is organized in this
framework and the authors describe, give case
examples, and discuss relevant theory and
literature for each consultation category. The
last two chapters are devoted to the theory,
technique and entrepreneurial aspects of
consulting. The authors, a psychologist and
social psychologist, present an applied
behavioral science perspective to the consulting
field.

RELEVANCE: This book is best suited to the
professional consultant, manager and expert in
organization development, individual and group
psychology. It is an excellent resource aid for
assessing and diagnosing the issues, relevant
background, most effective approaches, and
particular consultation problems in relation to
the whole field.

<<<<<<>>>>>>

CONSULTATION IN HIGHER EDUCATION
A Handbook for Practitioners and Clients
1979
Pilon, Daniel   -   Bergquist, William
Gary Quehl, Jean Brodsky
First
159
Council for the Advancement of Small Colleges
1 Dupont Circle
Washington, DC 20036
(202) 466-7230

Good
Guide

INCLUSIONS: Appendices: glossary; CASC
National Consulting Network; bibliography; sample
forms and consulting agreement

DESCRIPTORS: Consultation; higher education
consultation

SUMMARY: This book describes the
principles and process of consultation. It
presents from the points of view of the consultant
and the consultee. Topics include the roles and
functions of consultants, stages of consulting --
entry, contracting, information collection,
analysis and feedback, recontracting,
intervention, evaluation, and exit. It also
covers how to choose and evaluate consultants,
training programs and consultants, and ethical
considerations.

RELEVANCE: Although the title of this work
leads the reader to assume a focus on consultation
in higher education, there is no discussion of the
higher education setting and its attributes. This
book is no different than other books on how to do
consulting and choose consultants.

                    <<<<<<>>>>>>

CONSULTATION IN SOCIAL WORK
1977
First
Kadushin, Alfred
236
0-231-04124-1
Columbia University Press
526 West 113th Street
New York, NY 10025
(212) 316-7100
Order: Columbia University Press
136 South Broadway
Irvington on Hudson, NY 10533
(914) 591-9111
$24.00

Excellent
Book

INCLUSIONS: Index by subject; name of
individual; bibliography

DESCRIPTORS: Social work; consultation;
consultant

SUMMARY: This book provides an overview
of social work consultation, which began after
World War II. Social work consultation is defined
and differentiated from supervision, in-service
training, therapy, and collaboration. Discussion
of situations of social work as consultants and
consultees is followed by discussion of the
contribution of consultants and the structures in
which work is done. Five types of consulting are
delineated: client-centered, consultee centered,
program-centered administrative, and consultee-
centered administrative.

RELEVANCE: This book is an invaluable
guide to the subject of social work consulting,
and could be of interest to consultants in related
disciplines as well.

<<<<<<>>>>>>

THE CONSULTING PROCESS IN ACTION
1978
First
Lippitt, Gordon   -   Lippitt, Ronald
130
0-88390-141-2
University Associates, Inc.
8517 Production Avenue
San Diego, CA 92121
(619) 578-5900
$15.50

Very good
Primer

INCLUSIONS: Index; annotated bibliography;
appendices on suggestions for continued learning
and consulting organizations and resources

DESCRIPTORS: Consulting; consultant;
evaluation; ethics

SUMMARY: Readers are oriented to the
field of process consulting. The book emphasizes
process in the discussion of consulting phases;
consultant roles; relation of intervention
strategies, decisions and actions; and action
research and evaluation in the consulting process.
The phases in consulting are identified as: 1)
contact and entry; 2) formulating a contract and
establishing relationship; 3) problem
identification and diagnostic analysis; 4) goal
setting and planning; 5) taking action and cycling
feedback; and 6) contract completion: continuity,
support, and termination. It examines multiple
roles of the consultant from less to more
"directive" -- objective observer/reflector,
process counselor, fact finder, alternative
identifier and linker, joint problem solver,

trainer educator, informational expert, and
advocate. It examines consultant ethical codes,
dilemmas and guidelines, competencies, and
development. It discusses data collection and
evaluative methods.

RELEVANCE: This is a good introduction or
review of the consulting process written by
experienced, recognized consultants.

<<<<<<>>>>>

CONSULTING WITH HUMAN SERVICE SYSTEMS
1978
First
Goodstein, Leonard
172
Addison-Wesley Publishing Company
1 Jacob Way
Reading, MA 01867
(800) 447-2226
Out of print

Good
Book; textbook

INCLUSIONS: Index; bibliography

DESCRIPTORS: Consulting; process
consultation; mental health consultation;
organizational consultation; nonprofit
consultation; government consultation; clinical
psychology; diagnosis

IDENTIFIER: Addison-Wesley Series in
Clinical and Professional Psychology

SUMMARY: This book deals with
applications of clinical psychology to
organizational consultation. The first four
chapters are an overview of concepts and
approaches to organizational consultation. The
last four chapters present the process of
consultation from beginning to end. The chapters
cover: 1) specialized organizational issues in
working in public and nonprofit sectors; 2)

understanding the consultation process - mental
health consultation and consulcube (see abstract
on Consultation by Blake and Mouton); 3)
dimensions of process consultation; 4) approaches
to understanding organizations - the consulcube;
open-systems approach; Tavistock Institute and
psychoanalytic approaches; process consultation
approaches; differentiation-integration model; and
Weisbord's Six-Box model; 5) entry issues in
organizational consultation; 6) diagnosis in
consultation; 7) possible interventions; and 8)
later stages in consultation - evaluating and
terminating the relationship.

RELEVANCE: This could be used in academic
courses and by professional consultants. It tends
to be academic and theoretically oriented.

                    <<<<<<>>>>>>

DIRECTORY OF MANAGEMENT CONSULTANTS
1985 (The 1982 edition was abstracted.)
Fourth
Kennedy, James
Periodic
280
0-916654-37-0
Consultants News
Templeton Road
Fitzwilliams, NH 03447
(603) 585-2200
$58.50

Very good
Directory

INCLUSIONS: Appendix - bibliography;
indexes: basis of services classification;
services offered; basis of industries
classification; industries served; geographical
index; key principals index

DESCRIPTORS: Consultants; management
consulting; consultant directory

IDENTIFIER: Consultants News provides a
newsletter of that name for the consulting
profession.

SUMMARY: This lists and describes the
services of selected management consulting firms,
including solo practitioners. Firms tend to be
larger and accredited members of certain
professional associations. They are listed
alphabetically, with the following fields: company
name, address, telephone number, description,
contact, affiliates/branches, areas served, date
founded, staff, revenues, professional
affiliations, services, industries, and sometimes,
other key principals. The main categories of
basis of services are: general management,
manufacturing, personnel, marketing, finance and
accounting, procurement, research and development,
packaging, administration, international
operations, and specialized services. Each is
further subdivided into more specialized areas.
Industries classifications are: agriculture,
forestry and fishing; mining; construction;
manufacturing; transportation, communications,
electric gas and sanitary services; wholesale
trade; retail; finance, insurance and real estate;
services; public administration; and
nonclassifiable establishments. These are further
subdivided into specific industries. Both
services and industries are divided into
generalist and specialist categories of firms.

RELEVANCE: This can be helpful to
prospective personnel and customers of the large
management consulting firms in particular.

                     <<<<<<>>>>>>

HANDBOOK OF MANAGEMENT CONSULTING SERVICES
How You Can Effectively Deliver Top-Notch
Client Services in Today's Demanding,
Professional Consulting Practice
1986
First
Barcus, Sam - Wilkinson, Joseph
439

0-07-003658-6
McGraw Hill Book Company
1221 Avenue of the Americas
New York, NY 10020
(800) 262-4729

Very good
Guide; compendium

INCLUSIONS: Index; bibliography; appendix;
chapter notes; illustrations; tables; checklists;
forms; case examples

DESCRIPTORS: Management consulting;
consulting

SUMMARY: This is a book of eighteen
contributions to the basics of consulting
organized in four parts: 1) introduction to the
management consulting profession; 2) analytical
elements of the consulting process; 3)
administrative elements of the consulting process;
and 4) management of the practice. In addition,
are eighteen "checklists and work plans in key
practice areas," examples being: business
planning, evaluating and selecting a computer
system, software package evaluation; production
planning and control review, marketing audit,
financial management review, and merger and
acquisition analysis.

RELEVANCE: This is one of a number of how-
to be a consultant books. This one focuses on
management consulting and has specific work plans
and checklists.

                    <<<<<<>>>>>

HANDBOOK OF MENTAL HEALTH CONSULTATION
1986
Mannino, Fortune - Trickett, Edison - Shore,
Milton - Kidder, Margaret - Levin, Gloria
828
U.S. Department of Health and Human Services
National Institute of Mental Health
5600 Fishers Lane

Rockville, MD 20857
Superintendent of Documents
U.S. Government Printing Office
Washington, DC 20402
(202) 275-2051
$24.00

Excellent
Handbook; compendium

INCLUSIONS: Index by author; annotated
bibliography; chapter bibliographies

DESCRIPTORS: Mental health consultation;
consultation-mental health

SUMMARY: This compendium contains
contributions on the "theory, practice, training,
and research" of mental health consultation. It
is guided by these two principles: 1) it utilizes
the NIMH definition of mental health consultation:
"a triadic interaction among consultant,
consultee, and client involving indirect service
and concerning some aspects of mental health;" and
2) it gives preference to empirical material. The
volume has six main parts: 1) historical
perspective; 2) major models and orientations; 3)
mental health consultants -- psychiatrist,
nursing, social work, psychology; 4) organization
and process; 5) research and special areas; and 6)
annotated reference guide to the consultation
literature 1978-84.

RELEVANCE: This is one of the few works on
consulting to focus on a specific field, while
most of the consulting literature is generalist.
One chapter discusses organization development as
an approach to mental health consultation.
However, for what is called a "comprehensive"
handbook, is the absence of other than "mental
health disciplines," such as psychological and
medical anthropology and medical sociology.
Nevertheless, this is a significant work in the
mental health consulting specialty.

HOW TO BE YOUR OWN MANAGEMENT CONSULTANT
1978
First
Albert, Kenneth
207
0-07000-751-9
McGraw-Hill Book Company
1221 Avenue of the Americas
New York, NY 10020
(800) 262-4729
$14.95

Very good
Book

INCLUSION: Index, cross-referenced

DESCRIPTORS: Consulting; management
consulting; consultants

SUMMARY: This is a discussion of the
management consultant approach to problem solving
and advises under what circumstances to hire an
external consultant versus do it internally.
Management consulting is broken into four steps:
1) defining the problem; 2) gathering necessary
information; 3) analyzing and drawing conclusions;
and 4) making recommendations and effecting
implementation. It discusses the management
consulting approach to various areas - growth
planning, acquisitions, new products and ventures,
marketing strategy, sales forecasting,
organizational planning, executive search and
compensation, facilities planning, internal
organization of management consulting firms, how
they do business, and financial remuneration
systems. It discusses options for problem solving
internally: full-time consultant, special
assignment, task force, collaboration. It uses
actual consulting case studies to illustrate the
approach. An external consultant is recommended
when specialized expertise is needed, for a
politically sensitive issue, when impartiality is
necessary, time is critical, anonymity must be
kept, or when the prestige of an outside firm is
helpful.

RELEVANCE: This work can be useful to
aspiring and active consultants on the consulting
process and consulting firms and to business
owners and managers regarding internal as well as
external management consulting. It does not go
into the variation among consultants and
consulting firms.

<<<<<<>>>>>>

HOW TO MAKE IT BIG AS A CONSULTANT
1985
First
Cohen, William
209
AMACOM
135 West 50th Street
New York, NY 10020
(212) 586-8100
$17.95

Excellent
Guide

INCLUSIONS: Index by subject; appendices;
bibliography; sample brochure; company
questionnaire and audit; extensive consulting
proposal; charts; diagrams; forms; samples;
checklists; presentations

DESCRIPTORS: Consulting; proposal writing;
pricing; consulting contracts; consulting - legal
issues; consulting business; ethics; marketing;
proposal writing; contracts; pricing

SUMMARY: The author begins by defining
"the incredible business of consulting:" --
incredible largely because of its many advantages
in choice of work style, conditions, location,
associates, clients, and pay. He then covers: 1)
how to get clients through direct and indirect
marketing methods and public sector marketing; 2)
the initial interview; 3) how to write a proposal
or letter proposal and how to convert it into a
contract; 4) pricing strategies and billing; 5)
contracts; 6) planning and scheduling; 7) solving
client problems; 8) ethics; 9) professional

presentations; and 10) operating your business -
legal, record-keeping, and financial aspects. The
author has been a consultant, Professor of
Marketing, and Director of the Small Business
Institute at California State University, written
many books, served on boards of directors, and
received awards. He shares his experience and
that of others for whom he has provided a forum in
classes.

RELEVANCE: This Guide covers the basics of
consulting in a readable form. It is recommended
for potential and practicing consultants.

<<<<<<>>>>>>

MANAGEMENT CONSULTING
A Guide to the Profession
1986 (The 1983 edition was abstracted.)
Seventh
Kubr, Milan
611
02-2-101165-8
International Labor Office-Washington Branch
1750 New York Avenue N.W., Suite 330
Washington, DC 20006
(202) 376-2137
$25.65

Very good
Guide

INCLUSIONS: Bibliographies (6 - one for
each part); appendices (8 - associations of
management consultants in selected countries;
professional codes; terms of business; case
history of consulting in product management; case
history of process consulting; person-to-person
communication in consulting; consultant report
writing; and training films); illustrations

DESCRIPTORS: Consulting; consultants;
management consulting

SUMMARY: This Guide on management
consulting discusses the definition and nature of
management consulting; initiation and execution of
assignments; consultation in various areas of
management; organization of consulting services;
and career and training aspects of consulting. It
covers the following: the nature, purpose, and
profession of management consulting; management
survey and financial appraisal; fact finding and
analysis; presentation of proposal and
implementation; consultation in general;
marketing; production; personnel; small enterprise
management; and information systems and data
processing. It discusses types of consulting
organizations and their internal organization;
systems and services; and consulting as a career -
personal characteristics of consultants,
recruitment, selection, and career development;
and training of consultants, new and continuing.

RELEVANCE: This aims to aid and improve the
profession of management consulting. It is
written for new and experienced, private and
public, internal and external consulting
practitioners, management teachers, trainers and
researchers, and managers who use consultants.
This work takes a comprehensive, informative
approach. Aspiring consultants may find its most
important use is its identification of who is and
who is not likely to meet market specifications
regarding age, education, and experience for being
hired by a consultant firm.

<<<<<<>>>>>>

MANAGING THE CONSULTANT
A Corporate Guide
1981
First
McGonagle, John
210
0-8019-7016-4
Chilton Book Company
Chilton Way
Radnor, PA 19089
(215) 964-4729

$23.50

Excellent
Guide

INCLUSIONS: Index by subject; appendix;
samples; letters of agreement; forms; contracts;
case study; sources; references

DESCRIPTORS: Consultants; management;
contracts; legal issues; consulting fees;
corporate policy

SUMMARY: This book is about corporate
policy and management of consultants. It
emphasizes legal issues and contracts, providing
sample contracts and analysis of clauses. It
defines consulting and discusses how to find and
evaluate consultants. It covers management issues
-- budgeting and fees, conflict of interest,
insurance, and confidentiality. Separate chapters
are devoted to details of corporate policy, legal
issues, letter agreement, master consulting
contract, and disputes, remedies, and arbitration.

RELEVANCE: This book is written from a
corporate perspective for management. It focuses
on corporate policy, contractual and legal issues.
Thus, it raises many specific aspects related to
consulting which are usually not covered.
It also provides how-to information with sample
forms, letters, and contracts.

<<<<<<>>>>>>

OTHER PEOPLE'S BUSINESS
A Primer on Management Consultants
1977
First
Klein, Howard
202
0-88405-377-6
Mason/Charter Publishers, Inc.
641 Lexington Avenue
New York, NY 10022

Very good
Book

INCLUSIONS: Index; bibliography

DESCRIPTORS: Consulting; consultants;
management consulting; consulting firms;
management consultant professional associations

SUMMARY: Klein undrapes the world of
management consultancy, deals with definitions of
who is a consultant, negative stereotypes, and the
nature of consultant work. He discusses the
historical roots of consulting, types and styles
of consultants, distinguishing generalists and
specialists, consultants specializing in
personnel, marketing, financial, production,
logistics, and executive recruiters. He presents
a behind-the-doors picture of major firms -
McKinsey and Company; Booz, Allen and Hamilton;
Cresap, McCormick and Paget; and describes Peter
Drucker and John Diebold. He urges consultants to
"come out of the closet," organize, and share
knowledge to create major changes. This book
reveals the powerful place of the consultancy in
the running of America, concentrating on the elite
of the consulting industry.

RELEVANCE: This book combines research
(firsthand interviews) and knowledge of the
business and consultant world with a journalist's
writing skills. It advises hirers of consultants
as to the nature of consultants, their
differences, and how to find one to suit the job.
It examines different styles of how top
consultants get and do business and describes
elite management consultant professional
associations.

                    <<<<<<>>>>>>

PRIVATE CONSULTING
How to Turn Experience into Employment Dollars
1982
First
Johnson, Barbara

147
Prentice-Hall, Inc.
Rt. 9 West
Englewood Cliffs, NJ 07632
(201) 767-5049
Order: 200 Old Tappan Road
Old Tappan, NJ 07676
(201) 767-5054
$7.95

Good
Guide

INCLUSIONS: Index; personality test;
samples

DESCRIPTORS: Consulting; consultant
characteristics; contracts; pricing; marketing

SUMMARY: The author defines a private
consultant as a "self-employed individual, who,
for a fee, gives experienced and skilled advice or
service in a field of special knowledge or
training." The chapters cover: 1) the strengths
needed - talent, temperament, personality,
education, experience, ethics, finances; 2) nature
of the work - types of service, job examples,
specialist, generalist, clients, competitors,
advantages and pitfalls; 3) marketing - market,
resume, target clients, contacts; and ongoing
marketing program; 4) doing the job - contracts,
fees, billing, collection; 5) successful client
relations - methods of maintaining communication
and relating; 6) how to run a profitable business
- overhead, filing system, insurance, tax record-
keeping, expansion, forms of business and
incorporation; 7) future of consulting

RELEVANCE: This is a short overview of the
consulting business for the beginner.

<<<<<<>>>>>>

REAL ESTATE CONSULTANT'S HANDBOOK
1978
First

Rams, Edwin
367
0-87969-720-5
Reston Publishing Company, Inc.
A Prentice-Hall Co.
Order: P.O. Box 500
Englewood Cliffs, NJ 07632
(201) 592-2427
Out of print

Very good
Handbook

INCLUSIONS: Index by subject; tables; index
to functional methods of analysis; formulas

DESCRIPTORS: Real estate; consulting

SUMMARY: This source is specifically
oriented to real estate consulting. It assumes
the reader has a basic knowledge of real estate.
It is organized in a specific question-answer
format in three basic parts: basic concepts and
principles, urban area neighborhood studies, and
property dynamics and analysis. The text is
accompanied by many mathematical formulae and
tables of figures.

RELEVANCE: While there are many books on
real estate investing, this one specifically
includes a consultant point of reference. It is
not intended for the beginner. Besides the real
estate consultant it can be useful for the
investment advisor, other real estate industry
groups, and clients who may seek consultants. The
book is dated by the use of 1970s statistics (and
probably in other ways). Nevertheless it gives an
idea of the field and factors to be taken into
account.

<<<<<<>>>>>>

THE SHADOW GOVERNMENT
The Government's Multi-Billion Dollar Giveaway
of Its Decision-Making Powers to Private Government Consultants, 'Experts,' and Think Tanks

1976
First
Guttman, Daniel   -   Willner, Barry
354
0-39449-244-7
Pantheon Books
201 East 50th Street
New York, NY 10022
(212) 751-2600
$10.00

Very good
Book

INCLUSIONS: Index; introduction by Ralph
Nader; case studies

DESCRIPTORS: Consultants; consulting;
management consultants; consulting firms;
government contracts; influence spending

SUMMARY: The authors reveal the role and
power of the big private management consulting
firms and other organizational structures and
powerful individuals in the use, abuse, and
shaping of government policy. They trace the
interlaced development of firms, projects, key
individuals, and policies of government. They
show how large sums of money are misdirected and
wasted in the contracting process through private
control of public spending. They expose how
designs to promote efficiency in government and
industry feed corporate growth. They discuss the
background of influence spending in various
government programs and projects. Ideas are
backed by actual case illustrations of companies
and project involvements with government. They
discuss types of contractors for government
business which get most of the money granted -
industrial corporations (e.g. Westinghouse); the
"Big Eight" accounting firms; and Rand
Corporation, Battelle Memorial Institute,
Brookings Institute, Federal Contract Research
Centers, and Stanford Research Institute.

RELEVANCE: This is recommended for
consultants interested in how inside track and
personal influence methods of marketing by

powerful individuals and large firms and abuse of
consulting cast a critical light on the consulting
field.

<<<<<<>>>>>>

TIME IS MONEY
A Guide to Selling Your Professional Services
1980
First
Creedy, Richard
170
0-52593-114-7
E. P. Dutton
2 Park Avenue
New York, NY 10016
(212) 725-1818
$11.95

Very good
Book

INCLUSIONS: Index by subject; checklists;
samples

DESCRIPTORS: Pricing; service business;
professional services

SUMMARY: This book advises on how to
select a specific business idea or service based
on your practical experience, package it, market
it, and make it pay. It examines management of
time and money aspects of making your business
profitable. It discusses how to manage your
business by objectives and specific plans, choose
a location, find low-cost equipment, establish
financial records, deal with the IRS, and seek
accountant help. It discusses how to place a
price on your service that will cover overhead,
taxes, and profit; how to forecast your income,
discuss your price with clients, bill and collect.
It coaches in morale building and coping
techniques. It emphasizes identifying and
focusing on a particular market.

RELEVANCE: The book encourages
professionals interested in going into business
with how-to-do-it advice and practical pointers as
well as counsels in how to deal with worry,
disappointment and criticism while building
confidence and enthusiasm.

                    <<<<<<>>>>>>

WHO'S WHO IN CONSULTING
A Reference Guide to Professional Personnel
Engaged in Consultation for Business, Industry
and Government
1973; First Supplement 1981; Second 1983
Irregular
Second
Wasserman, Paul - McLean, Janice
1011; First Supplement 198; Second 450
Gale Research Company
Book Tower
Detroit, MI 48226
(313) 961-2242
$188.00

Very good
Directory

INCLUSIONS: General abbreviations; key to
subject field numbers; subject and location index

DESCRIPTORS: Consultants; biography

IDENTIFIER: Sub-subtitle of Supplement: A
Periodic Supplement to the Second Edition of Who's
Who in Consulting

SUMMARY: The first part is a
biographical listing of over 7500 consultants in
the United States and Canada. Arrangement is
alphabetical by last name. Information is based
on questionnaire response, including information
in these fields: name, business address and
telephone number, birth date and birth place;
education, career, present posts, memberships,
principle consulting specialties, publications,
and fields of activity. One-hundred forty-six

consulting specialties are identified for fields
of activity. Examples are: audio-visual aids,
automation, business writing, career guidance,
community relations, counseling, educational,
executive development, human relations, library,
management, personnel, planning, small business
development, etc. The second part is a cumulative
index. It contains: 1) cross references by
subjects and "see also" references; and 2) a
subject index of consultants by location.

RELEVANCE: This is the only directory of
individual consultants. It is a useful source for
purposes of searching for an appropriate
consultant, job hunting contacts, and marketing to
consultants. It is not comprehensive and a new
edition is called for. The supplement service was
to have three issues, each having approximately
1000 consultants and published in parts in order
to be timely. The cumulative index is helpful.
The publisher intends this resource to be used
along with its Consultants and Consulting
Organizations Directory (see abstract).

CHAPTER 9

CONTRACTS, COPYRIGHTS, PATENTS, AND TRADEMARKS

Materials in this chapter are related to materials in the chapter on law, such as the law of contracts and copyright law.

This chapter contains:

- how-to plan and use contracts, patents, copyrights

- selection and use of trademarks

- negotiation and writing of contracts.

CONTRACT AS PROMISE
A Theory of Contractual Obligation
1982 (The 1981 edition was abstracted.)
Second
Fried, Charles
176
0-674-16925-5
Harvard University Press
79 Garden Street
Cambridge, MA 02138
(617) 495-2600
$16.50

Very good
Legal guide; primer; textbook

INCLUSIONS: Index; examples (hypothetical
cases); notes (comments, legal cases); reference
citations

DESCRIPTORS: Agreements; contract law;
contracts

SUMMARY: This describes the basic legal
and socio-moral concepts, principles and doctrines
underlying contract law. It shows how parties to
a contract: 1) invoke each other's trust and good
faith; 2) promise to meet specific conditions; 3)
perceive offers, counter-offers, future assurances
and each other's rights; 4) propose, accept,
and/or reject offers made; 5) sometimes make
mistakes which nullify specific rights; and 6) are
subject to obligations of fair sharing,
compensation, and/or restitution when a breach of
contract situation occurs.

RELEVANCE: This is a good guide for
someone interested in understanding the basic
concepts and theory of contract law.

                    <<<<<<>>>>>>

CONTRACT REMEDIES IN A NUTSHELL
1981
First
Friedman, Jane

323
0-314-60373-5
West Publishing Company
P.O. Box 64526
St. Paul, MN 55102-1611
(800) 328-9352
$9.95

Very good
Book; legal guide; primer

INCLUSIONS: Indexes by subject, UCC;
advertisements; bibliographies

DESCRIPTORS: Indexes by subject, UCC;
contract law; breach of contract; legal remedies;
sales contracts; bibliographies; illustrative
examples (contracting problems and remedies)

SUMMARY: This book covers compensatory,
legal remedies available to those who have been
aggrieved, damaged from ill-conceived contracts or
breach of contract situations. Key sections
treat: compensations available when critical
expectations are not met; remedies bearing upon
the sale and exchange/nonexchange of goods; and
remedies for situations involving contracting
mistakes, unconscionable contract provisions,
and/or invalid, falsely-conceived provisions.

RELEVANCE: Emphasis is on legal remedies
for grievances. A glossary would help.

                    <<<<<<>>>>>>

CONTRACTS
1983 (The 1977 edition was abstracted.)
Third
first edition was in 1970.
Calamari, John   -   Perillo, Joseph
397
0-314-34698-8
West Publishing Company
P.O. Box 64526
St. Paul, MN 55102-1611
(800) 328-9352
$14.95

Excellent
Textbook; primer

INCLUSIONS: Indexes by cases, subjects,
UCC citations; bibliography (publisher's list: law
school publications); case studies

DESCRIPTORS: Contracts; contract law; law

SUMMARY: This treats and interprets
basic legal doctrines, concepts, and principles
bearing upon contracts made between two or more
parties. It covers: 1) the formation, performance,
enforcement and discharge (alteration,
cancellation, termination) of contracts; 2) common
types of contracts, e.g. bilateral/joint,
formal/informal, implied, unilateral,
enforceable/unenforceable, illegal,
nonperformable, voidable; 3) contracts involving
multiple obligors/obligees; 4) contracts involving
misconduct, mistake, and/or loss of sales or
goods; 5) breach of contract situations and
related legal remedies and damages; 6) the Statute
of Frauds; and 7) other topics.

RELEVANCE: This contains a good discussion
of types of contracts, is generally well-done and
makes a good reference book.

<<<<<<>>>>>>

CONTRACTS IN A NUTSHELL
1984 (The 1975 edition was abstracted.)
Second
Schaber, Gordon - Rohwer, Claude
425
0-314-78065-3
West Publishing Company
P.O. Box 64526
50 West Kellogg Blvd.
St. Paul, MN 55102-1611
$8.95

Very good
Legal guide; book; primer

INCLUSIONS: Index by subject;
bibliographies; illustrative examples; reference
citations (UCC)

DESCRIPTORS: Contract law; contracts

SUMMARY: This is an introductory
discussion of contract law treating the formation,
performance and enforcement of contracts. It
covers: the basic requirements of a valid contract
(offer, acceptance, consideration); factors and
conditions influencing the legality and
enforceability of a given contract; common types
of contracts (bilateral, unilateral, implied);
commonly encountered problems; breach of contract
situations and related compensatory remedies;
situations involving excusable obligatory
conditions; and other topics.

RELEVANCE: This is a good introduction to
contract law.

                    <<<<<<>>>>>>

CONTRACTS IN PLAIN ENGLISH
1976
First
Wincor, Richard
143
0-07070-966-1
McGraw-Hill Book Company
1221 Avenue of the Americas
New York, NY 10020
(800) 262-4729

Very good
Book; legal guide

INCLUSIONS: Index by subject; appendices
(3); glossary; evaluative comments; formulas
(language); illustrative examples (international
TV and foreign sales); samples

DESCRIPTORS: Contract language; contracts;
contract writing

SUMMARY: This is a definitive discussion
of key factors influencing the meaning and
interpretation of English language contracts. It
is designed to: 1) help persons involved in
proposing, negotiating and/or drafting contractual
agreements to accurately and clearly convey their
respective viewpoints, positions, intents, etc.;
and 2) prevent unnecessary disputes triggered from
poorly-worded contracts. It covers the basics of
contract law and the contract negotiation process;
and evaluates the practical utility of commonly
used terms and phrases.

RELEVANCE: The emphasis is on contract
language. It can be helpful in the writing and
interpretation of contracts.

<<<<<<>>>>>>

FORMS OF BUSINESS AGREEMENTS AND RESOLUTIONS
1984   (The 1979 edition was abstracted.)
Prentice-Hall Editorial Staff
3 Volumes
Prentice-Hall, Inc.
Rt. 9 West
Englewood Cliffs, NJ 07632
(201) 592-2000
Order: Old Tappan Rd.
Old Tappan, NJ 07676
(201) 767-5054

Good
Legal forms guide; serial; loose-leaf

INCLUSIONS: Indexes by subject, annual
cumulative, cross-referenced; checklists;
newsletters; notes; reference citations;
regulatory information (UCC and IRS codes);
samples (contracts and clauses)

DESCRIPTORS: Business agreements; contracts;
corporation law; forms of agreement

IDENTIFIERS: The 1979 edition was written
and published by the Institute for Business
Planning. Volume 3, Commercial Transactions,

includes Commercial Transactions Ideas, a monthly newsletter.

SUMMARY: This is a three-volume set of materials covering the following topics and transactions: corporate finance, organization, operation and liquidation; joint ventures; sole proprietorships; franchises; business transfers; settlements and compromises; copyrights and patents; nonprofit organizations; UCC regulations; and other topics.

RELEVANCE: This is useful for drafting a broad range of agreements.

<<<<<<>>>>>

THE GUIDE TO BUSINESS CONTRACTS
1980
Second
Howell, John
160
0-89648-056-9
Citizens Law Library
P.O. Box 1745
Leesburg, VA 22075
$5.95

Very good
Book; legal guide

INCLUSIONS: Glossary; checklists; forms (44); guidelines (contract preparation/writing); legal and regulatory information (UCC summary); samples (contracts and clauses)

DESCRIPTORS: Business contracts; commercial law; forms of agreement

SUMMARY: This book reviews the basic purposes, parts (10 articles), and emphases of the Uniform Commercial Code statutes. It illustrates and describes common types of contracts: acknowledgments, affidavits, assignments, baitments, deeds, employment contracts, guaranties, settlements, independent contractor

and sales agreements, and forms/instruments used
for arbitration, compromise, gift-giving,
indemnity, power of attorney, release,
satisfaction, and other arrangements.

RELEVANCE: This is a popular work designed
to help one negotiate and prepare commercial
contracts.

<<<<<<>>>>>>

LAW AND BUSINESS OF LICENSING
Licensing in the 1980s
1983 (The 1981 edition was abstracted.)
Annual updating via supplemental pages
Second
Goldscheider, Robert   -   Arnold, Tom
1300 (approximately)
0-87632-136-8
Clark Bordman Company Ltd.
435 Hudson Street
New York, NY 10014
(718) 929-7500
$195.00

Very good
Legal guide; serial; loose-leaf

INCLUSIONS: Index by subject; checklists;
forecast; guidelines (evaluative, misc.);
illustrations (charts, graphs); legal and
regulatory information (misc.); market information
(U.S. and foreign); notes; reference citations
(legal); samples (agreements)

DESCRIPTORS: Licenses; licensing business;
licensing law; opportunities; technology transfer

SUMMARY: This contains 20 chapters and
60 articles and reports. It covers: 1) the
domestic, foreign and international
licensing/technology-transfer industry; 2)
licensing of private, university, and government-
owned technology, inventions, copyrights, patents,
trademarks, trade secrets, know-how, computer
software, etc.; 3) the role of consultants; and 4)
many other topics.

RELEVANCE: This can serve as a useful
source for the creator and licenser of property
and for the consultant and user of consultants.

CHAPTER 10

CORPORATIONS, BIG BUSINESS AND INDUSTRY

This chapter contains:

- corporations

- business responsibility and social
  conscience

- executive and middle management

- corporate publications in print

CORPORATE AMERICA
A Historical Bibliography
1984
First
Schlachter, Gail
341
0-87436-3624
ABC-Clio Information Services
2040 Alameda Padre Serra, Box 4397
Santa Barbara, CA 93103
(800) 422-2546
$32.50

Excellent
Annotated bibliography

INCLUSIONS: Indexes by author, subject;
abbreviations

DESCRIPTORS: Corporations; corporate
bibliography

SUMMARY: This work contains 1368
abstracts of articles published between 1973 and
1982. It is organized into these chapter
subjects: multinationals, conglomerates, and big
business; banking, investments, and service
industries; transportation; communications;
energy; food and fiber; mining/ manufacturing and
merchandising; social effects and environmental
impacts; and government regulation and
intervention. The abstracts were selected from a
history database covering 2000 journals
internationally.

RELEVANCE: This is a well-organized source
useful for researching the periodic literature on
corporations.

                      <<<<<<>>>>>>

THE CORPORATE FINANCE BLUEBOOK
1988 (The 1983 edition was abstracted.)
Annual
Fifth
Patruno, Cathy

1850
National Register Publishing Company
3004 Glenview Rd.
Wilmette, IL 60091
(800) 323-6772
$350.00

Very good
Biographical directory

INCLUSION: Index of subsidiaries

DESCRIPTORS: Corporate officers; biography
of corporate officers

SUMMARY: This is the Who's Who of the
top 2000 non-financial corporations. It provides
information on: officers/managers, names, titles,
area of responsibility, and telephone numbers.
The finance functions covered include cash
management, corporate development, employee
benefits, general counsel, international finance,
investor relations, leasing, pension
administration, real estate, risk management, and
stock specialist. The Bluebook also includes
"outside firms currently providing financial
services.

RELEVANCE: This is where to find who is in
charge of specific financial functions in non-
financial corporations.

                    <<<<<<>>>>>>

THE CORPORATE FINANCE SOURCEBOOK 1988
1988
Annual
Peterson, Linda
1140
0-87217-927-3
National Register Publishing Company
3004 Glenview Rd.
Wilmette, IL 60091
(800) 323-4601
$212.00

Excellent
Loose-leaf directory

INCLUSIONS: Index of firms; advertisers

DESCRIPTORS: Corporate finance sources;
finance sources

SUMMARY: This source provides detailed
information on firms that are sources of corporate
financing. It is divided into these sections:
U.S. venture capital lenders, major private
lenders, commercial banks, foreign banks,
investment banks, foreign investment banks,
business intermediaries, pension managers, master
trusts, cash managers, business insurance brokers,
corporate real estate services, securities
analysts, and CPA accounting and audit firms.
There is also a chapter listing 10,304 corporate
public offerings in the last three years arranged
alphabetically by company name.

RELEVANCE: If you are a corporate owner,
finance officer, or consultant responsible for
seeking financing, this is where to turn for
sources.

                       <<<<<<>>>>>>

CORPORATE PUBLICATIONS IN PRINT
The Corporate Intelligence Source Book
1980
First
Norback, Craig
271
0-07047-140-1
McGraw-Hill Book Company
1221 Avenue of the Americas
New York, NY 10020
(800) 262-4729
$25.00

Very good
Bibliography

INCLUSION: Index

DESCRIPTORS: Corporate publications;
corporations

SUMMARY: This lists publications from top
U.S. corporations. It derives information from
mailings and direct contact. It categorizes
publications under corporation, employee, and
product. It supplies brief annotations on some
citations. Costs are given where relevant. It
contains 270 corporations, including Allied
Chemical, Anheuser-Busch, Atlantic Richfield,
Babcock and Wilcox, Boise Cascade, Burroughs, and
General Dynamics. Types of publications listed
are booklets, manuals, magazines, newsletters,
catalogs, brochures, kits, calendars, annual and
quarterly reports, financial reports, corporate
profile, proxy statements, in-house news, employee
news, career opportunities, product information,
sales promotion material, and factual reports.

RELEVANCE: This collects corporate
publications under one cover. Corporate
publications are a significant if neglected
resource. Annual reports provide information on
marketing and sales, for example. Users can find
out product information and identify competition.

                    <<<<<<>>>>>>

DESKBOOK FOR SETTING UP A CLOSELY-HELD
CORPORATION
1986 (The 1980 edition was abstracted.)
Second
Irregular
Hess, Robert
549
0-87624-114-3
Institute for Business Planning, Inc.
Eleanor Bridgida, Customer Services
200 Old Tappan Road
Old Tappan, NJ 07675
(201) 542-2015
$69.95

Excellent
Handbook

INCLUSIONS: Index; checklists; Directory
(state offices); financial information; guidelines
(incorporation, legal, tax planning, other);
sample forms (incorporation, IRS, DOL, other)

DESCRIPTORS: Incorporation; new
corporations; small business management; tax
planning

SUMMARY: This covers tax aspects,
consequences and benefits of establishing and
running a corporation. It shows how to: 1)
determine if and when incorporation is advisable;
2) gain maximum tax savings; and 3) draft all
necessary legal documents (articles of
incorporation, bylaws, minutes, pension and
profit-sharing plans, etc.).

RELEVANCE: This is a complete, step-by-
step legal guide for those who are considering
incorporating a business with a small number of
owners, including Subchapter "S" professional
corporations.

<<<<<<>>>>>>

DIRECTORY OF CORPORATE AFFILIATIONS 1988
Who Owns Whom, The Family Tree of Every Major
Corporation in America
1987
Annual, bimonthly supplements
Rotman, Inge
1300
National Register Publishing Company
3004 Glenview Rd.
Wilmette, IL 60091
(800) 323-4601
$349.00

Excellent
Directory

INCLUSIONS: Indexes by corporation, S.I.C.,
geographical; key to stock market abbreviations

DESCRIPTORS: Corporations; corporate
affiliations

SUMMARY: This lists U.S. corporations,
their affiliates, divisions, and subsidiaries.
The "alpha index cross references over 40,000
divisions, subsidiaries, affiliates, etc. with
their parent company." Section 2 lists "over 4000
parent companies in alphabetical order." Entries
include address, telephone number, ticker symbol,
stock exchange(s), transfer agents, approximate
sales, number of employees, type of business, top
officers, etc. It also contains new listings;
breakdown of companies by state; mergers,
acquisitions and name changes, 1987; mergers,
acquisitions and name changes, 1976-86; and other
products and services.

RELEVANCE: This is an excellent resource
on U.S. corporations. It can be useful for
consultants, business people, and librarians. A
companion, annual volume is International
Directory of Corporate Affiliations.

                    <<<<<<>>>>>>

HOW TO FORM YOUR OWN PROFESSIONAL CORPORATION
1980
Second
Nicholas, Ted
138
0-91386-440-6
Enterprise Publishing, Inc.
725 Market Street
Wilmington, DE 19801

Very good
Guide; handbook

INCLUSIONS: Advertisements (publications,
training materials); appendices (forms, list of
state statutes); bibliography (books,
periodicals); checklists; directory (state
offices); financial information (costs, income,
state filing fees); geographic listings; glossary;
guidelines (evaluation, procedural); index
(subject); legal information; mail order form;
samples (incorporation forms); tables

DESCRIPTORS: Corporation law; corporations;
incorporation; professional corporations

SUMMARY: This is a practical, corporate
planning and evaluation guide for licensed,
certified professionals (accountants, doctors,
engineers, etc.). It explores the pros and cons
of forming a professional corporation, and the key
question: "should I/we form a professional
corporation?" It treats essential planning and
implementation factors and tasks, including
articles of incorporation and bylaws.

RELEVANCE: This can be useful to
consultants who are considering forming a
professional corporation.

                       <<<<<<>>>>>

MILLION DOLLAR DIRECTORY "SERIES" 1987
1986
5 volumes
Annual
0-918257-24-7
Dun's Marketing Services
Dun and Bradstreet, Inc..
3 Century Drive
Parsippany, NJ 07054
(800) 526-0651
$1195.00

Excellent
Directory

INCLUSIONS: Index by companies
alphabetically; cross-reference volumes by
geography and by industry classification;
numerical index of SIC codes; alphabetical index
of SIC codes; list of symbols and abbreviations;
user's guide

DESCRIPTORS: Corporations

IDENTIFIER: The sixth volume is Top 50,000
Companies, with net worth over $1,850,000.

SUMMARY: This source lists 160,000 U.S.
firms with net worth of over $500,000. The set of
five volumes includes three alphabetical volumes
(A-F, G-O, P-Z) in which companies are listed with
the following information: business name, state
of incorporation, subsidiaries, DUNS number,
import, export, address, telephone number, telex
or TWX, annual sales, number of employees, bank,
divisions, SIC code, officers names, titles and
functions. The sixth volume on the Top 50,000
Companies also provides information on:
"accounting firm and legal counsel, company ticker
symbol on stock exchange and stock exchange
abbreviations, and names of directors." The
Cross-Reference volumes contain: 1) an index to
companies in alphabetical order with page
references to listings in the Series and in Dun's
Top 50,000 Companies, America's Corporate
Families, Dun's Industrial Guide, Dun's Business
Rankings, and Million Dollar Directory Logo
Advertisers; 2) an index arranged alphabetically
by states and towns with address and SIC codes;
and 3) an index by SIC codes arranged numerically.

RELEVANCE: The Directory is useful in
marketing, purchasing, public relations,
advertising, sales, etc. While not comprehensive,
it is extensive.

                <<<<<<>>>>>>

RATING AMERICA'S CORPORATE CONSCIENCE
A Provocative Guide to the Companies Behind
the Products
1987
First
Lydenberg, Steven - Marlin, Alice -   Stub, Sean
Council on Economic Priorities Staff
499
0-201-15886-8
Addison-Wesley Publishing Company, Inc.
1 Jacob Way
Reading, MA 01867
(800) 447-2226
Write for information on cost

Excellent
Guide

INCLUSIONS: Index; chapter notes; product
charts; appendices: methodology and sources of
information; references; resources and related
publications; company products and services

DESCRIPTORS: Corporate ratings; corporate
conscience; corporations; social investing

SUMMARY: This source rates the social
conscience of 130 U.S. corporations. Chapter one
contains a discussion of the concepts, approaches,
and historical background, with company examples,
applied to rating corporate conscience. Chapter
two focuses on "the social investing movement,"
its history and impact. Chapter three discusses
the issues upon which the product charts and
performance ratings are based -- charitable
contributions, participation of women and
minorities in top leadership positions, disclosure
of social information, involvement in South
Africa, conventional and nuclear weapons
contracting. Chapter four describes how to use
the book. Chapters five through eight present
discussion, information on particular companies,
and product charts on these areas: food, drugs,
transportation, and household products.

RELEVANCE: This source can aid the
consumer in making purchase and investment
decisions. It can also be useful to corporate
personnel and scholars in evaluating and
developing business ethics.

                    <<<<<<>>>>>>

REFERENCE BOOK OF CORPORATE MANAGEMENTS 1988
America's Corporate Leaders
1988
Dun's Marketing Services staff
6800, 4 volumes
0-918257-64-6
Dun's Marketing Services, Inc.
Three Century Drive

Parsippany, NJ 07054
(800) 526-0651
$695.00, $495.00 libraries

Excellent
Biographical Directory

INCLUSIONS: Indexes: volume 4; numerical
S.I.C. codes; alphabetical S.I.C. codes; user's
guide; abbreviations

DESCRIPTORS: Corporate personnel

SUMMARY: This reference provides
biographical information on officers and directors
of corporations. Volumes one through three list
companies alphabetically. Biographical
information is given for key officers, including
date of birth, college(s) attended, degree(s)
earned, marital status, military service, current
and previous positions. Other officers and
directors are listed but without further
information. The fourth, cross-reference volume
contains companies geographically, by industry
classification (S.I.C.), principal officers and
directors listed alphabetically, and roster of
companies.

RELEVANCE: This can be useful for anyone
seeking information on who to contact in a
corporation, and on particular individuals.

                    <<<<<<>>>>>>

STANDARD & POOR'S REGISTER OF CORPORATIONS,
DIRECTORS AND EXECUTIVES
1988
Annual
61st
3 volumes
0361-3623
Standard & Poor's Corporation
25 Broadway
New York, NY 10004
(212) 208-8702
Excellent
Directory

INCLUSION: Indexes

DESCRIPTORS: Corporations; subsidiaries;
divisions; executives; directors

SUMMARY: Volume one contains corporate
listings arranged alphabetically. Entries have
business name; address; phone; names, titles, and
roles of officers, directors and others; name of
accounting firm; stock exchange(s);
products/services; SIC codes; annual sales; number
of employees; divisions; subsidiaries; and other
affiliations of executives. Volume two contains
individual listings of information on directors
and executives arranged alphabetically. Volume 3
contains 7 indexes: 1) SIC codes in major groups,
arranged alphabetically and numerically; 2) four-
digit SIC codes arranged numerically; 3)
geographic index arranged by states and major
cities with business names arranged
alphabetically; 4) corporate family with cross-
referencing of subsidiaries, divisions and
affiliates arranged alphabetically and with an
Ultimate Parent Index arranged alphabetically; 5)
obituaries arranged alphabetically; 6) new
individual additions arranged alphabetically; and
7) new company additions.

RELEVANCE: These volumes can be used to
find corporate and executive information for a
variety of purposes, including job hunting and
marketing.

                    <<<<<<>>>>>>

WORLD'S LARGEST INDUSTRIAL ENTERPRISES 1962-1983
1985
Second
Dunning, John   -   Pearce, Robert
192
St. Martin's Press, Inc.
175 Fifth Avenue
New York, NY 10010
(800) 221-7945
$65.00

Good
Information sourcebook

INCLUSIONS: Appendices (2); tables

DESCRIPTORS: Corporations; industrial
enterprises; corporate statistics

SUMMARY: This draws on annual data from
Fortune to present data on the world's largest
corporations. Two presentations are the
"rationalised sample" of the largest firms in any
year, and the "equalised sample that consists of
an equal number of the largest enterprises for
each of the years (1962, 1967, 1972, 1982), drawn
from those in the rationalised sample." It is
divided into these parts: introduction; the data
for 1983; changes in the sample composition 1962-
1982; employment of the world's largest
enterprises; concentration, size, and
diversification profitability and growth 1962-82;
international operations; and research and
development expenditures of the world's largest
enterprises.

RELEVANCE: This might be useful to
corporations, libraries, or individuals for a
variety of purposes.

CHAPTER 11

EDUCATION, HIGHER AND VOCATIONAL

This chapter contains:

- higher education institutions
- higher education options/alternatives
- higher education support services
- vocational training
- vocational counseling and guidance
- management education programs

AMERICAN COMMUNITY, TECHNICAL, AND JUNIOR
COLLEGES
A Guide
1984
Ninth
Parnell, Dale   -   Peltason, Jack
956
0-02-904210-0
American Council on Education
One Dupont Circle
Washington, DC 20036
(202) 939-9300
Macmillan Publishing Company
866 Third Avenue
New York, NY 10022
(800) 257-5755
$85.00

Very good
Catalog; directory

DESCRIPTORS: Community colleges; two-year
colleges; junior colleges

SUMMARY: This source lists over 1500
public and private two-year colleges, also known
as community colleges. Thirteen percent of them
have "technical" and some have "junior" in their
title. Arrangement is alphabetical within states
arranged alphabetically. Entries include name,
address, and telephone number of school, general
description, history, governance, administration,
facilities, accreditation, academic calendar,
admission requirements, curricula, faculty, degree
requirements and conferrals, special training
facilities and media resources, enrollment,
student activities, fees, student aid, and school
finances.

RELEVANCE: More two-year schools and more
students indicates the increased importance of
these institutions. This source can be useful for
the educational counseling consultant and
prospective student.

BEAR'S GUIDE TO NON-TRADITIONAL COLLEGE
DEGREES
1985
Second
Bear, John
272
0-89815-149-X
Ten Speed Press
P.O. Box 7123
Berkeley, CA 94707
(415) 845-8414
$9.95

Excellent
Guide; catalog

INCLUSIONS: Index by subjects; schools;
"hello/goodbye"; glossary; bibliography; state
agencies for higher education; accrediting
agencies and associations; correspondence courses

DESCRIPTORS: Non-traditional college
degrees; higher education

SUMMARY: This lists all kinds of options
offering "non-traditional degrees":
correspondence, bachelor's, master's and
doctorate degrees, schools requiring a year or
less on campus, weekend colleges, high school
diplomas and associate degrees, law schools,
medical schools, bible schools, degree mills, and
honorary doctorates. It also discusses degrees,
titles, accreditation, how to evaluate a school,
scholarships and financial aid, equivalency exams,
credit for life experience, the Credit Bank, and
other topics.

RELEVANCE: This is an excellent overview
of the subject. It's very informative about
alternative as well as established educational
markets and what degrees, accreditation,
traditional and non-traditional education really
means and their value. The author has generously
contributed fearless commentary on topics and
schools.

BRICKER'S INTERNATIONAL DIRECTORY
University Executive Programs
1987 (The 1983 edition was abstracted.)
First
Pedolsky, Andrea
416
0-8103-0965-3
Gale Research Company
Book Tower
Detroit, MI 48226
(800) 223-4253
$195.00

Good
Catalog; directory

INCLUSIONS: Indexes by subject, name

DESCRIPTORS: Continuing education; seminars;
workshops; independent study programs; training
programs; audio-visual

SUMMARY: This lists 30,000 educational
offerings in business. It is organized in four
parts: 1) continuing education programs of
colleges and universities, arranged
geographically; 2) associations and organizations
offerings arranged alphabetically with a
geographic index; 3) independent study programs
arranged alphabetically with a geographic index;
and 4) sources of continuing education learning
materials, including audiocassettes, multimedia
kits, and programmed learning material. The
subject index covers these sixteen subjects:
accounting, banking and finance, bookkeeping,
communications, computer and data processing,
insurance, law, management, manufacturing,
marketing, personnel, quality control, real
estate, sales management, secretarial, and small
business management.

RELEVANCE: The need for continuing
education among the employed and self-employed is
well-recognized. This source is organized to
provide the information. However, continuing
education is an, ever-changing market, with
frequent course changes. For updated information,
check the schools/organizations involved.

CHRONICLE CAREER INDEX
For 1986-87 School Year
1986
Annual
Revised
Downes, Paul
160
0-912578-97-1
Chronicle Guidance Publications, Inc.
P.O. Box 1190
Moravia, NY 13118-1190
(315) 497-0330
$13.75

Excellent
Sourcebook

INCLUSIONS: Index

DESCRIPTORS: Career; vocational counseling;
vocational guidance

SUMMARY: This lists 816 sources of
publications and audio-visual materials for
vocational and educational guidance. It is
arranged alphabetically by source and contains
contact and ordering information and annotations.
Entries are cross-referenced by occupational,
educational and professional subjects. The
occupational information is compatible with the
Chronicle Occupational Library and Chronicle
Occupational Briefs. Entries also contain D.O.T.
(Dictionary of Occupational Titles) and G.O.E.
(Guide for Occupational Exploration) numbers. The
educational and professional information is
compatible with the Chronicle Educators'
Professional Guide.

RELEVANCE: This seems to be a useful
reference for vocational and educational
professionals in locating occupation-specific
materials for research, counseling, and teaching
purposes.

CHRONICLE VOCATIONAL SCHOOL MANUAL
For 1986-87 School Year
1986
Annual
Revised
Downes, Paul
330
0-912578-93-9
Chronicle Guidance Publications, Inc.
P.O. Box 1190
Moravia, NY 13118
(315) 497-0330
$15.50

Excellent
Manual; information source

INCLUSIONS: Appendices on additional
information and list of accreding associations

DESCRIPTORS: Vocational schools; vocational
training

SUMMARY: This lists 638 vocational
education programs in the United States, Guam and
Puerto Rico. Part one covers programs of study
and schools offering them. It is arranged
alphabetically by State and program name inside of
alphabetically arranged subject headings.
Examples of subjects are accounting, advertising
management, banking, electronics assembly, human
services, information systems, international
business, journalism, marketing, office
technology, production management, and technical
writing. In addition, vocational school charts
lists 4083 schools by state on: general
information, admissions, costs, enrollment,
government job training and financial aid, and
student services. Asterisked items have
additional information in an appendix.

RELEVANCE: This is useful for students
investigating information on accredited programs
which lead to an occupation in a variety of
subject areas. It can also be useful to
vocational counselors advising students or
educators seeking a job.

COLLEGE AND UNIVERSITY ADMINISTRATORS DIRECTORY
A Guide to Officers, Deans, Managers,
and Other Administrative Personnel in American
Colleges and Universities
1980
First
704
0-8103-1133-X
Gale Research Company
Book Tower
Detroit, MI 48226
(800) 223-4253
$160.00

Very good
Directory

DESCRIPTORS: College personnel; university
personnel

SUMMARY: This Directory provides access
to college and university administrative personnel
by name and function. The three major sections
are: college and university administrators
directory; administrators classified by function;
and geographical list of colleges and universities
in the United States and its possessions. It
enables the user to identify address and title of
a known administrator, identify administrators by
function, and identify the administrative
composition of a school. It also reports
available vacancies in an office. It bases
information on HEGIS surveys, U.S. Department of
Health, Education and Welfare's National Center
for Education Statistics (NCES), and
questionnaires from 3,173 institutions.

RELEVANCE: This is an easy-to-use source
of information for anyone seeking to identify
higher education personnel. It allows persons
interested in seeking administrative positions to
identify vacancies and individuals to query.
Check relevant schools for changes in
administrative personnel.

THE COLLEGE BLUE BOOK VOL. IV
Occupational Education
1987
21st
1057
0-02-695910-0
Macmillan Publishing Company
866 Third Avenue
New York, NY 10022
(800) 257-5755

Excellent
Catalog; directory

INCLUSIONS: Indexes by subject,
institution; abbreviations; accrediting
associations

DESCRIPTORS: Vocational education

IDENTIFIER: This is one of a five-volume
set of the College Blue Book. Occupational
Education was formerly a separate title and is now
in its eighth cumulation.

SUMMARY: This directory contains
information on over 9000 business, trade, and
technical schools. The volume is arranged
alphabetically by school within city within state.
Each state has an introduction with contact
information for state vocational education offices
and state legal regulations. Schools are
classified as: allied medical, art, barber,
business, correspondence, flight and ground,
nursing, trade and technical, or a two-year
college. Entries include this classification
along with name, address, and telephone number of
school, tuition, financial aid, and curricula.
The second half of the volume contains curricula
and programs of instruction arranged
alphabetically by school within state within
subject area.

RELEVANCE: Occupational education is an
important option for the public school dropout,
and individual in need of occupational training in
order to enter the work force. Almost all jobs
available today require specific education and

training. This source can be helpful to the
vocational counseling consultant and prospective
student.

<<<<<<>>>>>>

DIRECTORY OF MANAGEMENT EDUCATION PROGRAMS
1978
Second
Voss, Fred
744
0-8144-5525-5
AMACOM
135 West 50th Street
New York, NY 10020
(212) 586-8100
$25.00

Very good
Catalog; directory

INCLUSIONS: Indexes by subject,
contributor; program questionnaire

DESCRIPTORS: Management education programs;
management

SUMMARY: This provides information on
management education programs. The programs are
coded and can be found under a number of headings.
It includes programs which are non-credit,
recurring, and programs of interest and
availability to a broad range of audiences.
Subjects are classified into the following major
areas: finance, general administrative services,
human resources/personnel, insurance,
international operations, legal, management
systems, manufacturing operations,
marketing/sales, personal development, purchasing,
research and development,
transportation/distribution, programs outside the
U.S. and Canada, and programs directed to
field sales management, market research/sales
industries or groups. The section on
marketing/sales includes management of the
marketing/sales function, advertising/promotion,

forecasting, pricing, and principles of
marketing/sales. Entries include program
description; curriculum and teaching methods;
fees, awards and evaluation; instructional staff
profile; recent participant profile; additional
comments; and contact.

RELEVANCE: This is a resource to turn to for
information on management education programs. It
combines breadth and depth of coverage. However,
it is old.

                    <<<<<<>>>>>>

EDUCATION INDEX
A Cumulative Author Subject Index to a
Selected List of Educational Periodicals and
Yearbooks
1987, 1988
Annual, monthly cumulations
Hewitt, Marylouise
Variable
0013-1385
H. W. Wilson Company
950 University Avenue
Bronx, NY 10452
(800) 367-6770

Excellent
Index

INCLUSIONS: Abbreviations; abbreviations of
periodicals indexed; periodicals indexed

DESCRIPTORS: Education; education index;
education periodicals

SUMMARY: This source is an index to
educational materials, mostly periodicals, but
also yearbooks and monographs. It is
alphabetically organized by subject and author
entries. "See also" references are used.
"Subject areas indexed include administration and
supervision; pre-school, elementary, secondary,
higher and adult education; teacher education;
vocational education; counseling and personnel

service; teaching methods and curriculum. Subject
fields included are arts, audio-visual education,
comparative and international education, computers
in education, English language arts, health and
physical education, languages and linguistics,
library and information science, multi-
cultural/ethnic education, psychology and mental
health, religious education, science and
mathematics, social studies, special education and
rehabilitation, and educational research relative
to areas and fields indexed."

RELEVANCE: This is the resource to use for
researching and locating educational sources.

                    <<<<<<>>>>>>

EDUCATIONAL MEDIA AND TECHNOLOGY YEARBOOK
1983 (The 1981 edition was abstracted.)
Annual
Brown, James   -   Brown, Shirley
586
8755-2094
Libraries Unlimited
P.O. Box 263
Littleton, CO 80160
(303) 770-1220
$47.50

Excellent
Resources guide; yearbook

INCLUSIONS: Indexes (general and
classified); bibliographies (annotated, reference
materials, periodicals, media); classified
listings; directories (associations, grant
sources, organizations, publishers)

DESCRIPTORS: Educational media;
communications media; instructional materials;
library materials; training materials

IDENTIFIER: Co-sponsor: Association for
Educational Communications and Technology

SUMMARY: This resource has articles,
descriptive, market, survey, and state of the art
reports and other inclusions. It serves as a
guide to reference publications, periodicals,
communications media, organizations, and current
trends and developments useful to educational
media professionals and consumers. It covers all
types and forms of media: audio-visual, computer,
electronic print, photo, microform, radio,
television, and telecommunications.

RELEVANCE: This is a current awareness
tool for persons who select, evaluate, purchase
and/or produce software and hardware products for
educational, training and communication purposes.

                  <<<<<<>>>>>>

EVERYWOMAN'S GUIDE TO COLLEGES AND
UNIVERSITIES
An Educational Project of the Feminist Press
1982
First
Howe, Florence   - Howard, Suzanne   - Strauss,
Mary
512
0-9-35312-09-9
The Feminist Press
Box 334
Old Westbury, NY 11568
(800) 242-7737
$4.95

Excellent
Catalog; directory

INCLUSIONS: Index by school; sample entry

DESCRIPTORS: Colleges and universities;
women's studies programs; higher education;
educational institutions

SUMMARY: Florence Howe discusses the
development of feminist consciousness out of the
women's movement in the realm of higher education,
including Title IX and women's studies programs.
Everywoman's Guide to Colleges and Universities

contains "nearly 600 entries on American women's
colleges, public and private four-year colleges,
doctorate-granting universities, and public and
private two-year colleges." It includes
information which may have been left out of other
college catalogs and stars are used to indicate
important items and ratings. Data by sex on
enrollment, faculty, and degrees awarded are
included and used as indicators of sex equity
factors. Items receiving scores in stars include:
women in student leadership, women in top
administration, curriculum and sports. Other
factors -- minority women, childcare, special
services and programs, women returning women
students, special features, and institutional
description are also included. No school is
judged perfect, and different schools rate better
on different factors.

RELEVANCE: This catalog can mean the
difference between a healthy, happy, higher
educational experience for a woman and one fraught
with difficulties, struggle, and failure. At
$4.95 this is an incredible bargain! The Guide is
sponsored by ten women's, educational,
professional, faculty, and student organizations.

                    <<<<<<>>>>>>

GUIDE TO EXTERNAL DEGREE PROGRAMS IN THE
UNITED STATES
1983
Second
Sullivan, Eugene
120
American Council on Education
One Dupont Circle
Washington, DC 20036
(202) 939-9300
Macmillan Publishing Co.
866 Third Avenue
New York, NY 10022
(800) 257-5755
$16.95

Very good
Catalog; directory

INCLUSIONS: Indexes by institutions, areas
of study; appendices: joint statement on transfer
and award of academic credit; awarding credit for
extra-institutional learning; supplemental
references

DESCRIPTORS: External degree programs;
higher education; colleges and universities

SUMMARY: This lists external degree
programs alphabetically by state, which are
accredited by the Council on Postsecondary
Education, American Council on Education, and
American Association of Collegiate Registrars and
Admissions Officers. These programs are intended
for working and part-time students and they award
credit for prior college education. Entries
"include the institution's accreditation,
acceptance of out-of-state students and tuition
differential, minimum campus time, instructional
methods provided for off campus learning, and
student support services."

RELEVANCE: This does not include all the
options for alternative higher education, and the
number of schools meeting the criteria for
inclusion number just over 100. Some states and
areas of study are entirely excluded.

<<<<<<>>>>>>

HIGHER EDUCATION EXCHANGE
1980
First
Mitchell, Janet
766
Book Order Department
Peterson's Guides
P.O. Box 2123
Princeton, NJ 08540
(609) 924-5338
$60.00

Excellent
Directory; almanac, marketplace guide

INCLUSIONS: Indexes by institutions,
marketplace (firms and consultants, combined),
educational consultants

DESCRIPTORS: Higher education; educational
institutions; college and university personnel;
educational information sources

SUMMARY: This lists educational
institutions, professional groups, businesses,
consultants, governmental agencies, accrediting
agencies, foundations and other organizations
serving the post-secondary educational community
in the U.S. and Canada. It is designed
specifically to foster communication between the
business and educational sectors of the
marketplace. It also lists related federal and
private funding sources; federal, state and
foundation funding statistics; faculty and
administrator salary statistics; enrollment and
graduate statistics; congressional committees;
alternative education opportunities; college and
university radio stations; mailing list vendors;
university presses; other media and publishing
groups; academic consortia; accredited proprietary
institutions; about 500 education periodicals; and
over 100 educational guides/directories. It lists
over 200,000 names and facts.

RELEVANCE: This is an outstanding
reference book and excellent marketing tool for
consultants and firms providing relevant
services/products. Consultant specialization
categories are: education, testing and
counseling; educational writing/editing;
facilities planning and engineering; library and
publishing; management; public relations,
marketing, fund raising; and research.
Institution entries note the basic contracting
method used in obtaining goods and services from
vendors. Summary counts are given for about 70
product/service categories of the number of
firms/consultants who supply related
goods and services. This source accepts and lists
annotated product/service descriptions from
consultants and firms.

NICEM INDEX TO NON-PRINT SPECIAL EDUCATION
MATERIALS: MULTIMEDIA
LEARNER VOLUME; PROFESSIONAL VOLUME
1978
Varies: 2nd - 7th
Biennial with supplements
NICEM
Varies
0-89320-022-0
National Information Center for Educational
Media (NICEM)
University of Southern California
Los Angeles, CA 90007
(213) 746-6681
$24 Learner; $8 Professional

Very good
Directory; catalog

INCLUSIONS: Indexes by producers,
distributors; media descriptions (audiovisual
aids, educational media); classified listings;
directories (companies);

DESCRIPTORS: Audiovisual aids; educational
media; instructional materials; visual aids

SUMMARY: This is annotated catalogs (13)
of non-print media used for educational purposes.
It describes thousands of titles, preschool
through adult/college. Separate catalogs treat:
audio tapes, 8 mm motion cartridges; educational
films, filmstrips, overhead transparencies,
records, slides and videotapes; producers and
distributors; and subject-specific multimedia
(environment, health and safety, psychology,
vocational-technical). Other catalogs (7) cover
special education media.

RELEVANCE: This can be used by educators,
trainers and educational consultants to identify
nonprint media resources. However, updating is
called for.

THE RIGHT COLLEGE 1988
1987
Mazzari, Louis
1545
0-13-044868-0
ARCO Publishing
Gulf and Western Bldg.
One Gulf and Western Plaza
New York, NY 10023
(201) 767-5937
$24.95

Excellent
Catalog; directory

INCLUSIONS: Indexes by majors, colleges,
intercollegiate sports, competitiveness, test
scores, costs, enrollment, religious affiliation,
availability of military training, and Phi Beta
Kappa; tables, glossary

DESCRIPTORS: Colleges and universities;
educational institutions; higher education

SUMMARY: This is a catalog of 1540 four-
year colleges in the U.S. plus selected,
accredited schools in Canada, Mexico, and Puerto
Rico. Entries on each college include: profile,
accreditation, religious orientation, special
facilities/museums, athletic facilities, programs
of study, student life, athletics, admissions,
financial aid, student employment, foreign
students, computer/database facilities, graduate
career data, and prominent alumnae/i.

RELEVANCE: This is an up-to-date,
comprehensive catalog on B.A. granting
institutions, useful for students, counselors,
prospective employees, and educational
consultants.

                        <<<<<<>>>>>>

SELECTING AND DEVELOPING MEDIA FOR INSTRUCTION
1983 (The 1976 edition was abstracted.)
Second

Anderson, Ronald
192
0-442-20976-2
Van Nostrand Reinhold Co.
135 W. 50th Street
New York, NY 10020
(212) 265-8700
$26.95

Excellent
Handbook

INCLUSIONS: Index by subject; annotated
bibliography (reference materials); appendices;
charts; checklists; flowcharts; evaluation-
selection guidelines; illustrations; samples

DESCRIPTORS: Educational media;
instructional materials; media selection; training
materials; audiovisual aids

IDENTIFIER: American Society for Training
and Development (ASTD), (cosponsor)

SUMMARY: This is a basic reference tool
for persons who create and/or select materials
used for training or instructional purposes. It
provides a system for choosing materials best
suited to one's purposes. It gives criteria and
guidelines for designing, evaluating and selecting
still visuals, motion visuals, audio and printed
materials, and realia (physical objects). It uses
flowcharts to depict commonly-encountered media
selection decisions.

RELEVANCE: This is useful for professional
trainers in preparing for presentations by
identifying resources and giving evaluative
guidelines. New computer programs and technology
geared for presentation can usefully be added as
an important resource.

                    <<<<<<>>>>>>

TELEVISED HIGHER EDUCATION
Catalog of Resources

1984
First
Green, JoAnn
349
06-100-520-000-401
Western Interstate Commission for Higher Education
P.O. Drawer P
Boulder, CO 80301
(303) 497-0200

Good
Catalog

INCLUSIONS: Indexes by subject, key
work, producer and course title; appendices: other
sources of televised instruction; list of
distributors; list of producers

DESCRIPTORS: Televised higher education;
videocourses; audio-visual

IDENTIFIER: Former title: Televised Higher
Education: Catalog of Videocourses

SUMMARY: This lists "almost 1100
videocourses in a wide array of academic fields"
for postsecondary education.   It excludes
videocourses produced by large training companies.
The organization of the book is alphabetical by
videocourse within alphabetical subject area.
Major subject areas are: business, communications,
computer science, education, energy; engineering,
English and composition, foreign languages, health
sciences, humanities, law, library science, life
sciences, mathematics, personal development,
philosophy, physical sciences, psychology,
recreation, religion, social sciences, trades and
services, and visual and performing arts.   Entries
include a description, course and technical;
release date, level, prerequisite skills, course
description, instructor, producer, distributor,
rental fee, purchase price, and rights.

RELEVANCE: One can be truly amazed at the
diversity of videocourses available.   This is a
convenient way to learn, and especially relevant
for the homebound and rural student.   In what
surely must be a volatile market, however, this
could use an update.

WHO OFFERS PART-TIME DEGREE PROGRAMS?
1985
Second
Hegener, Karen
423
0-87866-285-5
Peterson's Guides, Inc.
P.O. Box 2123
Princeton, NJ 08543-2123
(800) 225-0261
$7.95

Very good
Catalog; directory

INCLUSIONS: Index to colleges; directories
of specialized information

DESCRIPTORS: Part-time degree programs;
external degree programs; higher education

SUMMARY: This provides information on
colleges offering part-time degree programs
arranged alphabetically by state. The entries
contain general information and information on
undergraduate and graduate programs, as
applicable. Part two, Directories of Specialized
Information, lists colleges offering: part-time
evening programs, part-time weekend programs,
part-time summer programs, and external degree
programs.

RELEVANCE: Schools have recognized the
importance of flexibility in schedule for today's
educational market. This resource is based on and
structured by schedule.

CHAPTER 12

ENTREPRENEURS AND ENTREPRENEURSHIP

This chapter's subjects include:

- start-up considerations
- key characteristics of entrepreneurs
- success criteria
- decision-making and motivation
- ventures

BUSINESS STARTUP BASICS
1981 (The 1978 edition was abstracted.)
Second
Dible, Donald
262
0-8359-0597-7
Reston Publishing Company
P.O. Box 500
Englewood Cliffs, NJ 07632
(201) 767-5049
$21.95

Good
Handbook

INCLUSIONS: Checklists; worksheets
(equipment, furniture and supplies; taxes);
illustrations

DESCRIPTORS: Entrepreneurship;
entrepreneurs; small business

SUMMARY: This is an introduction to what
the potential or new business person needs to know
about going into business. It discusses
financing, pricing, advertising, hiring employees,
and the use of lawyers, accountants, and sales
agents. It includes the following topics:
questions to ask yourself about yourself, legal
considerations, business operations planning and
knowledge; and small business insurance (fire,
liability, automobile, workers' compensation, and
others). It discusses managing cash flow for
manufacturing, retail, and service businesses. It
covers planning an advertising campaign, measuring
advertising effectiveness, and using signs to
attract business. Chapters include the following
topics: selecting a business name, locating,
franchising, incorporating, obtaining retail sales
tax and resale permits, record-keeping, borrowing,
budgeting, finding and distributing products, and
reducing bad check losses.

RELEVANCE: This work explains basic
considerations in starting and financing a
business. It is not scholarly, encyclopedic, or
concerned with state-of-the-art considerations.

ENTREPRENEUR'S GUIDE
1981
Second
Not established
Brown, Deaver
173
0-345-33596-1
Ballantine Books, Company, Inc.
201 East 50th Street
New York, NY 10022
(800) 638-6460
$2.95

Very good
Guide

INCLUSIONS: Appendix; index; product
selection guide

DESCRIPTORS: Entrepreneurship; business
entrepreneurs; marketing; packaging; promotion;
public relations; advertising

SUMMARY: Based on the experience of a
successful businessman, this Guide contains
discussion of the characteristics of successful
entrepreneurs, the need to insure survival and
earn a profit, and ways to avoid pitfalls. In an
extensive discussion of marketing, the author
advises a simple, basic approach and explains the
process of identifying market and customer needs.
Packaging, promotion, public relations, and low-
cost advertising considerations are also
discussed. Other topics are financial
considerations, venture money, collateralized
lending, and operations involving material and
equipment.

RELEVANCE: This is useful for
entrepreneurs involved in considering, planning,
operating and selling a business. It recommends
use of one-person consultants with quick fixes to
save company money.

THE ENTREPRENEURIAL WORKBOOK
A Step-By-Step Guide to Starting and
Operating Your Own Small Business

1985
First
Taylor, Charlotte
148
Venture Concepts
806 15th Street N.W., Suite 421
Washington, DC 20005
0-452-25660-7
New American Library
1633 Broadway
New York, NY 10019
(212) 783-1166
$9.95

Very good
Workbook

INCLUSIONS: Case studies; worksheets;
glossary; case study review questions; business
planning exercises

DESCRIPTORS: Entrepreneurship; small
business; business planning

SUMMARY: This Workbook presents
concepts, case studies and exercises in the areas
of business planning, financing, marketing,
decision-making, and operating a business. The
last section provides a summary case for a retail
business. The case studies are on one service
business. The Workbook is designed to help the
participant apply each step in the process of
making a business succeed. The emphasis is on
developing a business plan. Questions and
worksheets permeate the entire Workbook.

RELEVANCE: This is a useful aid for new
and aspiring entrepreneurs. It provides workspace
formats for various aspects of business planning.

ENTREPRENEURSHIP AND SMALL BUSINESS MANAGEMENT
1979
Schollhammer, Hans   -   Kuriloff, Arthur
608
0-471-76260-1
John Wiley and Sons, Inc.
605 Third Avenue
New York, NY 10158
(212) 850-6418
$40.95

Excellent
Textbook; primer

INCLUSIONS: Indexes by subjects, names;
appendices (2); bibliographies; case studies;
checklists; evaluation aids; financial data;
forecast; illustrations (charts, graphs, graphic);
samples; tables

DESCRIPTORS: Business startup;
entrepreneurship; new ventures; small business
management

SUMMARY: This textbook treats the
theory, general principles and practices involved
in successfully initiating (6 chapters) and
managing (8 chapters) a small business. It covers
entrepreneurial success-failure factors; legal
considerations and financial strategies for new
and growing businesses; and many other topics.
Detailed case studies (170 pages) focus on
strategic issues actually encountered by
entrepreneurs who formed a variety of business
operations.

RELEVANCE: This can be helpful to
entrepreneurs planning, initiating, and in the
beginning stages of a business. It helps to see
what problems others overcame.

<<<<<<>>>>>>

HANDBOOK FOR MANUFACTURING ENTREPRENEURS
1973
Morrison, Robert
558

0-912400-09-9
Western Reserve Press, Inc.
PO Box 675
Astabula, OH 44004
(216) 997-5851
$12.50 paperback

Very good
Handbook; guide

INCLUSIONS: Index; appendices (forms,
tables, other), charts; checklists; financial
data; glossary; samples

DESCRIPTORS: Entrepreneurs; manufacturing
enterprises; manufacturing management; new
ventures

SUMMARY: This is a complete
entrepreneur's guide for current and prospective
owners/managers of manufacturing enterprises.
Major sections treat these topics: 1) the
decision to become an entrepreneur; 2) the
establishment, financing, and operation of the
business; 3) general and financial management
skills; 4) the manufacturing and marketing
operations; and 5) research and development,
product engineering, and long-range planning
considerations.

RELEVANCE: This Handbook has special
relevance for manufacturing entrepreneurs and
consultants working with them. It gives a
convincing rationale for becoming a manufacturing
entrepreneur, and provides a wealth of practical
suggestions and advice.

<<<<<<>>>>>

HOW TO ORGANIZE AND OPERATE A SMALL BUSINESS
1988 (The 1979 edition was abstracted.)
Eighth
Irregular
Baumback, Clifford - Lawyer, Kenneth
608
0-13-424987-9

Prentice-Hall, Inc.
Rt. 9 West
Englewood Cliffs, NJ 07632
(201) 592-2352
Order: 200 Old Tappan Road
Old Tappan, NJ 07675
(201) 767-5049
$38.00

Very good
Textbook; primer

INCLUSIONS: Index by subject; appendices;
bibliography; checklists; illustrations (charts,
figures); samples; self evaluation aids; self
study aids; tables

DESCRIPTORS: Entrepreneurship; business
startup; management guides; small business
management

SUMMARY: This shows how to establish and
operate a small business. It treats these and
other topics: deciding to be self-employed;
justifying, financing, organizing and staffing the
business; setting up a record keeping system;
using outside sources of assistance; pricing,
advertising and sales promotion; and handling
regulations and taxes. Supplemental materials are
a study guide (workbook) and instructor's guide.

RELEVANCE: This is for the new
entrepreneur or instructor on small business.

                    <<<<<<>>>>>>

HOW TO START A SERVICE BUSINESS AND MAKE IT
SUCCEED
1987
First
Retzler, Kathryn
280
0-673-18591-5
Scott Foresman and Company
1900 East Lake Avenue
Glenview, IL 60025

(312) 729-3000
$14.95

Excellent
Guide

INCLUSIONS: Index by subject; bibliography;
appendices: financial reports; service business
list; charts; graphs; illustrations; case study
and samples; chapter notes; checklist

DESCRIPTORS: Service business; small
business; entrepreneurship; computers; business
plan; business financing; marketing

SUMMARY: This is a guide to creating a
successful service business. Service businesses
comprise over half of business startups. The
author explores the development of a business idea
and presents the "success formula" -- combine
planning, money, preparation, and luck. Major
topics covered are: 1) funding -- start-up,
operating expenses, funding sources and proposal;
2) marketing -- demographics, psychographics,
market strategy, delivery, advertising, sales, and
pricing; 3) legal issues -- form of business (sole
proprietor, partner, corporate), licenses, taxes,
and accounting; 4) the business plan; 5) "tools of
the trade" -- honesty, consistency, good record
keeping, and positive image; 6) money and time
management; 7) expansion; 8) buying a business; 9)
computerization; and 10) entrepreneur success
characteristics.

RELEVANCE: This is a helpful overview for
service business entrepreneurs. It is written in
a simple, down-to-earth style, while covering most
of the bases.

<<<<<<>>>>>>

HOW TO START AND OPERATE A MAIL-ORDER BUSINESS
1987 (The 1984 edition was abstracted.)
Fourth
Irregular
Simon, Julian

640
0-0705-7531-2
McGraw-Hill Book Company
1221 Avenue of the Americas
New York, NY 10020
(800) 262-4729
Price not set

Excellent
Handbook

INCLUSIONS: Index by subject; appendices
(9); annotated bibliographies; charts; consultant
listings; financial data; illustrations (ads,
figures, photographs); FTC regulations; sample
forms; statistics; tables; evaluation-selection
guidelines

DESCRIPTORS: Direct mail; mail order
business; new ventures; small business management

SUMMARY: This is a practical, step-by-
step guide for mail-order marketing and sales
advocates. It thoroughly teaches the mail-order
business. It show how to: handle all essential
business startup and management tasks; find a
select, salable product; create, test and use
advertising copy; use available mailing lists and
various mail-order media; avoid legal hassles;
and do other key tasks. It gives a wealth of
suggestions and information.

RELEVANCE: Mail-order is an important
aspect of many businesses and a business in itself
for others.

<<<<<<>>>>>>

INNOVATION AND ENTREPRENEURSHIP
Practice and Principles
1985
First
Drucker, Peter
256
0-06-015428-4
Harper and Row Publishers

10 E. 53rd Street
New York, NY 10022
(800) 242-7737
$19.45

Excellent
Book

INCLUSIONS: Index; suggested readings; case
examples

DESCRIPTORS: Entrepreneurship;
entrepreneurs; innovation; business management;
management

SUMMARY: Drucker presents information,
ideas, and examples based on his long experience
with business. The book is organized into three
parts: The Practice of Innovation, the Practice
of Entrepreneurship, and Entrepreneurial
Strategies. The Introduction "relates innovation
and entrepreneurship to the economy," and the
Conclusion "relates them to society." Drucker
presents innovation and entrepreneurship not as
mystique but as learnable and doable.
Entrepreneurship is described as a "practice" and
"the entrepreneur always searches for change,
responds to it, and exploits it as an
opportunity." Innovation is defined as "the
specific tool of entrepreneurs." Drucker
discusses the significance of purposeful
innovation and seven sources of innovative
opportunity: unexpected; incongruity; process
need; changes in industry or market structure;
demographics; changes in perception, mood, and
meaning; and new knowledge. Part two deals with
entrepreneurial management in the existing
business, the public-service institution, and the
new venture. Part three deals with
entrepreneurial strategies in the marketplace:
"fastest with the mostest," "hitting them where
they ain't," having a niche, and by changing
something in order to find the customer.

RELEVANCE: This is a book for the
theorist, entrepreneur, or existing business
owner/manager.

NEW VENTURE CREATION
A Guide to Entrepreneurship
1985
Second
Timmons, Jeffry - Smollen, Leonard - Dingee,
Alexander
0-256-03476-1
Richard D. Irwin, Inc.
1818 Ridge Road
Homewood, IL 60430
(800) 323-4560
$33.50

Very good
Handbook; guide

INCLUSIONS: Index; appendices (8);
annotated bibliography citations; charts;
exercises; exhibits; information sources (market
research); planning aids; samples (business plan,
first venture analysis, investment agreements);
self evaluation aids; suggested readings; tables;
worksheets; case examples

DESCRIPTORS: Entrepreneurial teams;
entrepreneurship; new ventures; small business
development

SUMMARY: This is an introduction and
thorough discussion of the creation and management
of new ventures. It treats entrepreneurial career
planning considerations; characteristics and
skills of successful entrepreneurs; formation and
use of entrepreneurial team, business plans and
action plans; and analysis and financing of new
ventures. Finally it discusses "the harvest" and
success. The appendices are: 1) Robert Morris
Associates Statement Studies; 2) "The Legal
Process of Venture Capital Investment" by Richard
Testa; 3) outline of an investment agreement; 4)
sample terms sheet; 5) sample vesting and stock
restriction agreement; 6) summary of state and
federal start-up requirements; and 8) solution to
"creative squares."

RELEVANCE: This is a useful resource for
the entrepreneur creating a new venture. It
encourages the use of a learn-by-doing approach.
There is a section on using consultants.

NEW VENTURE STRATEGIES
1980
Karl Vesper
303
0-13615-948-6
Prentice-Hall, Inc.
Rt. 9 West
Englewood Cliffs, N.J. 07632
(201) 592-2352
Order: 200 Old Tappan Road
Old Tappan, NJ 07675
(201) 767-5049

Very good
Handbook

INCLUSIONS: Index by subject; bibliography;
charts; checklists; evaluation-selection
guidelines; tables

DESCRIPTORS: Entrepreneurship; new ventures;
entrepreneurs; strategic planning

SUMMARY: This entrepreneur's guide is
distilled from the experience of hundreds of
entrepreneurs. It shows how one can discover new
venture opportunities, break into
entrepreneurship, and successfully evolve new
ventures into ongoing, competitive business
enterprises. It also describes common types of
entrepreneurs, ventures, and startup approaches;
sources of business acquisitions and how to
evaluate and negotiate the acquisition deal;
strategies for gaining competitive market entry
leverage; and key success factors.

RELEVANCE: Entrepreneurs of all kinds can
find relevance among the topics discussed.

<<<<<<>>>>>

THE SMALL BUSINESS SURVIVAL GUIDE
Sources of Help for Entrepreneurs
1980
Mancuso, Joseph
422

Prentice-Hall, Inc.
Rt. 9 West
Englewood Cliffs, NJ 07632
(201) 592-2000
Order: 200 Old Tappan Rd.
Old Tappan, NJ 07675
(201) 767-5054
$9.95

Very good
Catalog; resources guide

INCLUSIONS: Indexes by names, publication,
titles, sources; annotated bibliographies;
classified listings; consultant listings;
directories (11); geographic listings

DESCRIPTORS: Business information; business
publications; entrepreneurs; small business
management; women; minorities

SUMMARY: This subject guide lists and
describes business publications of all types and
organizational sources of help under these and
other subjects: advertising and public relations,
business plans, Canada, data processing,
entrepreneurial education, franchising,
government, management and planning, manufacturers
representatives, marketing, minority business,
patents and inventions, the SBA and DOC, taxes,
venture capital, and women entrepreneurs.

RELEVANCE: This is a good sourcebook for
entrepreneurs, women and minorities included.

                    <<<<<<>>>>>>

UP YOUR OWN ORGANIZATION
A Handbook on How to Start and Finance a News
Business
1986 (The 1974 edition was abstracted.)
Third
Dible, Donald
423
$17.95
Entrepreneur Press

3422 Astoria Circle
Fairfield, CA 94533
(707) 422-6822

Very good
Guide

INCLUSIONS: Index by subject; appendices
(6); recommended reading; checklist

DESCRIPTORS: Business startup;
entrepreneurship; business plan; money sources;
marketing; venture capital

SUMMARY: Written by an entrepreneur,
this handbook covers aspects of starting a
business. It covers the following: 1)
characteristics of a successful entrepreneur,
image, motivation, training, responsibility,
partner selection, product idea, and professional
assistance; 2) the business plan and proposal;
3) 40 money sources, including banks, finance
companies, investors, the Small Business
Administration, credit unions, foundations,
trusts, and customers; and 4) information on
markets and marketing concepts. The appendices
include: annotated list of directories and guides
to venture capital sources, seminars and
workshops; directory of membership of National
Association of Small Business; investment
companies; six business startup checklists; and
SBA and Department of Commerce field office
locations.

RELEVANCE: This is a good beginner book
for the business entrepreneur. It is male
directed, however.

CHAPTER 13

FINANCE AND MONEY

This chapter contains:
- financial planning
- strategies and choices
- sources of financing
- financial transactions
- international finance
- return on investment

2001 SOURCES OF FINANCING FOR
SMALL BUSINESS
1983
First
Holtz, Herman
173
0-668-05468-9
ARCO Publishing, Inc.
1 Gulf & Western Bldg.
New York, NY 10023
(212) 373-8931
$14.95

Good
Sourcebook; guide

DESCRIPTORS: Small business; finance;
venture capital

SUMMARY: This lists 2000 sources of
federal agencies and programs, state agencies and
sources of financing for small business. It
provides help in understanding appropriate sources
of funds and how to approach these sources. It
covers minority business funding opportunities and
programs and foundation support, help in doing
proposals and business plans, sales and marketing
issues, and the use of outside consultants and
brokers.

RELEVANCE: This book is good as an
introductory source. It is neither detailed nor
sophisticated.

<<<<<<>>>>>

CREATIVE BUSINESS FINANCING
How to Make Your Best Deal When Negotiating
Equipment, Leases and Business Loans
1983
First
Simmons, James
310
0-13-189142-1
Prentice-Hall, Inc.
Rt. 9 West

Englewood Cliffs, NJ 07632
(201) 592-2000
Order: 200 Old Tappan Road
Old Tappan, NJ 07675
(201) 767-5054
$12.95

Very good
Guide

INCLUSIONS: Index; tables; examples; forms;
checklists

DESCRIPTORS: Business financing; loans;
equipment financing; financial statements; leasing

SUMMARY: This book's focus is borrowing
and arranging equipment financing. Chapters cover
the importance of knowledge, how to make a good
presentation, the mathematics of financing, how to
negotiate a deal, credit and financial statements,
lender habits and how to protect yourself,
leasing, and accounts receivable financing. It is
full of how-to advice, tips and warnings. The
author is a retired banker and had extensive
experience in loans, leases, and contracts.

RELEVANCE: This is intended for the business
owner and manager. Written in simple,
conversational style for the lay person, this book
also provides step-by-step procedures, checklists
and examples. It attempts to give the reader the
inside scoop about what really goes on and how to
deal with this reality. It can be useful for its
focus on equipment financing.

<<<<<<>>>>>>

DIRECTORY OF BUSINESS AND FINANCIAL SERVICES
1984
Irregular
Eighth
Grant, Mary - Berleant-Schiller, Riva
200
0-87111-287-6
Special Libraries Association

1700 18th Street N.W.
Washington, DC 20009
(202) 234-4700
$35.00

Excellent
Information sourcebook

INCLUSIONS: Indexes by publisher, subject;
investment consultants; geography; appendix of
selected stock exchanges in different countries

DESCRIPTORS: Finance information services;
investments; business information services; online
database

SUMMARY: This Directory consists of
annotated lists of services providing continuous
information on facets of business and finance. It
is arranged alphabetically within categories of
print sources and online databases. It excludes
government publications, training courses,
periodicals, bank letters, brokerage services
unavailable to the public or available only for
commission, and legal and tax services without
special application to business decision-making.

RELEVANCE: The Directory provides lead
sources to find focused information, useful for
librarians, researchers, business persons, and
consultants.

                    <<<<<<>>>>>>

DIRECTORY OF STATE AND FEDERAL FUNDS FOR
BUSINESS DEVELOPMENT
1985 (The 1977 edition was abstracted.)
Levy, Robert
Pilot Staff
48
0-87576-116-X
Pilot Books
103 Cooper Street
Babylon, NY 11702
(516) 422-2225
$5.00

Good
Directory

DESCRIPTORS: Finance; business development;
business assistance; government support for
business

SUMMARY: This reference introduces
sources of state and federal financial assistance
for business and indicates where to go for further
information. It lists the agency which
administers each State's industrial development
program and provides a general description of the
available assistance program. It lists federal
government sources and describes the type of
assistance available. State and local government
assistance includes help in business location and
relocation. States provide assistance regarding
available sites and buildings, how to get
financing, conduct labor or market surveys, and
other information.

RELEVANCE: This is a simple guide for
identifying and comparing funds for business
development by geographic area for users seeking a
conducive market location for a business.

<<<<<<>>>>>>

GUIDE TO INTERNATIONAL VENTURE CAPITAL
1985
Third
Annual
Editors of Venture, The Magazine for
Entrepreneurs
283
0-6715-5698-3
Simon and Schuster, Inc.
Rockefeller Center
1230 Avenue of the Americas
New York, NY 10020
(800) 223-2348
$60.00

Very good
Guide

INCLUSIONS: Indexes by firms, domestic
locations industry preferences geographical
preferences

DESCRIPTORS: Venture capital-directories;
small business investment companies; international
financing; international venture capital;
entrepreneur financing

IDENTIFIER: Venture, the Magazine for
Entrepreneurs

SUMMARY: One section contains articles
on venture capital, how to write an effective
business plan, and hold onto equity. It lists
venture capital firms, their address, year funded,
amount of funds, investment history, number of
deals, average investment, project preferences,
principals and contact persons. This Guide
contains a directory of 780 venture firms in the
U.S. and Puerto Rico above and below $10 million;
small business investment companies above and
below $3 million; and minority enterprise small
business investment companies above and below $1.5
million. It contains foreign listings of 177
firms in Canada, the United Kingdom, Europe, Asia,
and Israel.

RELEVANCE: This has a useful listing of
venture capital sources.

<<<<<<>>>>>>

HANDBOOK OF BUSINESS FINANCE AND CAPITAL SOURCES
1985 (The 1979 edition was abstracted.)
Third
Annual
Rao, Dileep
650 (1985)
0-8144-5811-4
AMACOM
135 West 50th Street
New York, NY 10020
(212) 903-8087
$95.00 (1985)

Very good
Handbook

INCLUSION: Index by subject

DESCRIPTORS: Business finance; capital
sources

SUMMARY: This reference provides
information on sources for raising business funds.
Four major sections are on: 1) business finance,
including: fundamentals, financial instruments,
capital sources, and special interest topics; 2)
private financial institutions; 3) state
institutions and programs; and 4) federal
programs. It does the following: 1) discusses
types of financial institutions and instruments
used by businesses; fundamentals and aspects of
business finance; sources and credit criteria for
obtaining funds; different types of financial
institutions and their financing; (e.g. startup,
equipment, real estate, etc.); 2) provides names,
addresses, contact officers, and investment
criteria of private financial institutions,
arranged by type of institution (e.g. leasing
company), by state and city, and alphabetically
within the city; 3) provides contact information,
addresses and investment criteria of state
financial programs; and 4) provides information on
federal financial assistance programs to
businesses and farms.

RELEVANCE: This reference is written to
help business persons, financial officers, and
business professionals such as attorneys and
accountants identify sources of business
financing.

<<<<<<<>>>>>>

INTERNATIONAL FINANCE HANDBOOK
1983, 2 volumes
George, Abraham - Giddy, Ian
1833, 2 volumes
Vol. 1   0-471-81172-6
Vol. 2   0-471-81174-2

Set   0-471-09861-2
John Wiley and Sons, Inc.
605 Third Avenue
New York, NY 10158
(212) 850-6418
$95.00 per set, $50.00 per volume

Very good
Handbook

INCLUSIONS: Index, cross-referenced;
glossary; appendices on mathematics of
international finance, and sources of information;
chapter bibliographies

DESCRIPTORS: Finance; international finance

SUMMARY: This covers comprehensive and
detailed tasks and tools of international
financing, banking and investment. The volumes
are organized into parts: introduction; the
foreign exchange markets; the Eurocurrency
markets; national banking, money, and bond
markets; the international bond market;
international equity markets; special financing
techniques and sources; and the management of
international finance. The 59 contributors are of
authoritative standing in their fields.

RELEVANCE: This source provides much
important information about international finance
for anyone interested in doing business
internationally.

                    <<<<<<>>>>>>

MOODY'S ANALYTICAL OVERVIEW OF 25 LEADING U.S.
CITIES
1977
First
286
Moody's Investors Service, Inc.
99 Church Street
New York, NY 10007
(212) 267-8800
$10.95

Good
Reference

INCLUSIONS: Tables; statistical data;
budgets

DESCRIPTORS: Cities; U.S. cities; finances;
municipal bonds ratings

SUMMARY: This presents study data and
analysis of 25 cities (excepting Washington D.C.)
as measured by population in 1970.
Economic/social, government, and financial factors
are considered for each city. Each city is ranked
for overall economic health. It describes the
following kinds of information: rating of general
obligation bonds; history; opinion; SMSA (Standard
Metropolitan Statistical Area); data;
employment/unemployment; government factors -
property tax administration, income taxes, debt
factors, pensions, services, fiscal aid, capital
improvements, financial plans, programs, and
restraints, including information relevant for
different cities. Cities are viewed as "economic
units that together comprise a national urban
hierarchy in which the largest urban places offer
the highest level of service to the regional,
national and international markets."

RELEVANCE: This is written primarily for
investors in city bonds, and may be used by
investment consultants. The statistical data and
resultant analysis is woefully out of date. It is
out of print and a new edition is called for.

                    <<<<<<>>>>>

PRATT'S GUIDE TO VENTURE CAPITAL SOURCES
1988
Twelfth
Irregular
Morris, Jane
687
0-914470-23-X
Venture Economics, Inc.
16 Laurel Avenue

Box 348
Wellesley Hills, MA 02181
(800) 521-8110
$100.00

Very good
Guide

INCLUSIONS: Indexes by company name,
personal names of company officers; venture fields
of interest for included investment firms

DESCRIPTORS: Finance sources; venture
capital; entrepreneurship

SUMMARY: This contains sections on: 1)
background to venture capital and the successful
entrepreneur; 2) sources of business development
financing, including organized and informal
investors; seed capital; SBA programs; community
development corporations; MESBICs (minority
enterprise small business investment companies);
corporate and limited partnership capitalists; 3)
how to raise venture capital; 4) when and how to
go for the public market place; 5) venturing and
the relationship between the capitalist and the
entrepreneur; and 6) directories of U.S. and
Canadian venture capitalists and U.S. small
company underwriters.

RELEVANCE: This Guide provides an overview
on entrepreneurship and venture capital, as well
as detailed listings.

                  <<<<<<>>>>>>

PUBLIC FINANCE INFORMATION SOURCES
1964
First
Knox, Vera
142
0-8103-0803-7
Gale Research Company
Book Tower
Detroit, MI 48226
(800) 223-4253
$65.00

Very good
Bibliography

INCLUSIONS: Indexes by author, subject;
appendix of state taxpayer associations;

DESCRIPTORS: Public finance; bibliography;
information sources; fiscal administration;
government fiscal policy; international public
finance

SUMMARY: This is a bibliography of texts
on public finance, including government revenues,
expenditures, borrowing and indebtedness, and
fiscal administration. It emphasizes studies of
the 1960s and older studies which are "standards."
Some sections feature an introductory explanatory
note. There are nine sections to this broad but
not comprehensive source: public finance; public
revenues; public expenditures; public debt; fiscal
policy; fiscal administration; international
public finance; and periodicals, services and
indexes. Some examples of subsectional topics
are: specific taxes, e.g. on alcoholic beverages,
excise and sales, corporation, individual; tax
burden and exemption, public personnel, research,
social security, and country by country
publications.

RELEVANCE: This is written for students and
professionals in the field of public finance and
taxation and for library collections. It pulls
together the best of the available references as
of 1964, and is thus in need of an update though
it is useful for historical purposes.

<<<<<<>>>>>

ROI BASICS FOR NONFINANCIAL EXECUTIVES
1980 (The 1979 edition was abstracted.)
Sweeny, Allen
136
0-8144-5553-0
AMACOM
135 West 50th Street
New York, NY 10020

(212) 903-8087
$11.95

Very good
Annotated bibliography

INCLUSIONS: Index; compound interest tables;
present value tables

DESCRIPTORS: Capital investments-evaluation

SUMMARY: This book explains what return
on investment is. It covers basic methods,
including payback accounting, and present value,
and their advantages and limitations. ROI is
discussed as a measure of overall business
performance measured as return on shareholder's
equity, total investment, and total assets.
Specific applications and variations of ROI in
large, complex organizations are examined. ROI in
inflationary circumstances is considered.

RELEVANCE: This book is designed for
readers without prior knowledge of ROI and it
includes examples of how to do financial analysis.

                  <<<<<<>>>>>>

THE SMALL BUSINESS GUIDE TO BORROWING MONEY
1980
First
Rubin, Richard   -   Goldberg, Philip
265
0-07054-198-1
0-07-054198-1
McGraw-Hill, Inc.
1221 Avenue of the Americas
New York, NY 10020
(800) 262-4729
$19.95

Very good
Sourcebook; guide

INCLUSIONS: Appendices; glossary; indexes
by subject, organization, individual, cross-
referenced

DESCRIPTORS: Small business-finance; credit

SUMMARY: Topics discussed are: sources
of financing for small business, including banks,
venture capital, life insurance companies,
government sources, especially the various
programs of the Small Business Administration.
The book includes a section on getting started as
an entrepreneur and how to handle the money once
it is received, from advice about business
management to financial calculations. The
appendices contain a package for a bank-
participating SBA loan; venture capital companies;
and small business investment companies by state.

RELEVANCE: This is an introductory and
advisory book for entrepreneurs seeking and
approaching appropriate sources of financing. We
advise the reader to consult a more recent
publication (this is out of print) on this
subject.

<<<<<<>>>>>>

SUCCESSFUL TECHNIQUES THAT MULTIPLY PROFITS
AND PERSONAL PAYOFF IN THE CLOSELY-HELD CORPORATION
1980 (The 1977 edition was abstracted.)
Fourth
IBP staff
500
Institute for Business Planning
IBP PlazaMarking
Englewood Cliffs, NJ 07632
(201) 592-2040

Very good
Handbook

INCLUSIONS: Index by subject; appendix
(bulletin); checklists (many, indexed); financial
data (business, personal); guidelines (financial
planning); statistics; tables (information
summaries, data)

DESCRIPTORS: Business finance; closely-held
corporations; financial management; profit
planning; tax planning; business startup

SUMMARY: This is a planning guide
designed to enhance the financial management and
wealth-building skills of owners of small,
closely-held corporations.   It shows how to: 1)
set up, control and run the corporation; 2) raise
needed money; 3) gain optimal tax savings; 4)
increase benefits to one's family; 5) protect
against needless lawsuits, losses and liabilities;
and 6) interpret/apply the Tax Reform Act of 1976.
It suggests hundred of practical, money-saving
strategies.

RELEVANCE: This can be a useful guide for
small business owners/operators.   Changes is
taxation necessitate looking elsewhere for more
up-to-date information and advice.

CHAPTER 14

GENERAL PURPOSE

This chapter contains:

- general information sources

- guides

- directories to directories

- directories of contacts

- general purpose directories

- consumer guides

- research services

BIOGRAPHY AND GENEALOGY MASTER INDEX
1988
Annual
McNeil, Barbara
1200
0-8103-1514-9
0730-1316
Gale Research Company
Book Tower
Detroit, MI 48226
(313) 961-2242
$220.00

Very good
Biographical index

INCLUSION: Index by name

DESCRIPTORS: Bibliographical index

SUMMARY: This provides information on
sources of biographical sketches listed in Who's
Whos and Biographies. It specifies relevant
edition(s) of published listings of individuals.
Listings include living, deceased, domestic and
foreign individuals. Emphasis is on living
individuals prominent in the United States. The
first edition lists more than 725,000 sketches in
Who's Who biographies. The supplements
considerably extend the number of listings.

RELEVANCE: This resource allows the user
to find a desired biographical sketch. In many
cases the index indicates multiple listings for
the same person. The user can then choose
whichever source is available to them or make
comparisons between the various sources available
to them. This source may be the key to unlocking
information about a person that may help you make
or same money in your consulting business.

<<<<<<>>>>>>

COMPLETE SPEAKERS AND TOASTMASTERS LIBRARY
1965
First

Braude, Jacob
8 volumes
0-13-164616-8
Prentice-Hall, Inc.
Rt. 9 West
Englewood Cliffs, NJ 07632
(201) 592-2000
Order: 200 Old Tappan Rd.
Old Tappan, NJ 07675
(201) 767-5054
$49.95

Very good
Sourcebook

DESCRIPTORS: Speech material; public
speaking

SUMMARY: These eight volumes are
intended to provide material for speeches. The
volume contents are: 1) speech openers and
closers; 2) business and professional pointmakers;
3) definitions and toasts; 4) human interest
stories; 5) origins and firsts; 6) proverbs,
epigrams, aphorisms, sayings, and bon mots; 7)
remarks of famous people; and 8) rhyme and verse.
Each volume is alphabetically arranged by topic.

RELEVANCE: These small volumettes can come
in handy when speech-writing and even writing in
general. It can help you say what you want on
particular occasions for particular purposes. It
is unique.

<<<<<<>>>>>>

CONSUMER SOURCEBOOK
A Directory and Guide
1983 (The 1978 edition was abstracted.)
Third
Irregular
Wasserman, Paul - Morgan, Jean
1622
0-8103-0371-X
Gale Research Company
Book Tower

Detroit, MI 48226
(800) 223-4253
$68.00

Excellent
Directory

INCLUSION: Bibliography

DESCRIPTOR: Consumer information

IDENTIFIER: 1987 Supplement

SUMMARY: This is a comprehensive
compilation of printed and unprinted information
sources useful to consumers, in six major
sections, each with subject fields. The sections
are: government organizations; associations,
centers, institutes, etc.; media services; and
companies and trade names. The fields are
consumer finance, action, health, safety,
environment, social welfare, law, transportation,
etc. The 1978 edition lists over 1,200 non-
governmental organizations; 200 federal; 500
state, county and city consumer offices and state
public utility commissions, and more than 17,000
companies producing consumer goods and services.

RELEVANCE: This is a guide to resources
with all types of information from the consumer
interest standpoint, including consumer resources,
offices, programs, government and media services,
and organizations. It enables the user to
identify a problematic trade name and company.

                    <<<<<<>>>>>>

DATAPRO REPORTS ON OFFICE SYSTEMS
1988
Updated monthly
Patterson, Robert
3 volumes
Datapro Research Corporation
1805 Underwood Boulevard
Delran, NJ 08075
(609) 764-0100

Very good
Catalog; loose-leaf resources guide

INCLUSIONS: Indexes; appendices; calendars;
classified listings; data; directories (products
and services); evaluation-selection aids
(checklists, guidelines, survey); glossaries;
illustrations (charts, photographs); newsletters;
specifications (equipment, systems); reports;
tables

DESCRIPTORS: Equipment; equipment
manufacturers; equipment suppliers; office
equipment

IDENTIFIER: McGraw-Hill Company is the
parent firm.

SUMMARY: This is a comprehensive, three-
volume buyer's guide to office equipment, systems,
and related manufacturers, vendors, and suppliers.
It describes in detail, hundreds of commonly used
products: addressing and labeling devices,
dictation machines, calculators, collators,
copiers, duplicators, facsimile units, postal
scales, small business computers, telephone
systems, typewriters, etc.

RELEVANCE: This can keep you up-to-date on
office equipment products and services and help in
the selection process.

                    <<<<<<>>>>>>

THE DIRECTORY OF DIRECTORIES
An Annotated Guide to Approximately 9600
Business and Industrial Directories,
Professional and Scientific Rosters, Directory
Databases, and Other Lists and Guides of All
Kinds
1987
Biennially in even years and supplemented with
three issues of the Directory Information Service
Fifth
Marlow, Cecilia   -   Thomas, Robert
1800

Gale Research Company
Book Tower
Detroit, MI 48226
(800) 223-4253
$195.00

Excellent
Directory; annotated guide

INCLUSIONS: Indexes by title; combined
subject-title. Both are cross-referenced.

DESCRIPTORS: Directories; lists; rosters;
databases

SUMMARY: This is an annotated guide to
publications and other documents containing useful
name-and-address lists of all kinds and subjects
available from local through international
sources. Between editions it is supplemented by
the Directory Information Service. It describes
9560 titles, covering a comprehensive range of
subjects and marketplace sectors. It includes
general business and industrial directories;
general and specialized lists of cultural
institutions; directories of individual
industries, trades and professions; rosters of
professional and scientific organizations;
membership lists of special-interest groups of all
kinds -- social, political, cultural,
recreational, religious, etc., state and
government publications listing their own
activities or the programs supported by them; and
a wide variety of lists and information guides on
other subjects. Directory descriptions are listed
alphabetically within 16 subject categories,
including these and others: business, industry and
labor; banking, finance, insurance and real
estate; law, government and military; education;
health and medicine; science and engineering.
Entries include publisher, compiler; editor;
address and phone number of producer; subject
matter coverage and scope; number of listings and
pages; organizational arrangement; entries; type
of indexes; frequency of publication; advertising
accepted; former title; price; ordering source;
and other supplemental information.

RELEVANCE: This is an outstanding reference
book. Every serious consultant should become
familiar with its subject index and general
content. It can be used to identify many
directories and companion documents useful in
building one's practice. It is a valuable
marketplace guide. The subject index can be used
for several purposes to quickly identify: 1)
current lists of contacts bearing upon a given,
defined marketplace sector or target population;
2) titles of comprehensive, special-interest
oriented marketplace guides and reference books
which supply both directories and other useful
information; 3) titles of directories which are
"hidden" within complex documents (this
publication lists and indexes unique sections of
comprehensive directories as separate titles).
The publication also enables one to: 1) compare
the relative merits of directories unavailable for
direct inspection, which focus upon the same
marketplace segments/targets; and 2) identify
marketplace directories which list consultants and
consulting firms.

<<<<<<>>>>>>

ENCYCLOPEDIA OF GEOGRAPHIC INFORMATION SOURCES
A Detailed Listing of Publications and
Agencies of Interest to Managerial Personnel,
with a Record of Sourcebooks, Periodicals,
Guides to Doing Business, Government and Trade
Offices, Directories, Handbooks, Bibliogra-
phies, and Other Sources of Information of
Each Location
1987
Fourth
Mossman, Jennifer
450
0-8103-0415-5
Gale Research Company
Book Tower
Detroit, MI 48226
(800) 223-4253
$130.00

Very good
Sourcebook

INCLUSIONS: Bibliographies; directories

DESCRIPTORS: Geographic information sources;
statistics sources

IDENTIFIER: Volumes for 1970-78 issued as
Volume 2 of the Encylopedia of Business
Information Sources

SUMMARY: This lists sources of
information, emphasizing economic and financial
materials on particular geographic areas, regions,
counties, and cities. It covers over 390
geographic locations and regions and breaks down
into multinational, continental, regional (East
Africa, Arctic region, Europe, Pacific region),
individual countries, regions within countries
(South Australia, Queensland), and cities. It
includes abstracting and indexing services,
almanacs and yearbooks, bibliographies,
biographical sources, directories, directories of
newspapers and periodicals, geographic sources,
gazetteers and guides, government and trade
offices, guides to doing business, periodicals,
statistic sources, and others.

RELEVANCE: This source enables the user to
locate sources of information relevant to business
and to identify specific geographic markets.

<<<<<<>>>>>>

HANDBOOK OF BUSINESS LETTERS
1965
Second
Frailey, Lester
918
0-13-375972-5
Prentice-Hall Inc.
Rt. 9 West
Englewood Cliffs, NJ 07632
(201) 592-2000
Order: 200 Old Tappan Road
Old Tappan, NJ 07675
(201) 767-5054
$32.50

Excellent
Handbook; manual

INCLUSIONS: Index; sample letters

DESCRIPTORS: Letter writing; business
letters

SUMMARY: This volume describes what, why
and how to write effective business letters. It
covers all sorts of common business areas and
provides hundreds of sample letters. The volume
is organized into 14 subject sections with each
subject further subdivided. Sections discuss
business letter rationale, language, "carpentry,"
mechanics, and personality. It includes sections
on these types and purposes of letters: sales,
supplementary sales, regain lost buyers, win
goodwill, human relations, sales manager,
adjustment, credit and collection.

RELEVANCE: This is a well-written, well-
organized how-to manual which contains scores of
helpful information and examples as well as
mistakes to avoid. It captures the spirit as well
as the letter. It can be useful to anyone in
business needing help with how to say what to
whom.

                    <<<<<<>>>>>>

INFORMATION FOR EVERYDAY SURVIVAL
What You Need and Where to Get It
1976
First
Gotsick, Pricilla
403
Appalachian Adult Education Center,
Moorehead State University
0-8389-0211-1
American Library Association
50 East Huron Street
Chicago, IL 60611
(800) 545-2433
$10.00

Very good
Sourcebook

INCLUSION: Index by subject, cross-
referenced

DESCRIPTOR: Information sources

SUMMARY: This list of information
sources for solving problems of everyday life
includes books, pamphlets, films, tapes, games,
and records from various sources (professional
associations, special interest groups, businesses,
publishing companies). Materials are mostly free
or inexpensive and easy to read and use. Major
categories are aging, children, community
education, family, free time, health, home, jobs,
law and government, money management, self and
others, and transportation. Over 200
subcategories include the following: aging -
employment, finances, retirement, etc.; children -
adolescence, adoption, child care, discipline,
etc.; community - busing, environment and ecology,
libraries, news media, social action, etc.;
education - adult, colleges and universities,
credit for experience, GED, vocational and
technical, etc.; jobs -- advancement, career
planning, training, unemployment, etc.

RELEVANCE: Written for the public,
librarians, teachers and counselors, this is a
useful guide to materials evaluated by a staff of
adult educators.

                    <<<<<<>>>>>

NATIONAL DIRECTORY OF ADDRESSES AND TELEPHONE
NUMBERS
1986 (The 1981 edition was abstracted.)
Tenth, revised edition
Annual
Spaeth, Steven
1072
Concord Reference Books, Inc.
Whitney Communications Corp.
850 Third Avenue

New York, NY 10022
0-940994-27-5
B. Klein Publications
P.O. Box 8503
Coral Springs, FL 33065
(305) 752-1708
$24.95

Good
Directory

INCLUSIONS: Index, alphabetical by category
and place, cross-referenced; SIC categories and
subcategories arranged in numerical order with
page references

DESCRIPTORS: Telephone directory; address
directory; corporations

IDENTIFIER: This has been put out by
different people in different editions.

SUMMARY: This is a business directory in
three major parts. The first part contains names
and numbers arranged variously in sections on:
banks, brokerage and investment; accounting; law;
advertising; consultants; media; associations and
unions; political parties; federal government
congress; state government; top 50 cities;
hotels/motels; air travel; car, rail, bus; toll-
free; international travel; postal courier; and
office equipment. The second part lists the top
50,000 U.S. corporations alphabetically. The
third part, The Business Yellow Pages, cross-lists
the 50,000 corporations and classifies them by
Department of Commerce SIC numbers to identify
type of economic activity.

RELEVANCE: The 1977 edition included
consultants, embassies and better business
bureaus. This source is not comprehensive and
seems to have decreased in quality in more
recent editions. It is good as a general
resource. The 1986 edition can be accessed by
computerized database.

SPEAKERS AND LECTURERS
How to Find Them
1981
Second
Not established
Wasserman, Paul   -   Bernero, Jacqueline
350
0-8103-0393-0
Gale Research Company
Book Tower
Detroit, MI 48226
(800) 223-4253
$160.00

Very good
Directory

INCLUSIONS: Indexes by speaker; lecture
title and keyword; geographic; combined, subject
and institution; cross-referenced

DESCRIPTORS: Speakers; lecturers

SUMMARY: This is a sourcebook for
finding speakers and lecturers on a broad range of
topics. The major section is an alphabetic
listing of speakers and speaker bureaus. Sources
include commercial lecture booking agencies,
college and university speakers bureaus, company,
government agency, and professional societies and
trade associations. Listings are based on
response to a questionnaire and include entries on
name, address, telephone, description of speaker
bureau sponsorship, titles of lectures and
subjects covered.

RELEVANCE: This helps speakers and
lecturers to market themselves as well as enables
those seeking speakers to locate appropriate
persons.

<<<<<<>>>>>>

STATISTICAL REFERENCE INDEX ANNUAL
A Selective Guide to American Statistical
Publications from Sources Other Than the
U.S. Government

1987, 1988
Annual, compiled monthly, multiple year
cumulations
Jover, Susan
2 volumes
0-88692-135-X
0278-694X
Congressional Information Service, Inc.
4520 East-West Highway
Bethesda, MD 20814
(800) 638-8380

Excellent
Abstracting service; index; current awareness
statistical guide

INCLUSIONS: Indexes by subjects and names;
categories; issuing sources; titles; user's guide

DESCRIPTORS: Statistics sources; United
States statistics

SUMMARY: This provides abstracts and
indexes of statistical sources from U.S. private
organizations and State government agencies. It
also has a companion microfiche collection of
"statistical portions of the publications
covered." The 1987 annual edition contains
abstracts and indexing of 1960 publications. The
SRI is cumulative since 1980. It provides
national, statewide, foreign countries, and local
data. The index volume contains subject and
names, categories, issuing sources, and titles
indexes. The Guide to Selected Standard
Classifications includes: census regions and
divisions, outlying areas of the U.S., federal
reserve districts, metropolitan statistical areas,
consolidated metropolitan statistical areas,
cities with population over 100,000, consumer
price index cities, standard industrial
classification, standard occupational
classification, standard international trade
classification, and uniform crime reporting.

RELEVANCE: Related CIS services are
American Statistics Index, covering the U.S.
Federal Government statistical publications, and
the Index to International Statistics. They are

the most complete references to statistics sources
available. The abstract for the Statistics
Reference Index for the Federal Government can be
found in the CRG chapter on Government.

<<<<<<<>>>>>>

STATISTICS SOURCES
A Subject Guide to Data on Industrial,
Business, Social, Educational, Financial, and
Other Topics for the United States and
Internationally
1986 (The 1983 edition was abstracted.)
Eleventh
Irregular
Wasserman, Steven
2700 (2 volumes)
Gale Research Company
Book Tower
Detroit, MI 48226
(800) 223-4253
$280.00

Excellent
Guide

INCLUSION: Bibliography

DESCRIPTORS: Statistics sources; U.S.
statistics; international statistics

SUMMARY: This identifies statistical
sources of unpublished information, deriving
citations from publications as well as
organizations, government agencies, trade and
professional groups, and international bodies.
Listings for countries include statistical sources
from the national statistical office, if
available, the primary statistical source(s), and
the primary financial statistical source. It
includes dictionaries of terms, general sources,
guides, and almanacs; non-governmental
publications; publications of the U.S. Bureau of
the Census and other government agencies and
departments; guides to machine-readable data
sources; guides to online database; and

international sources and publications of the
United Nations and affiliated organizations.

RELEVANCE: This enables the user to
procure statistics on people, products, and
services in domestic and foreign markets.

CHAPTER 15

GOVERNMENT

This chapter contains:

- the government market

- contracts and bidding

- how to do business with government

- government statistics

- statistical services and
  publications

AMERICAN STATISTICS INDEX 1987
A Comprehensive Guide to the Statistical
Publications of the U.S. Government
1988
Annual
14th
Jover, Susan
2 volumes
0091-1658
Congressional Information Service
4520 East-West Highway, Suite 800
Bethesda, MD 20814
(800) 638-8380
$1090.00; $765.00 for current subscribers

Excellent
Abstracts; index

INCLUSIONS: Indexes by subjects and names;
categories; titles; agency report numbers;
Superintendent of Documents numbers; guide to
selected standard classifications; user's guide;
acronyms and abbreviations; detailed tables of
contents

DESCRIPTOR: Government statistics
publications

SUMMARY: This two-volume set contains:
1) abstracts volume of statistical publications;
and 2) index volume with indexes by subjects and
names, categories, titles, agency report numbers,
Superintendent of Documents numbers, and guide to
selected standard classifications. The index by
categories has geographic breakdowns (by census
division, county, foreign country, outlying area,
region, SMSA or MSA, state, urban-rural and metro-
nonmetro), economic breakdowns (by commodity,
federal agency, income, individual company or
institution, industry, and occupation), and
demographic breakdowns (by age, disease,
educational attainment, marital status, race,
ethnic group, and sex).

RELEVANCE: This has the greatest level of
indexing and breadth of coverage available (5000
titles) of government statistics reference
sources. It has in-depth abstracts, and gives

tables and select listing of major articles.
It also has "see also" references. This is the
source to use for serious federal government
statistics research. Two other sources of the
same excellent coverage put out by CIS cover non-
federal government and international statistics.
This is available by online database.

<<<<<<>>>>>>

BUSINESS SERVICES AND INFORMATION
The Guide to the Federal Government
1978
First
Weckesser, Timothy — Whaley, Joseph — Whaley,
Miriam
391
0-471-05366-X
John Wiley and Sons, Inc.
605 Third Avenue
New York, NY 10158
(212) 850-6418
$37.50

Very good
Sourcebook

INCLUSIONS: Index; chapter abstract;
finders'guide; checklist

DESCRIPTORS: Federal government; business
information; business resources; business
services; marketing

SUMMARY: This offers access to
information and services for business by the
federal government. It contains four major parts:
1) introduction; 2) annotations of items; 3)
appendix on addresses and telephone numbers of
departments and agencies; and 4) how to use census
data and index. Chapters treat the following
subjects: starting a business; money and financial
management; business administration; human
resources management; affirmative action; OSHA and
product safety; exporting; energy and the
environment; technical information and data bases;

and minorities and disadvantaged. The chapter on
market research, marketing, and government
procurement lists publications and films on
marketing and sales management. It includes:
measuring markets; practical business use of
government statistics; business service checklist,
marketing and low-income consumers; free
publications on marketing and sales; selecting
advertising media; training salesmen; small
business in the U.S.; data sources for specific
industry marketing; and films on advertising and
public relations.

RELEVANCE::   This source supplies the user
with access to government sources of information
and business opportunities.

                    <<<<<<>>>>>>

CIS ANNUAL 1987
Index to Congressional Publications and
Legislative Histories; Abstracts of
Congressional Publications; Legislative
1988
Annual
3 volumes
0-88692-138-4
Congressional Information Service
4520 East-West Highway, Suite 800
Bethesda, MD 20814
(800) 638-8380
$750.00; $375.00 for current subscribers

Excellent
Index; abstracts

INCLUSIONS: Indexes volume: indexes of
subjects and names; supplementary indexes; titles,
bill numbers, report numbers, document numbers,
senate hearings numbers, Senate print numbers,
Superintendent of Documents numbers, committee and
subcommittee chairmen; Legislative Histories
volume: indexes of subjects and names; bill
numbers; Also user's guides; acronyms and
abbreviations

DESCRIPTORS: Congressional legislation;
congressional publishing

SUMMARY: This is a comprehensive guide
to all the publications of Congress. It is an
index to the publications and public laws of
Congress. The CIS Annual provides beautiful
abstracts and indexing. It covers: 1) House and
Senate reports; 2) House and Senate hearings; 3)
House and Senate documents; and 4) committee
prints. The user can find people's names,
witnesses, and organizations represented, chairs
and sub-chairs, and "see also" references.
Abstract entries include: title, date of
publication, pages, price, microfiche information,
item number, Superintendent of Document
classification number, monthly catalog entry
number, and Library of Congress card number.
There is a summary of statement and discussion.
The Legislative Histories volume traces the
development of laws from their beginnings to end.
All significant laws barring some which are
"ceremonial" or "housekeeping" are covered. "Each
history contains an abstract of the public law and
bibliographic citations (title, date, collation,
congressional committee, Superintendent of
Documents classification number, and CIS accession
number where appropriate) for all relevant
documents from the current and prior congresses."

RELEVANCE: This is an excellent reference
to congressional publications. It can be useful
for researchers of congressional legislation as
well as particular legislation.

<<<<<<>>>>>>

CIS FEDERAL REGISTER INDEX
A Comprehensive Index to the Daily Federal
Register of the U.S. Government
Legislative Histories of U.S. Public Laws
1987
Weekly, cumulated semi-annually
Jover, Susan
2 volumes
Congressional Information Service

4520 East-West Highway, Suite 800
Bethesda, MD 20814
(800) 638-8380
$400.00; $295.00 current subscribers

Excellent
Index

INCLUSIONS: Indexes by subjects, names;
CFR section numbers; agency docket numbers;
calendar of effective dates; user's guide;
acronyms and abbreviations

DESCRIPTOR: Federal Register index

SUMMARY: This index to the Federal
Register covers rules, proposed rules, notices,
and presidential documents. It provides many
avenues of approach by: general policy area;
specific subject matter, commodity, or chemical
name; responsible Federal agency; authorizing
legislation; affected industries, organizations,
corporations, individuals, or geographic areas;
affected sections of the CFR; and agency-assigned
docket numbers for specific actions.

RELEVANCE: This is an excellent index to
complicated information. Compared to the Federal
Register Index put out by the Government, it is
far and away a superior index. It has a good
introduction and user's guide to other CIS
publications. This can be a useful source for
consultants, business people, librarians,
government personnel, researchers, students and
citizens.

                <<<<<<>>>>>>

DIRECTORY OF FEDERAL STATISTICS FOR LOCAL AREAS
A Guide to Sources
1980 (The 1978 edition was abstracted.)
Third
McCall, John
359 (1978)
U.S. Department of Commerce
Bureau of the Census

Washington, D.C. 20402
$4.50

Very good
Sourcebook

INCLUSIONS: Index by subject, cross-
referenced; bibliography of sources cited;
appendices: unpublished data for local areas;
population and rank of standard SMSA with map;
cities of 100,000 or more population, by rank,
1970-75; guides to federal and municipal
statistics

DESCRIPTORS: Statistical information;
federal statistics

SUMMARY: This Directory presents
statistical sources by subject in tables for over
100 areas smaller than states. Sources are
primarily published or sometimes processed
(photocopies, printouts), federal data. This
source covers major subject areas such as
agriculture, banking and finance, and sub-topics,
such as agriculture - farms, land use and acreage,
etc. It covers subject areas of commerce and
trade, crime communication and transportation, law
enforcement, education, environmental climate,
governments and revenue sharing, housing and
construction, income and earnings, labor and
employment, manufacturing, mineral industries,
population, prices, and vital statistics and
health. Types of areas covered are cities,
counties, SMSAs, air quality monitoring stations,
and flow-measuring locations on major waterways.
It covers many kinds of areas and specific areas,
such as the five largest cities, counties with
over 400 Blacks, or SMSAs in states requiring the
marital status of mother on the birth certificate.

RELEVANCE: This source contains subjects
and sources relevant to research and marketing for
specific areas of the U.S.

GOVERNMENT REFERENCE SERIALS
1988
First
Schwarzkopf, LeRoy
400
0-87287-451-6
Libraries Unlimited, Inc.
P.O. Box 3988
Englewood, CO 80155-3988
(800) 237-6124
$45.00

Excellent
Annotated bibliography

INCLUSIONS: Indexes by author; subject;
title; and Superintendent of Documents class
number

DESCRIPTORS: Government reference serials;
government publications

IDENTIFIER: Companion and supplementary
guide to Government Reference Books: A Biennial
Guide to U.S. Government Publications

SUMMARY: This covers government
publication serials transferred from Government
Reference Books, especially annual reports, and
biennial, semiannual, and quarterly publications,
as well as monthly and daily publications. Items
published less frequently than biennially continue
to be in Government Reference Books. The volume
is divided into four main parts: 1) general
library reference (directories; guides, handbooks,
manuals; audio-visual materials catalogs,
telephone directories); 2) social sciences; 3)
science and technology; and 4) humanities. Each
part is arranged by subject headings and
subheadings. Entries include: entry number,
title, corporate author, imprint statement,
edition statement, collation, series statement,
publication number, frequency of issue,
Superintendent of Documents classification number,
Library of Congress card number, LC classification
number, Dewey classification number, OCLC number,
ISSN number, Monthly Catalog entry number,
depository item number, stock number for GPO sales

publications, list identification number, order
number for NTIS items, price, and Superintendent of
Documents class number for the serial title.

RELEVANCE: This is a well-respected
bibliography of government serials.

                    <<<<<<>>>>>>

GOVERNMENT REGULATION OF BUSINESS
An Information Sourcebook; ORYX Sourcebook
Series in Business and Management
1987
First
Wasserman, Paul
Goehlert, Robert   -   Gunderson, Nels
464
0-89774-261-3
The Oryx Press
2214 North Central at Encanto
Phoenix, AZ 85004-1483
(800) 457-6799
$55.00

Very good
Bibliography; information sourcebook

INCLUSIONS: Indexes by author, subject,
title

DESCRIPTORS: Government regulation; business
regulation

SUMMARY: This is a bibliography on
government regulation of business. The most
important, first and sixth sections, are annotated
and arrangement is alphabetical. The first
section is titled "core library collection" and
consists of four parts: 1) economics of
regulation; 2) politics of regulation; 3)
regulatory activities; and 4) regulatory agencies.
The next four sections are on each of these four
parts broken down into subheadings, e.g. economics
of regulation -- government intervention, industry
and state, market regulation, and public good.
The sixth section is on reference works with

subheadings such as: research guides, handbooks,
directories, bibliographies, citators, reporters,
indexes, databases, etc. The title index contains
items cited in sections one and six. The author
index contains items in all sections, and the
subject index contains items in sections one
through five.

RELEVANCE: This is intended for
librarians, researchers, government personnel and
business people, and we can add consultants.

<<<<<<>>>>>

GUIDE TO POPULAR U.S. GOVERNMENT PUBLICATIONS
1986
Second, revised
Schwarzkopf, LeRoy
425
0-87287-452-4
Libraries Unlimited, Inc.
P.O. Box 3988
Englewood, CO 80155-3988
(800) 237-6124
$29.50

Excellent
Annotated bibliography; resources guide;
information sourcebook

INCLUSIONS: Indexes by subject; title;
appendix of publications catalogs; abbreviations;
user's guide

DESCRIPTOR: Government publications

IDENTIFIER: This is a revision of the
second edition, New Guide to Popular Government
Publications, 1978. The first edition was titled,
A Guide to Popular Government Publications for
Libraries and Home Reference, 1972.

SUMMARY: This is an annotated
bibliography of some 2900 publications, largely
dated since 1978. "Popular" is defined as a
"topic of broad interest to a large segment of the

the general public." There are 83 main topic
areas, which include: aging; archives,
genealogical and vital records; business,
economics, and industry; careers and occupations;
computers and data processing; constitution and
historic documents; copyrights, patents, and
trademarks; demography and statistics; education;
energy; foreign area studies; health and medical
care; labor and employment; maps; postal services;
social security; U.S. government; veterans and
military retirement; and women. Entries are
alphabetically arranged by title under topics and
subtopics and include: title, date of publication,
pagination, illustration, stock number, price, and
Superintendent of Documents classification number.
In addition these are included as available:
issuing agency, series, publication number,
charts, maps, and tables.

RELEVANCE: While this is intended for use
by the general public, consultants may find useful
sources listed. Items selected also are intended
to be inexpensive or free.

                    <<<<<<>>>>>>

GUIDE TO U.S. GOVERNMENT PUBLICATIONS
1988
Annual (formerly irregular)
Andriot, John
1459
Box 195
McLean, VA 22101
Documents Index, Inc.
(703) 356-2434
$275.00

Very good
Annotated bibliography

INCLUSIONS: Indexes by agency; title;
agency class chronology

DESCRIPTORS: Government publications;
Superintendent of Documents classification

SUMMARY: This is a shelf-listed
arrangement of United States government
publications. It includes important series and
periodicals currently published by U.S. government
agencies. It has a complete listing of
Superintendent of Documents numbers, an archival
organization which groups by subject agency rather
than content. The agency class chronology is used
to trace call number changes for specific titles.

RELEVANCE: This is a standard reference
tool for library specialists in government
documents, and would be difficult to use for
someone else. There is no table of contents or
cataloging in publication (CIP) data, and
according to a librarian specialist, there are
some errors.

<<<<<<>>>>>>

A GUIDE TO U.S. GOVERNMENT SCIENTIFIC AND
TECHNICAL RESOURCES
1983
First
Aluri, Rao   -   Robinson, Judith
259
0-87287-377-3
Libraries Unlimited, Inc.
P.O. Box 3988
Englewood, CO 80155-3988
(800) 237-6124
$23.50

Excellent
Guide; information sourcebook

INCLUSIONS: Index; illustrations and list
of illustrations; tables; chapter references;
further reading references

DESCRIPTORS: Government publications;
government scientific and technical resources

SUMMARY: This is a guide to scientific
and technical government publications. Non-
government sources are included which reference

government sources on subjects covered in the
chapters. The volume is organized into chapters
according to the process by which research is
undertaken and published: applying for funding,
research in progress, technical reports,
periodicals, patents, scientific translations,
standards and specifications, audio-visual and
non-book resources, indexes and abstracts, data
bases, information analysis centers, and reference
sources. Primary sources thus get covered before
secondary and tertiary sources. Major sources of
information on the subject area of each chapter
are provided.

RELEVANCE:.   This can be useful for
consultants, librarians, and others researching
scientific and technical subjects. The government
is a prime source for these materials, especially
patents and technical reports. This Guide
attempts to bridge the gap between sources
oriented to either library government documents
classification and subject oriented
classification.

                    <<<<<<>>>>>>

GUIDE TO U.S. GOVERNMENT STATISTICS
1987
Annual
Andriot, Donna   -   Andriot, Jay   -   Andriot,
Laurie
709
Documents Index, Inc.
Box 195
McLean, VA 22101
(703) 356-2434
$215.00

Good
Annotated bibliography

INCLUSIONS: Indexes by agency; title; area-
world; area-U.S.; subject; appendix; sample entry

DESCRIPTOR: Government statistical
publications

SUMMARY: This covers 12,599 United
States government statistical publications.
Titles are arranged by Superintendent of Documents
classification.   Each entry has a documents index
catalog number.   Entries contain: documents index
catalog entry number; document title; issuing
agency; collation; item number; stock number;
Library of Congress classification number; Dewey
classification number; Superintendent of Documents
classification number; date, price; notes; ISSN;
LC card number; and OCLC. The table of contents
has headings and subheadings for government
department and agencies within departments.

RELEVANCE: This is intended for government
document librarians and their public. It might be
useful for consultants, researchers, students and
business people.   However, more complete sources
for statistics are put out by Congressional
Information Service (abstracts for these are
included in the CRG).

<<<<<<<>>>>>>

INTRODUCTION TO UNITED STATES PUBLIC DOCUMENTS
1983
Third
Morehead, Joe
309
0-87287-359-5
Libraries Unlimited, Inc.
P.O. Box 3988
Englewood, CO 80155-3988
(800) 237-6124
$28.50

Excellent
Information sourcebook; guide; textbook

INCLUSIONS: Index by subject/name; index by
title/series; chapter summaries; chapter
references; illustrations and list of
illustrations; appendices: selected online
databases for federal government information; and
abbreviations, acronyms, and citations used in
this text

DESCRIPTORS: Government publications

SUMMARY: This book narrates key areas
and sources to search for government documents.
Chapters contain: 1) overview of government
documents; 2) government printing office; 3)
Office of Superintendent of Documents; 4)
depository library system; 5) technical report
literature; 6) selected information sources to
government publications (guides, catalogs,
indexes, checklists); 7) legislative branch
materials (legislative process, tracing
legislation, legislative histories, congressional
serial set, and other); 8) publications of the
presidency (White House Office, Executive Office
of the President, Office of the Federal Register,
Department of State, and other); 9) executive
branch and independent agency publications
(administrative rulings, statistical information,
government periodicals, geographic sources, audio-
visual information); and 10) legal sources of
information (research aids, federal court system,
computerized systems).

RELEVANCE: This is an introduction to
government bibliographic sources that are
"exemplary rather than definitive." It can be
very useful for anyone looking for sources of
government information.

                    <<<<<<>>>>>>

ONE HUNDRED BILLION DOLLAR MARKET
How to Do Business with the U.S. Government
1982
First
Holtz, Herman
272
0-8144-7570-1
AMACOM
135 West 50th Street
New York, NY 10020
(212) 903-8087
$10.95

Very good
Guide

INCLUSIONS: Index by subject; appendices
(8)

DESCRIPTORS: Government contracts; proposal
writing; government markets; contract bidding

SUMMARY: A successful practitioner reveals
the intricacies of how to be successful at
providing goods or services to the large complex
of federal government markets. He does the
following: 1) explains how government agencies
and markets work, what government looks for, and
how you can meet government needs; 2) exposes the
myth that only the large and rich can win
government contracts; 3) presents information,
resources, and ingenious methods geared to
success; 4) sifts out and shares with the reader
what works and what does not; 5) analyzes proposal
writing in terms of what is being asked for,
providing it, making it credible, and presenting
it as a sales strategy, as well as discusses steps
and fine points in writing successful proposals;
6) provides information on getting free help from
the government in the forms of resources and
literature; 7) informs and provides examples of
government forms, procedures, and terminology; 8)
gives tips on the significance of being in the
right place at the right time; and 9) explains how
to analyze and present costs in terms the
government wants and how to outbid and beat the
competition.

RELEVANCE: This cleverly written book
makes the subject of doing business with the
government interesting and even enticing...and
perfect fare for the consultant.

                      <<<<<<>>>>>

STATISTICAL ABSTRACT OF THE UNITED STATES 1988
National Data Book and Guide to Sources
1987
Annual
108th
990
0081-4741

U.S. Department of Commerce
Bureau of the Census
Washington, DC 20233
(202) 783-3238
U.S. GPO
Washington, DC 20402

Excellent
Reference; statistical report

INCLUSIONS: Index by subject; appendices
(f); tables; charts; state ranking; telephone
contact list; map of U.S.; user's guide

DESCRIPTORS: ·   United States statistics;
statistics sources

IDENTIFIER: USA Statistics in Brief, 1988,
insert available separately

SUMMARY: This is described as "the
standard summary of statistics on the social,
political, and economic organization of the United
States." There are 31 main subject areas with
subheadings. Each subject area begins with
introductory text. Select subject areas are:
population; vital statistics; health and
nutrition; education; state and local government
finances and employment; insurance and human
services; labor force, employment, and earnings;
income, expenditures, and wealth; prices; banking,
finance, and insurance; business enterprise;
communications; manufacturers; foreign commerce
and aid; and comparative international statistics.
Subheading topics are represented through one or
more statistical tables. The appendices are: 1)
guide to sources of statistics -- state and
foreign; 2) metropolitan area concepts and
components and population of metropolitan
statistical areas; 3) statistical methodology and
reliability; 4) index to tables of historical
statistics -- colonial to 1970 series; and 5)
index to tables having State and Metropolitan Area
Data Book Series.

RELEVANCE: This is a handy source of U.S.
statistics, and good for looking up one quick
source. (For greater coverage, see the abstract

for American Statistics Index.)   It can be useful
to consultants and business people for purposes of
locating desirable business sites, marketing, and
hosts of other information uses. It is also a
guide to other statistics sources.

<<<<<<>>>>>>

STATISTICAL SERVICES OF THE U.S. GOVERNMENT
1975
Revised
Irregular
234
Statistical Policy Division
Government Printing Office
Washington, D.C. 20402
$3.40

Very good
Reference

INCLUSION: Appendix foldout chart on
Federal Statistical System

DESCRIPTORS: Federal statistics; government
statistics; statistical programs; statistical
services; statistical publications

SUMMARY: This describes the statistical
programs of the Federal Government. The
Statistical Policy Division of government provides
policy guidance on development of an integrated
system of statistics for government agencies.
Major parts of this reference are: 1) the
statistical system of the federal government; 2)
principal social and economic statistical programs
- criminal justice; education; energy and energy-
related; environmental; health and vital; income
maintenance and welfare, labor; national economic
and business financial accounts; construction and
housing; population; and production, distribution
and service; and 3) principal statistical
publications of federal agencies - Office of the
President; Departments of government; and
independent agencies.

RELEVANCE: This source provides
information on federal statistics of possible use
to business persons. For example, the Bureau of
Economic Analysis has accounts on national income
and products, balance of payments with foreign
countries, and regional economic activity by
state, metropolitan area, and county. Most of
this information is published in BEA's monthly,
Survey of Current Business.   This source has good
scope but lacks an index and bibliography.

                    <<<<<<>>>>>>

WASHINGTON INFORMATION DIRECTORY
1988
Annual
1988-89
Davies, Ann
1019
0-87187-462-8
Congressional Quarterly Inc.
1414 22nd Street NW
Washington, DC 20037
(202) 887-8500
$25.00

Excellent
Directory

INCLUSIONS: Indexes by subject; name;
reference lists of names with addresses and
telephone numbers; list of state elected officials

DESCRIPTOR: Government officials

SUMMARY: This reference is for quickly
identifying the right person to contact in
Washington D.C. about your concerns. Each entry
provides address, telephone number, name of
department or organization and the name of a
contact person. It is a directory to all
individuals in the federal government located in
Washington DC.

RELEVANCE: This source is useful for any
consultant involved with federal government grants

or contracts. You can be sure your request for
information or assistance will be directed to the
appropriate source.

CHAPTER 16

GRANTSMANSHIP AND FUNDRAISING

This chapter contains:

- government, corporate, and
  foundation support

- fundraising for the nonprofit sector

- grants and research proposals

ANNUAL REGISTER OF GRANT SUPPORT
A Directory of Funding Sources 1987-88
1987
Biennial
Peterson, Linda
998
0-87217-102-7
National Register Publishing Co.
3004 Glenview Rd.
Wilmette, IL 60091
(800) 323-6772

Excellent
Directory; catalog

INCLUSIONS: Indexes: subject; entry listing
by chapter; organization and program; geographic;
personnel name

DESCRIPTORS: Grants; grantsmanship; proposal
writing

SUMMARY: This book is a comprehensive
guide to grants available to individuals in a
variety of fields. Types included are: academic
and scientific research, project development,
travel and exchange programs, publication support,
equipment grants, in-service training grants, and
competitive awards and prizes. Each entry
contains: a description, duration of the grant,
dollar amount, eligibility requirements, number of
applicants and recipients in most recent year,
application instructions, deadlines, and address.
The indexes allow the user to approach this
information by subject, program name, personal
name, and geographic location. Donors include
government agencies, public and private
foundations, corporations, community trusts,
unions, educational and professional associations,
and special interest groups.

RELEVANCE: This directory has 2679 entries
and many entries represent more than one grant,
meaning this is an excellent source of information
on grants available to U.S. or Canadian citizens
from various types of donors.

THE ART OF WINNING CORPORATE GRANTS
1980
First
Hillman, Howard
192
0-8149-0822-5
Vanguard Press, Inc.
424 Madison Avenue
New York, NY 10017
(212) 753-3906
$12.95

Very good
Guide

INCLUSIONS: Appendices include: history and
trends, sample copy of a corporate contributions
policy, tips to students seeking grants, and tips
on how to obtain tax exempt status for non-profit
corporations from the IRS; sample proposal

DESCRIPTORS: Grantsmanship; corporate
funding; proposal writing; grant research tools;
corporate grants; information services;
information sources; educational resources

SUMMARY: This grant seeker's primer is
on getting corporate grants, which total over four
billion dollars each year. It is part of a three-
part series on obtaining grants from private
foundations, government sources and foundations.
It provides humorous suggestions for developing
successful proposals, approaching funding
agencies, and evaluating one's overall efforts,
including follow through. It describes many
valuable grant research tools and information
resources. The sample proposal includes a budget
with appropriate spending categories. It explains
why, to whom, for what purposes, and how
corporations give grants, then discusses the
components of researching corporate donors: their
past giving patterns, their funding guidelines,
their funding vehicle, their evaluation and
decision making processes. A tip sheet for
successful communication during a fund seeking
meeting with a company representative and step-by-
step guidelines to writing the proposal enhance
the volume.

RELEVANCE: This source is sure to help you
understand corporate philanthropy and how to
obtain financial support from this sector. If you
are new to or experienced in grantsmanship this
source conveniently lays out the field and
strategies which can be used successfully time
after time.

<<<<<<>>>>>>

THE ART OF WINNING FOUNDATION GRANTS
1975
First
Hillman, Howard   -   Abarbanel, Karin
188
0-8149-0759-8
Vanguard Press, Inc.
424 Madison Avenue
New York, NY 10017
(212) 753-3906
$12.95

Very good
Guide

INCLUSIONS: Bibliography; sample proposal;
appendices: history and trends; most-funded
fields; government agencies; scholarship funds;
IRS Form 990 AR sample; applying for tax-exempt
status

DESCRIPTORS: Grantsmanship; foundation
funding; foundation grants; proposal writing;
fundraising

SUMMARY: This grant-seeker's primer and
guide describes how to get foundation grants,
which total $25 billion in annual contributions by
the private sector. This complements the Art of
Winning Government Grants and the Art of Winning
Corporate Grants. It provides a step-by-step,
how-to approach to seeking and obtaining grants.
Major sections describe the author's ten step
approach: goal definition, assessment of one's
chances, resources organization, prospect
identification, prospects research, initial

contact, meeting with foundation, proposal
writing, submission, and follow-up. Five types of
foundations are identified as: general-purpose,
company-sponsored, community, family, and special-
purpose. It describes useful professional
services and self-help publications.

RELEVANCE: This source can help you to
identify basic information sources and show you
how to approach funding sources.

<<<<<<>>>>>>

THE ART OF WINNING GOVERNMENT GRANTS
1977
First
Hillman, Howard
246
0-8149-0784-9
Vanguard Press, Inc.
424 Madison Avenue
New York, NY 10017
(212) 753-3906

Excellent
Handbook

INCLUSIONS: Index; appendices; glossary;
bibliography; checklist

DESCRIPTORS: Government funding;
grantsmanship; fundraising

SUMMARY: This is a grant-seekers' primer
and guide to annually-awarded U.S. government
grants totaling billions of dollars. Based on
interviews of grants seekers, funding officials,
congressmen and senators, and a literature review,
it summarizes numerous information sources and
resources, and gives grant-seeking techniques and
advice. Major sections cover grant-seeking phases
(preliminary, research, application preparation,
application submission, application review, and
post-decision phases), governmental departments
and agencies, and specific information
sources/resources. It provides information on the

Department of Health Education and Welfare, other
government agencies, quasi-governmental agencies,
state and local agencies. The section on
information sources includes general tips on
getting information through the Catalog of Federal
Domestic Assistance and Federal Register, federal
information centers, federal regional councils,
federal circulars, and other sources.

RELEVANCE: Competition for government
grants is getting keener, and this attempts to
help prospective grant seekers obtain knowledge
and skills necessary for success. This
complements The Art of Winning Corporate Grants
and The Art of Winning Foundation Grants (see
abstracts in this volume) in the private sector.

                <<<<<<>>>>>

CHARITIES AND CHARITABLE FOUNDATIONS
1974
First
Fish, Edith
869
0-9603140-0-8
Lond Publications
Pomona, NY 10970
(914) 354-3521
$35.00

Good
Resource book

INCLUSIONS: Index; tables of cases; table
of statutes

DESCRIPTORS: Nonprofit organizations;
charities; taxation; grants

SUMMARY: This book covers the laws which
govern the management, regulation, and taxation of
charities, be they organized as trusts,
corporations, or associations. The historical
development of charity from the Greeks to present
day is also discussed in one chapter. Topics
included are: definitions of various charitable

entities, how to set up a charity, how to operate
and purchase a charitable organization, and the
laws and regulations which impact how charities
solicit funds, etc. Footnotes abound and
references to court cases and the legal codes of
various states are so numerous that a special
index is provided at the back of the book for easy
reference.

RELEVANCE: This work is written to aid
persons who are interested in how to set up and
manage a charity under the laws of their state and
the regulations of the federal government.

<<<<<<<>>>>>>

THE CORPORATE FUND RAISING DIRECTORY 1987-1988
1986
Triennial
Cali, Joanna
408
0-914756-94-X
Public Service Material Center
5130 MacArthur Blvd. NW, Apt. 200
Washington, DC 20016-3316
(800) 424-3761
$85.00

Very good
Directory; catalog

INCLUSIONS: Indexes: corporations by
headquarters state; corporations by geographical
preference; corporations by subject areas of
interest, contact persons; corporations that issue
guidelines

DESCRIPTORS: Grants; corporate funding

SUMMARY: This directory provides
information on over 500 corporations which make
charitable contributions. Each entry provides:
name, address, telephone number, contact person's
name and title, application process, geographic
areas of interest, subject areas of interest,
amount given in a particular year, if the company

sends out guidelines for applicants, and
additional information of significance to grant
seekers. The indexes located at the back of the
volume help the researcher identify from what
companies they are most likely to receive funding.

RELEVANCE: This is a relatively
inexpensive directory containing the often hard-
to-come-by information on corporate contributions
in the United States.

<<<<<<>>>>>>

FOUNDATION DIRECTORY
1987
Biennial
Eleventh
Renz, Loren
1001
0-87954-199-7
0071-8092
Foundation Center
79 Fifth Avenue
New York, NY 10003
(800) 424-9836
$70.00

Excellent
Directory

INCLUSIONS: Indexes: personal name of
donors, officer; geographic, types of support;
subject; foundation name; tables; glossary

DESCRIPTORS: Grantsmanship; foundations

SUMMARY: This directory contains entries
for over 5000 foundations, which represent over 20
percent of all grant making foundations. Each
entry includes: name, address, date of founding,
name of initial donors, financial data, purpose
and activities, types of support, limitations,
application information, names of officers, number
of staff, and employee identification number. The
many indexes help the reader identify likely
funders. The lengthy introduction is chock full

of statistical information, advice on how to
research foundations, and trends in foundation
giving.

RELEVANCE: The standard reference work for
information on private and community foundations
in the United States, this work is relevant for
fund seekers, foundation and governmental
officials, scholars, journalists, and anyone
interested in foundation giving.

                    <<<<<<>>>>>>

FOUNDATION GRANTS TO INDIVIDUALS
1986
Fifth
Renz, Loren
288
0-87954-158-X
The Foundation Center
79 Fifth Avenue
New York, NY 10003
(800) 424-9836
$18.00

Excellent
Sourcebook; directory

INCLUSIONS: Indexes: foundation names;
subject and types of grant support; geographic
area funders serve; grants available to company
employees; educational institutions associated
with specific grants; bibliography

DESCRIPTORS: Foundation grants;
grantsmanship

SUMMARY: This is a comprehensive listing
of private foundations located in the United
States, which give grants to individuals.
Multiple indexes allow the reader to pinpoint
those likely to give. Over one thousand donors
are included. Each entry has: contact name, name
of organization, address, telephone number, any
geographic or other eligibility limitations,
financial information about the number and dollar

amounts of the grant, program description,
publications of the donating foundation, and
application procedures and deadlines.

RELEVANCE: Individuals will find this work
to be the only one of its kind. Here you quickly
find out which private foundations in the United
States make grants to individuals for a variety of
purposes.

                    <<<<<<>>>>>>

GETTING GRANTS
1981 (The 1980 edition was abstracted.)
Second
Smith, Craig - Skjei, Eric
286
Public Service Materials Center
5130 MacArthur Blvd. N.W., Apt. 200
Washington, DC 20016-3316
(800) 424-3761
$16.00

Very good
How-to guide; resource guide; textual document

INCLUSIONS: Index by subject; directories;
glossary; research tools; information sources;
bibliography

DESCRIPTORS: Grantsmanship; grants;
grantsmanship process; proposal writing; grant
research tools; foundation funding; governmental
fundiNG

IDENTIFIERS: Grantspeople, Inc.; Federal
Assistance Program Retrieval System (FAPRS);
COMSEARCH; Foundation Center

SUMMARY: This is a general guide to the
grants economy and grantsmanship process. It
discusses the characteristics of successful grant
seekers and the operational dynamics of the
overall grants economy. It is helpful for
refining one's skills in: 1) designing and
packaging proposals; 2) finding relevant funding

sources, programs, and technical assistance
services; 3) seeking governmental and foundation
funds; and 4) approaching funding sources. It
gives suggestions for seeking corporate,
philanthropic, private and community foundation
grants as well as federal, state and local
government funds. It describes current funding
trends and program thrusts likely to be prevalent
during the coming decade for projects dealing with
these areas: the arts, education, social
rehabilitation, science and technology research,
religion, health care, urban and rural
development, economic development and
international issues. It briefly describes the
Federal Assistance Program Retrieval System
(FAPRS) and the Foundation Center's (COMSEARCH)
computer databases. It discusses how to become
more believable, by using third parties to support
one's project and to enhance one's credibility.
It gives many suggestions and insights useful in
planning and marketing effective grantsmanship
efforts. For example, it discusses the grant
seeker's role as entrepreneur in developing
grantsmanship strategies; how to find and select
an appropriate sponsor for a given project if not
affiliated with a nonprofit organization; and
mistakes to avoid in approaching funding sources.

RELEVANCE: This source provides unique
insights into the grants economy and the overall
grantsmanship and strategic planning processes not
covered by other publications. It can be useful
for the neophyte and the advanced grant seeker
alike.

                    <<<<<<>>>>>>

GRANTS
How to Find Out About Them and What to Do Next
1976
First
White, Virginia
354
0-686-24205-X
Public Service Material Center
5130 MacArthur Blvd. N.W., Apt. 200

Washington, DC 20016-3316
(800) 424-3761
$22.50

Excellent
Handbook

INCLUSIONS: Index; appendices (8)

DESCRIPTORS: Grantsmanship; government
funding; foundation funding; corporate funding

SUMMARY: This is a comprehensive guide
to identifying and obtaining grants from
government, foundation, and corporate sources.
Major sections are on types of grants, how to find
out about them, and who gives them, pre-
application, application, and post-application
phases; and comments on the art and craft of
grantsmanship. It treats programs which fund
billions of dollars -- government, corporations,
foundations, contracts, fellowships, and
scholarships. It identifies basic information
sources: libraries, institutional grants offices,
subscription information services, workshops, news
media, word-of-mouth sources, and sources specific
to government, foundations, business and industry.

RELEVANCE: This source is useful for
identifying specific types and sources of grants
and specific techniques for winning them. It
discusses various consultant roles involved in
gransmanship -- proposal writers, advisors on
funding sources, and influence peddlers. It is
straightforward and helpful in interpreting the
art and craft, political, ethical, and personal
considerations involved in obtaining grants. The
author's perspective is broad ranging.

                    <<<<<<>>>>>>

HOW TO PREPARE A RESEARCH PROPOSAL
1988 (The 1965 edition was abstracted.)
Third
Krathwohl, David
304

1600 Jamesville Avenue
Syracuse, NY 13244-5160
(315) 423-2596
$29.95

Good
Guide

INCLUSIONS: Appendix (with comments on proposals for experimental; survey; predictive; methodological; equipment instrument, and material development; philosophical and historical; and longitudinal studies); checklist

DESCRIPTORS: Government funding; proposal writing; research proposal; grantsmanship

SUMMARY: This discusses the presentation aspect of a successful research proposal that gets a small grant. Sections are on general comments, problem statement, related research, objectives, procedure, personnel, facilities, budget, and abstract.   The table of contents is a checklist, which also covers subsidiary points. It includes the following questions: Is the proposal within the scope of the grantor's program? Does the proposal flow logically section to section? Is there enough detail? Does the problem statement convince the reviewer of the proposal's importance?   Is the problem one that has generality beyond the local scene? Have primary and secondary sources been examined? Do the hypotheses or questions flow from the problem statement? Are the objectives clean-cut, specific, achievable? Are the hypotheses stated in a form which indicates what is expected to happen? The procedure subsections treats: population and sample, design, data and instrumentation, analysis, time schedule, and end-product.

RELEVANCE: This small document is geared for the new or experienced academic researcher, student or faculty doing educational research. While its emphasis is on the experimental study, comments in the appendix are on other types of research proposals.

SUCCESSFUL FUNDRAISING TECHNIQUES
1985
Second
Conrad, Daniel
356
0-916664-03-1
Public Management Institute
358 Brannan Street
San Francisco, CA 94107
(415) 896-1900
$39.00

Very good
Handbook

INCLUSIONS: Bibliography; charts; sample
letters; sample forms

DESCRIPTORS: Fundraising; grantsmanship

SUMMARY: This work provides practical
methods of raising funds for nonprofit
organizations. It covers the how and what of
direct mail, capital campaigns, grants,
endowments, memorial and honor giving, major gift
solicitation, and why donors give. It provides an
extensive bibliography of books organized into 16
subject areas.

RELEVANCE: This book is an excellent
working tool for anyone needing practical advice
on how to raise funds from various types of
donors.

CHAPTER 17

HEALTH AND MEDICAL

This chapter contains:

- self-help resources

- employee assistance and support
  programs

- toxicology and pharmaceuticals

THE CONSUMER HEALTH INFORMATION SOURCE BOOK
1984
Second
Rees, Alan   -   Janes, Jodith
530
0-8352-1877-5
R. R. Bowker Company
245 West 17th Street
New York, NY 10011
(800) 521-8110
$39.95

Excellent
Annotated bibliography; information sourcebook

INCLUSIONS: Indexes by author, subject,
title; appendices: directory of pamphlet
suppliers; directory of publishers

DESCRIPTORS: Health bibliography; health
information services; popular medicine

SUMMARY: This is basically an annotated
bibliography of selected references for the
medical consumer. The first chapter is an
introduction. Chapter two covers reference and
research aids -- general bibliographies, and
special topics bibliographies, e.g. aging,
arthritis, human sexuality, children's health,
women's health. Chapter three is on health and
consumer periodicals, chapter four is on
professional literature, and chapter five lists
health information clearinghouses and hotlines.
Part two chapters six through nineteen cover
specific health topics: physical fitness and
self-health care, medical consumerism; alternative
medicine, human sexuality, health of children,
health of women, pregnancy and childbirth, health
of the elderly, cancer, heart disease, diabetes,
mental health, substance abuse, and other health
problems and concerns. Some chapters have
introductory narratives. Annotations include
descriptive and evaluative statements.

RELEVANCE: This is relevant to any
adult concerned about their own or others' health.
The authors attempted to choose publications of
high quality and to deal with present-day health
concerns and topics.

DEVELOPING CONSUMER HEALTH INFORMATION
SERVICES
1982
First
Rees, Alan
296
0-8352-1473-7
R. R. Bowker Company
245 West 17th Street
New York, NY 10011
(800) 521-8110
$34.95

Good
Compendium

INCLUSIONS: Index; chapter summaries,
notes, and bibliographies

DESCRIPTORS: Health information services;
health education; consumer information; libraries;
networking

SUMMARY: This is a collection of
articles by health sciences information
specialists. It is divided into four parts. Part
one is on "the new medical consumerism," which has
developed since the mid-1970s, and the role of
libraries in providing consumer information. Part
two is about the seven main library-based consumer
health information programs in the United States
and Canada. They include public library,
hospital, health maintenance organization,
academic medical center, and school of information
and library science settings. Part three is
"program development and management," and part four
is about the importance of "networks and
networking."

RELEVANCE: This is a companion volume to
The Consumer Health Information Source Book (see
abstract). It is written for the librarian and
information specialist. It can also be useful for
health consultants in locating pertinent
information sources and services.

A GUIDE TO HEALTH DATA RESOURCES
1985
First
Singer, Ira - Myerhoff, Allen - Schiffman,
Susan
92
0-930177-00-2
Project Hope Center for Health Affairs
Millwood, VA 22646
(703) 837-2100

Very good
Annotated bibliography; abstracts; resource book

INCLUSIONS: Index by subject; publications
listing by title

DESCRIPTORS: Health data resources; health
information sources

SUMMARY: This is an annotated
bibliography of health data resources, which have
been published since 1976, are reference works
(excluding journal articles), and contain health
or social science related data for the U.S.
Entries include the following information:
reference number, author and title, general
description, pages and figures, data sources, data
period, frequency, availability, price, and
abridged table of contents. Seven chapters cover
these subject areas: general references, health
characteristics of selected population groups,
health status and determinants, health care
facilities, health care personnel, pharmaceuticals
and health care products industry, and health
programs and expenditures.

RELEVANCE: This is a good guide to the
health data literature. The print is small, the
abstracts quite thorough.

<<<<<<>>>>>>

A GUIDE TO SOURCES OF HEALTH CARE DATA
Clearinghouse on Business Coalitions for
Health Action
1986

First
99
Coalition Clearinghouse
U.S. Chamber of Commerce
1615 H Street N.W.
Washington, DC 20062
(301) 468-5128
$15.00

Good
Information sourcebook

INCLUSIONS: Bibliographies; glossary;
appendices: graphs, tables of selected data

DESCRIPTORS: Health data sources; health
information sources

IDENTIFIER: A Project of the U.S. Chamber
of Commerce

SUMMARY: This contains listings of
public and private organizations and publications
that provide health care data. It includes
chapters on: associations, federal and state
agencies, reference books, periodicals, research
institutes, foundations, a bibliography of
selected references from 1980-86, and special
health issues -- AIDS, alcoholism, and drug abuse.
Chapters contain introductory narratives.

RELEVANCE: This is put out with the
intention to "help purchasers and providers of
health care obtain health care data."

                         <<<<<<>>>>>>

HEALTH CARE ADMINISTRATION
A Guide to Information Sources
1988
First
Morris, Dwight - Morris, Lynne
264
0-8103-1378-2
Gale Research Company
Book Tower

Detroit, MI 48226
$65.00

Very good
Annotated bibliography; resources guide;
information sourcebook

INCLUSIONS: Indexes by author and title,
subject; appendices (5)

DESCRIPTORS: Hospital management; health
administration

IDENTIFIER: Volume 1 of Health Affairs
Information Guide Series

SUMMARY: This is an annotated
bibliography of sources on health care
administration. Its contents are grouped into the
following main sections: 1) general references;
2) statistical sources; 3) education for health
care administration; 4) administrative research;
5) organizational and inter-organizational
relationships; 6) management processes; 7)
institutional staffing and productivity; and 8)
social responsibilities. Appendices contain:
1) libraries and information centers;
2) associations; 3) audio-visual sources;
4) publishers; and 5) graduate schools in health
care administration.

RELEVANCE: This is intended for the
hospital executive and manager. It may also be
useful for the health care consultant doing
background research.

<<<<<<>>>>>>

HEALTH ORGANIZATIONS OF THE U.S., CANADA, AND
THE WORLD
A Directory of Voluntary Associations,
Professional Societies and Other Groups
Concerned with Health and Related Fields
1981
Irregular
Fifth

Wasserman, Paul - Kaszubski, Marek
500
0-8103-0466-X
Gale Research Company
Book Tower
Detroit, MI 48226
(800) 223-4253
$90.00

Excellent
Directory

INCLUSIONS: Selected keyword index of
organizations; list of subjects and cross
references; subject index of organizations

DESCRIPTORS: Health organizations; voluntary
associations

SUMMARY: The bulk of this reference
consists of an alphabetic, annotated listing of
health organizations. Entries include:
organization name, address, phone number, date
established, key contact person, statement of
purpose, membership, finances, meetings, and where
relevant -- publications, affiliations, former
name, and library. The keyword subject index and
subject index of organizations are important
components of this work.

RELEVANCE: As stated in the Introduction,
this work can help consultants and business people
as well as others locate relevant health
organizations. It is on purpose and easy to use.

                   <<<<<<>>>>>>

HEALTH SCIENCES AND SERVICES
A Guide to Information Sources
1979
First
Lunin, Lois
613
0-8103-0836-3
Gale Research Company
Book Tower

Detroit, MI 48226
(800) 223-4253
$65.00

Very good
Annotated bibliography; resource book

INCLUSIONS: Indexes by author, title,
topic; data base; organization; user's guide;
acronyms and abbreviations; sources used

DESCRIPTORS: Health sciences literature;
medical literature

SUMMARY: This is a select, annotated
bibliography to health sciences, including mental
health sources. Its major sections are: health
sciences and services-general; basic health
sciences, medicine-clinical sciences; dentistry;
nursing; public health; animal medicine; allied
health sciences and services; hospitals and
nursing homes; health insurance; pharmacy and
pharmaceutical industry; health information-
communication; core libraries for health sciences
and services; publishers, database distributors,
and suppliers. Arrangement within a section is in
order by publications, databases, and
organizations.

RELEVANCE: This is an important resource
book, however, it needs to be updated.

                    <<<<<<>>>>>>

HEALTH SCIENCES - INFORMATION SOURCES
1981
First
Chen, Ching-Chih
808
0-262-03074-8
MIT Press
28 Carleton Street
Cambridge, MA 02141
(617) 253-2884
$80.00

Excellent
Sourcebook; bibliography

INCLUSIONS: Indexes by title, author,
subject; list of review sources; subject guide;
subject classified reference list

DESCRIPTORS: Medicine; medical information
sources

SUMMARY: This reference includes over
4000 post-1970, primary and secondary, mostly U.S.
sources in 24 categories: selection tools; guides
to the literature; bibliographies; encyclopedias;
dictionaries; handbooks; tables, almanacs,
databooks, statistical sources; manuals,
laboratory manuals, and workbooks, source books;
guides; atlases; directories, yearbooks,
biographical sources; history; important series
and other reviews of progress; treatises;
monographs; abstracts, indexes, current-awareness
services; periodicals; technical reports and
government documents; conference proceedings,
translations, dissertations, research in progress,
preprints, reprints; classifications, standards,
patents; trade literature; nonprint materials;
professional societies and their publications; and
data bases. Sources are then grouped by subject
within each of the categories. Entries are by
title and most are briefly annotated with review
sources. The structure of medical subject
literature and other topics are also discussed.

RELEVANCE: This is quite comprehensive,
covering more than bio-medical topics. It
includes health services administration,
psychiatry, pharmacy, public health, veterinary
medicine, etc.

                    <<<<<<>>>>>>

HEALTH STATISTICS
A Guide to Information Sources
1982
First
Weise, Frieda

137
0-8103-1412-6
Gale Research Company
Book Tower
Detroit, MI 48226
(800) 223-4253

Very good
Annotated bibliography; information sourcebook;
resource guide

INCLUSIONS: Indexes by author, title,
subject; glossary; appendices (5)

DESCRIPTORS: Health care information; health
statistics

IDENTIFIER: Volume 4 in the Health Affairs
Information Guide Series

SUMMARY: This is an annotated
bibliography of health information sources
covering the following areas: 1) general
reference; 2) vital statistics; 3) morbidity;
4) health resources (facilities, personnel,
education); 5) health services utilization;
6) health care costs and expenditures; and
7) population characteristics. The appendices
are: 1) newsletters and journals; 2) government
agencies (state, federal, international);
3) associations; 4) regional depository libraries;
and 5) suppliers of bibliographic data files.

RELEVANCE: The Series is intended to help
find information about the health care system and
delivery of services, especially on social and
information aspects. Chapters begin with
introductory remarks.

<<<<<<>>>>>>

HOSPITAL ASSOCIATION GUIDE TO THE
HEALTH CARE FIELD
Annual Directory of Hospitals, Multihospital
Systems, and Health-Related Organizations
1987

Annual
0-87258-452-6
American Hospital Association
840 North Lake Shore Drive
Chicago, IL 60611
(800) AHA-2626
$60.00 AHA members; $150.00 non-members

Very good
Directory

INCLUSIONS: Index by subject; user's guide;
definitions of facility codes; abbreviations; maps

DESCRIPTORS: Health care market; hospitals;
hospital personnel; health organizations; health
care providers

IDENTIFIER: AHA Abridged Guide on diskette

SUMMARY: Based on an annual survey of
hospitals, this lists: 1) health care institutions
in the U.S. by state, U.S. hospitals
alphabetically, hospitals associated with and out
side the U.S., accredited long-term care
facilities; 2) multihospital systems and alliances
-- hospitals by state and headquarters, their
alliances, networks, and members; 3) maps (state,
metropolitan area); 4) AHA members -- classified
into membership categories, e.g. institutional,
hospital schools of nursing, contracting
hospitals, associate members of a number of types
and personal members of a number of types; and 5)
health organizations, agencies, and providers.
Detailed information and codes, e.g. on hospitals
are provided.

RELEVANCE: Lots of information is
presented in small print and not always easily
accessible. Several addresses for ordering
various things are provided. Nevertheless, this
could be valuable for business people and
consultants attempting to reach certain health
care markets.

HOSPITAL LITERATURE INDEX
1988

Quarterly; fourth quarterly in annual cumulation
Staff of Hospital Literature Service
638 (1987 volume 43); first and second quarter
1988 unbound volume 44
0-87258-462-3
American Hospital Association
840 North Lake Shore Drive
Chicago, IL 60611
(312) 280-6000
$135.00 members; $168.75 non-members

Excellent
Bibliography; index

INCLUSIONS: Indexes by author, journal, and
subject; recent acquisitions

DESCRIPTORS: Hospital literature index;
hospital administration index

IDENTIFIERS: Published since 1945, it was
semiannual until 1961, then quarterly from 1962.
Quinquennial cumulations were done for 1945
through 1974, with the last multi-year cumulation
covering 1975 through 1977.   Since 1978 the AHA
and NLM (National Library of Medicine) have
cooperatively produced the Index.

SUMMARY: This is a bibliography of
journal articles dealing with hospitals and other
health care facilities, health planning, and
administration. It excludes clinical aspects of
medicine. It includes coverage of homes for the
aged, hospices, mobile health units, nursing
homes, skilled nursing facilities, rehabilitation
centers, and health centers of all types,
including mental health, community, and academic.
Subject areas emphasized include: structure and
management of facilities; equipment and physical
plant; financial management; planning and
construction; insurance; legislation, regulation,
and accreditation; personnel; education; patient
care services; quality assurance; reimbursement;
risk management; and utilization review.
Arrangement is in author and subject sections and
entries include: subject heading, subheading,
author, article title, journal title abbreviation,
date of issue, volume number, issue number, and
pagination.

RELEVANCE: This is where to look up
journal articles on hospital literature. It
indexes any and all journals for relevant
articles, including those journals not
specifically health related.

<<<<<<>>>>>>

HOSPITAL STATISTICS
1986 American Hospital Association Annual
Survey Data on Hospital Utilization, Revenue,
Expense, Service Units, Personnel, and Other
Subjects
1987
Annual
245
0-87258-453-4
American Hospital Association
840 North Lake Shore Drive
Chicago, IL 60611
(800) AHA-2626
$40.00 AHA members; $100.00 nonmembers

Good
Statistical report

INCLUSIONS: Index to statistical tables;
survey questionnaire; glossary; technical notes;
tables; maps

DESCRIPTORS: Hospital statistics; hospital
utilization; hospital finances; hospital personnel

IDENTIFIER: Annual survey data published in
Hospitals J.A.H.A. part 2 of August 1 edition from
1946-1971.

SUMMARY: Based on the 1986 Annual Survey
of Hospitals, in which over 6000 responded, this
presents statistical tables on: trends in United
States hospital and multihospital systems; trends
in utilization, personnel, and finances for
selected years; short-term hospitals and long-term
hospitals; utilization personnel per census and
finances per inpatient day; utilization of
hospital units and nursing-home-type units

operated by hospitals and by community hospitals
by state; personnel and finances in hospital units
and nursing-home-type units operated by hospitals
and community hospitals by State; and utilization,
personnel, and finances in: U.S. registered
hospitals, census divisions, states, U.S.-
associated areas, and Puerto Rico; utilization,
personnel, and finances in community hospitals by:
Metropolitan Statistical area, 100 largest central
cities, affiliated with medical school;
utilization, personnel per census, and finances
per inpatient day in accredited hospitals; AHA
membership, approval, and affiliation status in
the U.S. and in states; revenue in community
hospitals; facilities and services in the U.S. and
in census divisions and states; hospital units,
and beds, by inpatient service area in the U.S.
and in census divisions and states; and
utilization, personnel, and finances in U.S. non-
registered hospitals.

RELEVANCE: This could be useful for
medical, business, and hospital consultant
personnel. This is straight, small-print
statistical data wanting for meaningful
interpretation and use.

                    <<<<<<>>>>>>

INDEX MEDICUS
1988
Monthly, cummulated annually
Multiple volumes
0019-3879
U. S. Department of Health and Human Services
Public Health Service
National Institutes of Health
National Library of Medicine
Superintendent of Documents
Government Printing Office
Washington, DC 20402
(202) 275-2051
$179.00 per year

Excellent
Index

INCLUSIONS: Other resources; NLM
publications; NLM recurring bibliographies

DESCRIPTORS: Medical index; health care
index; medical periodicals index

SUMMARY: Index Medicus is an index of
biomedical literature found in journals. Its two
main sections are author and subject listings.
The subject section is arranged alphabetically by
subject headings. Subject entries contain:
article title, first or sole author, journal title
abbreviation, date, volume, issues, and pages.
The author section is arranged alphabetically by
author's last name. Author entries contain the
same information as subject entries except author
is listed before title. Included with Index
Medicus are: 1) List of Journals Indexed in Index
Medicus; 2) Medical Subject Headings, which
provides descriptors for Index Medicus; and 3)
Bibliography of Medical Reviews. The Cumulated
Index Medicus consists of author index and subject
index volumes.

RELEVANCE: This is the most complete index
to periodical medical literature and is available
in medical libraries. It is a must when
conducting biomedical research, though planning,
management, administration, and consulting are not
its focus.

                    <<<<<<>>>>>>

INFORMATION RESOURCES IN TOXICOLOGY
1982
First
Wexler, Philip
333
0-444-00616-8
Elsevier North Holland, Inc.
52 Vanderbilt Avenue
New York, NY 10017
(212) 370-5520
$59.00

Excellent

Resource guide; information sourcebook

INCLUSIONS: Indexes by subject, journal
article; appendices: poison control centers;
abbreviations; additional reference sources

DESCRIPTORS: Toxicology; health hazards;
chemical toxins; toxic substance legislation and
regulation

SUMMARY: This is an annotated resource
book in toxicology -- chemical, physical, and
biological hazards to humans -- with emphasis on
commercial chemicals. The focus in on health
effects. Materials are English language and
organizations mostly United States, with one
chapter on international activities. Contents are
organized into these sections: 1) reference
sources -- historical perspective; books;
monographs; annual reports; fugitive literature;
popular literature; periodicals; audio-visuals;
microforms and card files; abstracts, indexes,
current awareness; databases; directories; 2)
organizations -- governmental, non-governmental,
federal coordinative groups; 3) legislation and
regulations; 4) international activities -
organizations; representative legislation; 5)
education -- universities with graduate programs
in toxicology; 6) information handling; and 7)
journal articles. The parts begin with
introductory narratives.

RELEVANCE: This is relevant for the
toxicologist, environmentalist, consultant, or
employee dealing with questions of occupational
and environmental health and safety.

<<<<<<>>>>>>

MEDICAL AND HEALTH INFORMATION DIRECTORY
A Guide to More Than 43,000 Associations,
Agencies, Companies, Institutions, Research
Centers, Hospitals, Clinics, Treatment
Centers, Educational Programs, Publications,
Audiovisuals, Data Banks, Libraries, and
Information Services in Clinical Medicine,

Basic Bio-Medical Sciences, and the
Technological and Socio-Economic Aspects of
Health Care
1988
Fourth, revised
Backus, Karen
3 volumes
0-8103-2519-5

Gale Research Company
Book Tower
Detroit, MI 48226
(800) 223-4253
$440.00

Excellent
Directory

INCLUSIONS: Master name and keyword index
to volume 1, volume 2, volume 3; chapter scope
notes; index notes

DESCRIPTORS: Health information; medical
information; health associations; health agencies;
health institutions; health libraries; health
services

SUMMARY: Volume one contains over 15,000
entries organized into 18 chapters and is
subtitled: "Organizations, Agencies, and
Institutions." It includes national and
international associations, state and regional
associations organized by subject categories;
foundations and funding organizations; government
agencies; consultant and consulting organizations;
etc. The consulting chapter is organized in order
by state, city, and consultant name, including
information on firm name, address, telephone
number, purpose and activity. Volume two is
subtitled: "Publications, Libraries, and Other
Information Services." It includes journals,
newsletters, annuals, abstracting and indexing
services, directories, publishers, audio-visual
and computer services, libraries and information
centers. Volume three is subtitled: "Health
Services."

RELEVANCE: This is a key resource for
medical and non-medical purposes, including
marketing and locating a consultant. If you are a
consultant this can help you ascertain what firms
exist in an area for the purposes of job-hunting
or assessing need for a new firm of a particular
specialty. If you are a librarian, this will help
you locate medical libraries and other sources.

<<<<<<>>>>>>

NATIONAL HEALTH DIRECTORY
1987 (The 1985 edition was abstracted.)
Ninth
Grupenhoff, John
670
0-87189-852-7
Aspen Systems Corporation
1600 Research Boulevard
Rockville, MD 20850
(800) 638-8437
$64.50

Very good
Directory

INCLUSIONS: Indexes; lists; maps;
organization charts; photographs

DESCRIPTORS: Health agencies; health
officials; government officials

SUMMARY: This is designed to help locate
health and government officials. The ten parts
are: 1) table of contents/agency index; 2)
congressional name index; 3) name index; 4) key
congressional health subcommittees and staff; 5)
congressional delegations by state; 6)
congressional full committees and subcommittees
dealing with health matters; 7) federal agencies
(23) personnel; 8) federal regional officials; 9)
state officials; and 10) city and country health
officers.

RELEVANCE: The Directory be useful for
anyone wishing contact information about personnel

and legislative officials, especially those
concerned with health issues.

<<<<<<>>>>>>

PHYSICIAN'S DESK REFERENCE
PDR Supplement
1988
Annual
42
Barnhart, Edward
2354
0-87489-848-7
Medical Economics Company, Inc.
680 Kinderkamack Road
Oradell, NJ 07649
(800) 223-058L
Order: P.O. Box C-779
Pratt Station
Brooklyn, NY 11205-9066
$36.95

Excellent
Reference

INCLUSIONS: Indexes: manufacturers; product
name; product category; generic and chemical name;
participating manufacturers; poison control
centers; product identification pictures

DESCRIPTORS: Drugs; drug product
information; pharmaceuticals; controlled
substances; drug manufacturers

SUMMARY: The bulk of this volume
contains drug product information supplied by
manufacturers. Sections contain: 1)
manufacturers' index -- addresses, phone number,
available products; 2) product name index --
alphabetical list of products; 3) poison control
centers; 4) product category index -- listing by
generic and chemical name by principal
ingredients; 5) product identification by pictures
under company names; 6) product information -- "an
alphabetical arrangement by manufacturer of over
2500 pharmaceuticals which are fully described as

to indications and usage, dosage, administration,
description, clinical pharmacology, supply,
warnings, contraindications, adverse reactions,
overdosage and precautions, and other information
concerning their use, including common name,
generic compositions, or chemical names;"
7) diagnostic product information arranged
alphabetically by manufacturer; 8) key to
controlled substances categories; 9) key to FDA
use-in-pregnancy ratings; 10) discontinued
products; 11) conversion tables; and 12) guide to
management of drug overdose.

RELEVANCE: This is a key resource for
physicians in the selection and use of
pharmaceuticals. It can be useful to others from
business and consumer perspectives.

                    <<<<<<>>>>>>

PSYCHOLOGICAL ABSTRACTS
Nonevaluative Summaries of the World's
Literature in Psychology and Related
Disciplines
1988
Annual, monthly updates, three-year cumulative
indexes
Granick, Lois
Variable
0033-2887
The American Psychological Association, Inc.
1400 N. Uhle Street
Arlington, VA 22201
(202) 955-7600
$750.00 institutions and nonmembers; $375.00
members

Excellent
Annotated bibliography

INCLUSIONS: Indexes by author, subject

DESCRIPTORS: Psychological literature;
periodical abstracts

SUMMARY: Psychological Abstracts
contains abstracts on psychological and social
science periodical literature. Abstracts are
arranged alphabetically in these major sections:
general psychology, psychometrics, experimental
psychology (human), experimental psychology
(animal), physiological psychology, physiological
intervention, communication systems, developmental
psychology, social processes and social issues,
experimental social psychology, personality,
physical and psychological disorders, treatment
and prevention, professional personnel and
professional issues, educational psychology, and
applied psychology. PA is also available online.

RELEVANCE: This is the resource to use in
searching for psychologically-related articles.

CHAPTER 18

HUMAN RESOURCE DEVELOPMENT AND TRAINING

This chapter contains:

- training and professional
  development

- communication skills

- international training

- training opportunities

- hosting seminars and conferences

- concepts and skills

- training methodology

- organization development

ASPA HANDBOOK OF PERSONNEL AND INDUSTRIAL
RELATIONS
1979
Second
Yoder, Dale   -   Heneman, Herbert
1000
0-87179-307-5
Bureau of National Affairs, Inc.
2550 M Street N.W., Suite 699
Washington, DC 20037
(800) 372-1033
Order: BNA Books
300 Raritan Ctr. Pkwy.
CN94
Edison, NJ 08818
(202) 225-1900
$60.00

Excellent
Guide; compendium

INCLUSIONS: Indexes by subject, name;
bibliography; annotated part references;
appendices (2); list of tables; list of
figures; list of exhibits; footnotes; chapter
outlines

DESCRIPTORS: Personnel management;
industrial relations; training and development;
employee relations; labor relations

IDENTIFIERS: Official handbook of the
American Society for Personnel Administration;
Each of the eight sections were previously
published as paperbacks.

SUMMARY: This volume contains 51
chapters to which 72 authors contributed
information on conceptual and practical aspects of
the personnel field. The volume is organized into
these eight parts: 1) PAIR (personnel and
industrial relations) policy and program
management; 2) planning and auditing PAIR; 3)
administration and organization; 4) staffing
policies and strategies; 5) training and
development; 6) motivation and commitment; 7)
employee and labor relations; and 8) professional
PAIR. The volume includes such topics as

performance appraisal, motivation, productivity, grievances, job design, pension, pay plans, safety, strikes, and unions.

RELEVANCE: This is a handy overview for personnel managers and other managers, unionists, trainers and organization development and management consultants.

<<<<<<>>>>>

BRAVE NEW WORKPLACE
1985
First
Howard, Robert
240
0-670-18738-0
Viking
40 West 23rd Street
New York, NY 10010
(800) 631-3577
Order: 299 Murray Hill Pkwy.
East Rutherford, NJ 07073
(201) 933-1460
$16.95

Very good
Book

INCLUSIONS: Index; case examples

DESCRIPTORS: Organizational change; human resource development; unions; workers' rights; occupational safety and health; workplace; human resource development; high technology

SUMMARY: The author questions that the expectations and promises of the "brave new workplace" of new technology will deliver. In Part one, the Computerization of Work, he argues that while computer technology is new, its management is based on old principles and values, and its contribution is to Taylorism, one of greater managerial control over work and workers. It also deals with the discouraging of employee self-development and the refusal to grant

occupational safety and health rights to workers.
Part two, The Reenchantment of the Workplace,
deals with the gap between visionary work
redefinition and the realities of managerial
control over decisions and design. The author
characterizes new approaches and concepts --
theory Z, corporate culture, excellence,
transformation, participatory teams, quality
circles, quality of work life -- as ways to "win
employee commitment to and participation in the
corporations' goals for working life." The
enchanted Silicon Valley corporate life is raised
as an example par excellance "of firms [that]
weave a cocoon of institutional attachments around
work" in an industry which must rely heavily on
its bright, young, volatile personnel. Howard
demonstrates how this "cocoon" can also be a
burden, especially for Silicon's low-paid workers,
while hazards of occupational health and safety
associated with the semiconductor, electronics
industry are ignored. Part three, the Social
Control of Technology, deals with the changing
role of labor unions. High technology has
unionism in a passive, defensive position. The
author's recommendation is that a social movement,
unions and the federal government exert control of
the new technology. He discusses ideas and
developments along these lines.

RELEVANCE: This book provides perspective
and vision on workers' rights, the workplace, and
high technology. It is recommended reading for
anyone who works and lives in Corporate America,
and especially for organizational theorists and
consultants, high technology decision makers, and
unionists.

                <<<<<<>>>>>

BUSINESS NOT AS USUAL
Rethinking Our Individual, Corporate, and
Industrial Strategies for Global Competition
1987
First
Mitroff, Ian
194

1-55542-030-3
Jossey-Bass Publishers
433 California Street
San Francisco, CA 94104
(415) 433-1740
$19.95

Very good
Book

INCLUSIONS: Index; references; tables;
diagrams; case examples

DESCRIPTORS: Organizational change;
organization development; global economy; career
development; innovation; international business;
systems approach; ethics

SUMMARY: This presents a view of global
change processes and the need for paradigm shifts
to deal with the new realities of global business.
The author discusses the demise of United States
competitive advantage and "slack." He discusses
the inexorable impact of change and a changing
world and the need for new thinking and
strategies. He compares and examines old and new
assumptions, conceptual frameworks, and "less is
more" and "more is more" approaches. He uses a
metaphors of world as garden and complex system as
hologram. He looks at U.S. and Japanese business
models and aesthetics, and states that while
Japanese take a global garden, hologram metaphor,
the West takes an abstract, intellectual,
technical metaphor. He asks: "What will it take
to shift our society's predominant metaphor so
that it can truly compete in a global
environment?"

RELEVANCE: This is an idea book for those
looking at models for organizational
change...consultants and organization development
theorists and practitioners. Given the success of
Japanese business, this is an important look at
the differences between Japanese and U.S. models,
and what might be done to improve business
concepts and strategies in the U.S.

COMMUNICATING WHEN YOUR COMPANY IS UNDER SIEGE
Surviving Public Crisis
1987
First
Pinsdorf, Marion
171
0-66911-790-0
Lexington Books
125 Spring Street
Lexington, MA 02173
(800) 235-3565
$21.95

Very good
Book; guide

INCLUSIONS: Index; bibliography; chapter
notes; case examples

DESCRIPTORS: Organization development;
corporate communications; organizational
communication; communication; public relations;
corporations; organizational change; crisis
management; crisis planning

SUMMARY: The author acknowledges the
pressures and crises of the modern corporate world
and the bottom line yet emphasizes the importance
of communications. She outlines ten significant
business and social trends for companies and
communication as well as four specifically of
concern to communicators. Topics discussed
include: corporations and the media; crisis
planning; crisis planning; mergers; "eruptive
disasters," with Love Canal, Tylenol, and Bhopal
being prime examples; communications as winning
solution, cabbage patch dolls being an example;
communicators in corporations -- history,
characteristics, and skills; and recommendations
for avoiding disasters.

RELEVANCE: The subject area of this book
is an important and complex one, involving many
players utilizing different skills in different
departments of a corporation or organization.
There are not cookbook answers and even clear-cut
guidelines are hard to come by, though they are
communicated about in this book.

A CONFERENCE AND WORKSHOP PLANNER'S MANUAL
1979
Hart, Lois - Schleicher, Gordon
150
0-911777-11-3
Leadership Dynamics Inc.
875 Poplar Avenue
Boulder, CO 80302
(303) 440-0909
$26.95

Very good
Manual; workbook

INCLUSIONS: Bibliography; forms; lists;
charts; diagrams; samples

DESCRIPTORS: Conferences; conventions;
meetings

SUMMARY: This is a systematic, how-to
approach to conference and workshop planning. It
covers topics of needs analysis, setting
objectives, and the Gantt Chart. It also covers
committee workbook sections for program,
arrangements, promotion, registration, exhibits,
fiscal, and evaluation committees. It includes who
does what, when and how. It provides many
different samples and aids, which can be of actual
use in planning.

RELEVANCE: Many professionals at one time
or another find themselves responsible for
planning a conference or workshop. This work can
be used for planning other events as well. It is
geared for organizational, committee-based
planning and it has detailed information on a
variety of pertinent topics planners and
organizers find useful to know about.

<<<<<<>>>>>>

DIRECTORY OF HUMAN RESOURCE MANAGEMENT
INSTRUMENTATION
1985
First

Peters, Douglas
370
0-8839-0188-9
University Associates, Inc.
8517 Production Avenue
San Diego, CA 92121
$105.95

Excellent
Resource book; directory

INCLUSIONS: Index (alphabetical of
instruments); subject index; theory base index;
vendor index

DESCRIPTORS: Instrumentation; assessment;
training tools; human resource development; needs
assessment

SUMMARY: This contains 300 instruments
from 63 vendors divided into six categories --
career planning, behavioral style,
managerial/leadership style; communication;
personal growth, and other. The subject index
provides a detailed breakdown. Each area begins
with tables assessing the instruments by details
within the categories: organization level,
functional class, data source, facilitator
training, scoring, interpretation, and validity.
This is followed by information sheets on each
instrument on: vendor/publisher, author, date,
purpose, design, facilitator training, data
source, theory base, intended audience, time to
complete, items and scales, scoring,
interpretation, validity/reliability, and typical
use. University Associates recommends the
following guidelines for selection and use of
instruments: establish a specific purpose,
examine the theory base, specify target audience
and training events, experience the instrument
yourself, collect normative data, establish
administrative requirements, and determine
actionable outcome.

RELEVANCE: This is a useful directory for
personnel managers, trainers and organization
development professionals seeking instruments in a
variety of areas. Instruments such as these are a

useful adjunct to other approaches in human
resource development for assessing a situation,
and with the benefit of information, making better
training and development decisions. Instruments
can be interesting or threatening to those being
"tested."

<<<<<<<>>>>>>

ENCYCLOPEDIA OF ORGANIZATIONAL CHANGE METHODS
1987
First
Huczynski, Andrjei
345
Gower Publishing Company
Old Post Road
Brookfield, VT 05036
(802) 276-3162
$62.95

Excellent
Directory; reference

INCLUSIONS: Index of methods;
bibliographies; charts; diagrams; information
sources (bibliography; journals; organizations)

DESCRIPTORS: Organization development;
organizational development methods; organizational
change

SUMMARY: The author introduces the
subject of organization development and reviews
four frameworks for interventions (French and
Bell, Blake and Mouton, Harrison, Schmuck and
Miles). The bulk of the book is the directory of
OD concepts/methods arranged alphabetically. Each
method is defined/described with references cited.
Examples of methods included are: appraisal,
early retirement, encounter groups, factory of the
future, gestalt, goal setting, harmonization,
interface groups, job sharing, Likert's levels
meetings, management by objectives, networking,
norm formation, organizational mirror, polling,
psychodrama, quality circles, recognition
programs, sabbaticals, survey feedback

interventions, sensitivity (T-group) training,
team mapping, theory Z management, union-
management committees, wellness programs, and zero
defects.

RELEVANCE: This is a handy reference for
the OD practitioner and student. It helps clarify
the wide-raining concepts and methods of the
field.

                    <<<<<<>>>>>

THE FRONTIERS OF MANAGEMENT
Where Tomorrow's Decisions Are Being Shaped
Today
1986
First
Drucker, Peter
416
0-525-24463-8
E. P. Dutton
2 Park Avenue
New York, NY 10016
(800) 526-0275
$19.95

Very good
Book; collection

INCLUSIONS: Index; case examples

DESCRIPTORS: Organizational change;
management; business management; entrepreneurship;
multinationals; international business

SUMMARY: This book begins with an
interview of Peter Drucker ranging from questions
of what is entrepreneurial to Ronald Reagan's
effect on it. Drucker replies with such answers
as -- large organizations "bore me to tears" and
"I'm an old- not a neo- conservative. The book
also contains 37 chapters and 35 essays and
articles in four parts: economics, people,
management, and organization. Its themes are: 1)
"the future is being made by totally anonymous
people" -- people who continue to make decisions

that run things despite "the daily crisis;" and 2)
"change is opportunity". The book includes such
topics as: world economy, multinationals, OPEC,
the Germans and Japanese, trade, entrepreneurship,
executives, supervisors, managers, workers,
education, labor unions, takeovers and
acquisitions, automation, IBM, Bell, etc. An
Afterword deals with "social innovation" (rather
than technological), with management as the focus.

RELEVANCE: This book is written for
executives. It can be interesting to others
willing to take the time.

                    <<<<<<>>>>>>

GUIDE TO CORPORATE SURVIVAL AND GROWTH
The New Thinking
1986
First
Business International Corporation
117
Business International Corporation
One Dag Hammarskjold Plaza
New York, NY 10017
(212) 750-6384

Very good
Book

DESCRIPTORS: Organization development;
organizational change; corporations; multinational
corporations; international business

SUMMARY: This consists of 19 essays in
six sections which document changes and new
approaches to the changing environment of
multinational companies. The six sections cover
the nature of the new problems, corporate
reactions, preparing for success in the future,
human issues, and what types of companies there
will be. The authors emphasize the importance of
"awareness and adaptability." They write that "no
fixed set of rules can be applied to all
companies." The three types of company of the
future are described as: "the biological company"

-- smaller and freer than companies today; "the
clipper ship" -- more efficient and adaptable; and
"the mayfly company" -- which will quickly arises
and dies. The West is predicted to do better in
the new environment than centralized, Eastern,
communist systems due to better use of economics
of scale, flexibility, and speed of response.

RELEVANCE: This is relevant for theorists
and potential people leaders and workers in the
multinational companies of the 1990s. Projected
characteristics for multinational companies are
along similar lines to those projected for
companies generally as well.

<<<<<<>>>>>>

GUIDEBOOK FOR INTERNATIONAL TRAINERS IN
BUSINESS AND INDUSTRY
1979
Miller, Vincent
249
0-442-25392-3
Van Nostrand Reinhold Company
7625 Empire Drive
Florence, KY 41042
(606) 525-6600
$24.95

Very good
Guide

INCLUSIONS: Index; bibliography checklists;
tables; charts; decision tables; grids

DESCRIPTORS: Training; international
training

IDENTIFIER: American Society for Training
and Development

SUMMARY: This work examines basic
training needs, functions, concepts, limitations,
personnel and techniques and international
applications, especially in developing countries.
It gives suggestions for preparing for cross-

cultural contact and home country re-entry. It
discusses training systems and techniques, and
selection, development and evaluation of trainers.
It discusses different roles of training
specialists: conductor, designer, administrator,
and consultant. It discusses evaluation
considerations: planning, measuring, getting
feedback, post training. It examines funding and
budgeting. It analyzes apprenticeship, in-service
training, on the job training, vestibule training,
vocational technical and trade schools training,
cooperative education and training, home study,
self study, etc.

RELEVANCE: This guidebook is ground in the
theory and practice of training and development as
represented by the American Society for Training
and Development. It generates opportunity and
awareness of the international market in terms of
training specialists, training programs and
skills. It is useful for new and experienced
trainers, consultants, and human resource
developers, especially those is government,
corporations and organizations.

<<<<<<>>>>>>

HANDBOOK OF LEADERSHIP
A Survey of Theory and Research
1981 (The 1974 edition was abstracted.)
First
Stogdill, Ralph
613
0-02931-660-X
The Free Press
866 Third Avenue
New York, NY 10022
(212) 935-2000
$19.95

Very good
Handbook

INCLUSIONS: Indexes by author, subject;
bibliography

DESCRIPTORS: Leadership; executives;
business leaders; organizational behavior

SUMMARY: This presents and reviews the
research literature on leadership. Major parts
are on leadership theory, leader personality and
behavior, leadership stability and change,
emergence of leadership role, leadership and
social power, leader-follower interactions, and
leadership and group performance. It also covers
situational determinants of leadership, work
performance of leaders, persistence and transfer
of leadership, leadership training, leadership and
power relations, democratic and autocratic
patterns, and participative and directive
patterns.

RELEVANCE: Examples of relevant findings
for business persons are that business leaders
exhibit similar performance profiles, and
executives in business organizations vary as much
within their organization as between types of
organizations.

<<<<<<>>>>>>

HANDBOOK OF MODERN PERSONNEL ADMINISTRATION
1972
First
Famularo, Joseph
1268
07-019912-4
McGraw-Hill Book Company
1221 Avenue of the Americas
New York, NY 10020
(800) 262-4729
$27.50

Good
Guide; compendium

INCLUSIONS: Index; chapter bibliographies;
illustrations

DESCRIPTORS: Personnel management; personnel
administration; employees; employee benefits;

training and development; labor relations;
personnel records

SUMMARY: This is intended as a handbook
and overview of personnel administration. There
are 81 article contributions organized in the
following chapter subjects: 1) management and
personnel administration; 2) organization and
operation of the personnel administration
department; 3) development of personnel resources;
4) recruitment, selection, and placement; 5)
training and development; 6) wage and salary
administration; 7) employee benefits; 8) employee
appraisal and assessment; 9) employee services,
safety, and health; 10) government controls; 11)
labor relations; 12) international personnel
management; 13) acquisitions and mergers; 14)
special personnel problems; 15) special employee
groups; 16) communicating to employees; 17)
records, reports, and statistics; and 18)
personnel research.

RELEVANCE: This is a companion to the
volume, Handbook of Personnel Forms, Records, and
Reports (see abstract). This volume is older and
the print is very small.

                    <<<<<<>>>>>>

HANDBOOK OF PERSONNEL FORMS, RECORDS, AND
REPORTS
1982
First
Newton, William - Gelatt, Esther
Joseph Famularo
640
0-07-019913-2
McGraw Hill Book Company
1221 Avenue of the Americas
New York, NY 10020
(800) 262-4729
$89.95

Excellent
Handbook

INCLUSIONS: Index; forms; checklists;
questionnaires

DESCRIPTORS: Personnel records; employee
records

SUMMARY: This is a book of forms and
records intended to aid in the personnel function.
An Introduction discusses the need for forms,
computerization, confidentiality, and the
employee's right-to-know through access to
records. Chapters begin with a discussion of the
subject followed by sample forms. The chapters
are: 1) recruitment; 2) internal placement
systems; 3) basic personnel records; 4)
development of personnel resources; 5) wage and
salary administration; 6) employee benefits; 7)
employee services; 8) succession plans; 9)
employee health; 10) equal employment opportunity;
11) safety and employee work injuries; 12)
overseas employees; 13) time off the job; 14)
employee communications; and 15) termination of
employment.

RELEVANCE: This contains useful discussion
of legalities and examples. It is intended as a
companion volume to Handbook of Modern Personnel
Administration (see abstract).

<<<<<<>>>>>>

HANDBOOK OF TRAINING EVALUATION AND
MEASUREMENT METHODS
1983
First
Phillips, Jack
316
0-87201-877-6
Gulf Publishing Company
P.O. Box 2608
Houston, TX 77252
(713) 529-4301
$27.00

Very good
Handbook

INCLUSIONS: Index; appendices (5);
examples; status test; tables; tools; forms;
checklists; chapter summary; chapter references

DESCRIPTORS: Training evaluation; evaluation

SUMMARY: Part one is an examination of
the myths about and need for evaluation, and the
trend toward measurement. Part two is on a
results-oriented approach and 18-step human
resources development (HRD) model, instrument
design, participant selection, evaluation design,
and program costs. Part three is on data
collection methods, data analysis and measurement,
and the evaluation of outside resources --
seminars, packaged programs, and consultants.
Part four is on the effect of management on HRD
program results and communication of results. The
appendices contain additional information,
questionnaires, and a performance contract.

RELEVANCE: This can be useful to internal
and external HRD professionals in designing,
implementing and analyzing system and specific
aspects of evaluation programs.

                      <<<<<<>>>>>>

HOW TO MAKE THE TRANSITION FROM AN
ENTREPRENEURSHIP TO A PROFESSIONALLY MANAGED FIRM
1986
First
Flamholtz, Eric
231
0-87589-069-0
Jossey-Bass Publishers
433 California Street
San Francisco, CA 94104
(415) 433-1740
$22.95

Very good
Guide

INCLUSIONS: Index; annotated bibliography;
diagrams; tables; case studies

DESCRIPTORS: Organizational change;
organization development; entrepreneurship;
management

SUMMARY: This book looks at why
entrepreneurships fail or succeed in progressing
to a professionally managed firm.   In Part one the
author presents and discusses: 1) "a pyramid of
organizational development" for success: identify
and define a market niche, develop products and
services, acquire resources, develop operational
systems, develop management systems, and develop a
corporate culture; 2) four stages of
organizational growth: new venture, expansion,
professionalization, and consolidation; and 3)
ten organizational growing pains.   Part two
presents management strategies for each stage of
organizational growth.   Part three chapters are on
management tools -- strategic planning and
organizational control systems.   Part four deals
with issues of the entrepreneur and CEO.

RELEVANCE: This book is relevant for
entrepreneurs, owners, CEOs, managers, and
scholars of these subjects.

                    <<<<<<>>>>>>

HOW TO ORGANIZE AND MANAGE A SEMINAR
What to Do and When to Do It
1983
Murray, Sheila
204
0-13-425199-7
Prentice-Hall, Inc.
Rt. 9 West
Old Tappan, NJ 07675
(201) 767-5054
Order: 200 Old Tappan Road
Englewood Cliffs, NJ 07632
(201) 592-2000
$14.95

Very good
Guide; manual

INCLUSIONS: Checklists; flow charts; index
by subject, organizations, individuals,
publications; resources list

DESCRIPTOR: Seminars

SUMMARY: This is a what and when to do
it guide to producing successful seminars arranged
with a chronological frame of reference. It takes
the reader step by step through states and
sections of planning, advance work, communication
with participants, the seminar, evaluation,
follow-up and debriefing. Each section has
subheadings on specifics and each subsection
contains one or two interviews with professionals.
Some subject areas discussed include theme and
objectives, participants' profile format and
design, staging and logistics, how to find a
speaker/trainer, how to shop for suppliers, audio-
visual equipment, room setup, facility issues, and
registration.

RELEVANCE: This work is useful for
individuals or organizations presenting seminars,
especially when outside speakers are involved.

                       <<<<<<>>>>>>

HUMAN RESOURCES MANAGEMENT AND DEVELOPMENT
HANDBOOK
1985
First
Tracy, William
1568
0-317-1734-8
AMACOM
135 West 50th Street
New York, NY 10020
(212) 903-8087
$85.00

Very good
Handbook

INCLUSIONS: Index; chapter summary

DESCRIPTORS: Human resources development;
human resources management; personnel management

SUMMARY: This covers all aspects of
human resources development (HRD) in 18 parts with
108 chapter contributors. Topics covered include:
discussion of the HRD function...its management,
organization, staffing, evaluation, improvement,
plant and facilities, support services, program
elements, employee and public relations, employee
services, organization and management development,
training, and HRD systems design, implementation
and evaluation. The editor points out that HRD is
a complicated function with many aspects.

RELEVANCE: This is a comprehensive
overview of HRD directed toward executives,
managers, human resources managers, trainers and
developers, and students. Chapter subtitles and
summaries and the index are helpful aids in wading
through this thick volume.

                    <<<<<<>>>>>>

IMPLEMENTING ORGANIZATIONAL CHANGE
A PRACTICAL GUIDE TO MANAGING CHANGE EFFORTS
1984
First
Lippitt, Gordon - Langseth, Petter - Mossop,
Jack
185
0-87589-622-7
Jossey-Bass Publishers
433 California Street
San Francisco, CA 94104
(415) 433-1740
$21.95

Very good
Book; guide

INCLUSIONS: Index; references

DESCRIPTORS: Organizational change;
organization development

SUMMARY: This book describes the change
process and a two-year case-study of planned
change at the Administrative Department of the
World Bank. The approach taken was eclectic,
combining different schools of thought. Chapter
topics are: 1) how to diagnose organizational
need for change of context, outputs, and
organization culture; task, formal organization,
people; physical setting and technology; 2) how to
initiate and plan change -- preconditioning,
setting up task forces, collecting data, data
analysis, planned action based on the data,
implementation of action, and evaluation; 3) how
to involve people in change; 4) how to identify
and choose opportunities for change; 5) how to
manage change; and 6) how to evaluate results.
The last chapter is a discussion of lessons
learned, and each chapter has end-of-chapter
"reflective comments."

RELEVANCE: This book is intended to be of
use for line managers, staff specialists,
organization development practitioners,
consultants, and evaluators. It is a book of
learnings and gleanings from an actual planned
change experience.

                     <<<<<<>>>>>>

IN SEARCH OF EXCELLENCE
Lessons From America's Best-Run Companies
1982
First
Peters, Thomas   - Waterman, Robert
360
0-06-015042-4
Harper and Row Publishers
10 E. 53rd Street
New York, NY 10022
(800) 242-7737
$21.45

Excellent
Book

INCLUSIONS: Index; chapter notes; case
examples

DESCRIPTORS: Organization development;
business management; management; corporate culture

SUMMARY: The authors examine the
attributes of what constitutes "excellence" in
companies: a bias for action," "close to the
customer," "autonomy and entrepreneurship,"
"productivity through people," "hands-on, value
driven," "stick to the knitting," "simple form,
lean staff," and "simultaneous loose-tight
properties." They studied 43 companies (high
technology, consumer goods, general industrial,
service, project-management, and resource based),
which evidenced success in financial performance.
They carried out structured interviews and did a
25-year literature review. They argue that the
rational model of management has serious
drawbacks, and people aren't always rational.
They review theories and theorists. They
underline the importance of culture and "managed
evolution" in a company.

RELEVANCE: This book has influenced a
turnaround in ideas and literature about what
leads to company success. It is relevant to
theorists, business owners/managers and
consultants.

                    <<<<<<>>>>>>

MANAGING PRODUCTIVITY IN ORGANIZATIONS
A Practical, People-Oriented Perspective
1986
First
Koplman, Richard
336
0-07-035329-8
McGraw-Hill Book Company
1221 Avenue of the Americas
New York, NY 10020
(800) 262-4729
$16.95

Very good
Book; research report

INCLUSIONS: Index; chapter notes; tables

DESCRIPTORS: Productivity; reward systems;
employee selection; goal setting; management by
objectives; training and development; participative
leadership; job enrichment; performance feedback;
job design; alternative work schedules

SUMMARY: This is an empirical study and
discussion of productivity factors. The author
defines "productivity," why it's important, and
factors involved in it. He provides the
conceptual framework and research methods used to
test ten theories of what improves productivity.
The ten areas are discussed in subsequent chapters
and are: reward systems, goal setting, management
by objectives, selection of employees, training
and development, leadership and participation,
organization structure and decentralization,
performance feedback, job design, and alternative
work schedules. The results show that the two
approaches contributing most to increased
productivity are output-based reward systems and
tests for employee selection. The two least
effective approaches found were job enrichment and
participative leadership. The author cautions
that the effectiveness of the different approaches
may vary situationally, and that organizational
diagnosis is important. The author also examines
the role of a productivity department. He
concludes that "productivity has to be planned and
systematically pursued; it has to be managed."

RELEVANCE: This can be useful to internal
or external productivity specialists/consultants
and managers.

                    <<<<<<>>>>>>

THE NEW UNIONISM
Employee Involvement in the Changing Corporation
1988
First

Hechscher, Charles
302
0-465-05098-0
Basic Books, Inc.
10 East 53rd Street
New York, NY 10022
(800) 242-7737
$22.95

Excellent
Book

INCLUSIONS: Index; bibliography; chapter
notes; case examples

DESCRIPTORS: Organizational change; trade
unions; associational unionism; unionism;
associations; industrial relations; employee
rights; employee participation; quality of work
life; collective bargaining; Wagner Act; National
Labor Relations Board; women; minorities

SUMMARY: This book deals with the
reality of the declining labor union movement on
the one hand and the legitimate need for employee
representation on the other. The author traces
the rise and decline of labor unions, the Wagner
Act, and the reasons for the decline: e.g.
increased, non-union oriented, white-collar
population, failure to be flexible, and
unpopularity of confrontation tactics. This
change is likened to the order of change of the
1920s and '30s when craft unionism transitioned
into industrial unionism. The author also traces
the birth of new style "associational unionism,"
which "opens the system of worker representation
to a multiplicity of groups and interests," and
which the author sees as more congruent with the
current situation of "rapid economic change,
flexible systems of management, and shifting
employee loyalties." While associations are
characterized as moving closer to a union model of
organized pressure, especially noting the impact
of women and minorities organizations, unions are
seen as losing power of uniform contracts and
moving toward local participation and diversity.
The author presents a vision of associational
unionism, necessary criteria and traps to avoid.

RELEVANCE: This is a new look at the
realities of what's happening to unions and new
directions in worker-management relations. It is
an important piece of the puzzle, which can be
read in relation to trends in work life and works
in the organization development and management
literatures.

                    <<<<<<>>>>>>

NEW WORLD, NEW WAYS, NEW MANAGEMENT
1983
First
Harris, Philip
324
0-8144-5755-X
AMACOM
135 W. 50th Street
New York, NY 10020
(212) 903-8087
$22.95

Very good
Book

INCLUSIONS: Index; bibliography; source
notes and references; appendices: organizational
culture survey instrument; management
communications inventory; change inventory for
leaders; inter-cultural relations inventory;
leadership motivation inventory

DESCRIPTORS: Organizational change;
organization development; organizational
transformation; organizational behavior;
leadership; corporate culture; communication;
computerization; telecommunications; career
development; reward systems

SUMMARY: This book is about what future
organizations will be like -- their requirements,
characteristics, personnel, and processes. It
takes an anthropological, culture model. Its
thesis is that technological change,
computerization, telecommunications, technology
transfer, and the global marketplace are fueling

corporate organizational change. The author
describes "metaindustry," characterized by new
organizational culture, horizontal power and
authority, and synergistic personnel. Harris
discusses the impact of culture on organizational
behavior. He discusses new patterns of corporate
rationale and identity, purposes and standards,
look and style, corporate processes and
activities, communications, career development
patterns, organizational relationships, and
recognition and reward systems. Other topics are
the relationship of technology to work culture and
the role of leadership in developing
organizational potential.

RELEVANCE: This book takes a look at the
future of organizations as influenced by
technological change. It is geared for the
organization development professional reader.

                    <<<<<<>>>>>>

ORGANIZATION CHANGE AND DEVELOPMENT
A Systems View
1980
First
Beer, Michael
367
0-8302-6416-7
Goodyear Publishing Company, Inc.
1640 5th St.
Santa Monica, CA 90401

Very good
Textbook; primer

INCLUSIONS: Index; references; appendix
(case studies); diagrams

DESCRIPTORS: Organization development;
organizational change; systems approach;
consultants; intervention

SUMMARY: Beer defines and traces the
development of organization development (OD). He
presents an open system approach and a systems

model of organizations. Part one is about organizations and organizational change. Part two is on OD intervention strategies. Part three is on intervention methods -- diagnostic interviews, process interventions, structural innovations and interventions, and individual interventions. Part four is on strategic issues in system change. The appendix has case studies in organization development for Corning Glass Works, Datavision, and May Department Stores Company.

RELEVANCE: This presents an overview of the field of organization development and is aimed at managers and students of management. It is also a good review or introduction for new OD consultants.

<<<<<<>>>>>>

ORGANIZATION DEVELOPMENT
A Total Systems Approach to Positive Change in
Any Business Organization
1983
First
Albrecht, Karl
254
0-1364-1696-9
Prentice-Hall Inc.
Rt. 9 West
Englewood Cliffs, NJ 07632

(201) 592-2000
Order: 200 Old Tappan Road
Old Tappan, NJ 07676
(201) 767-5054
$18.45

Very good
Guide; primer

INCLUSIONS: Bibliography; professional organizations; case studies

DESCRIPTORS: Organization development; organizational change; systems approach

SUMMARY: Albrecht presents basic
concepts and approaches to organization
development, group dynamics, behavior-
modification, and systems theory. He takes a
systems approach. He discusses four key systems
in separate chapters: technical, social,
administrative, and strategic. He then presents
the OD process in four phases and chapters:
assessment, problem-solving, implementation, and
evaluation. He makes predictions about the future
of organization development and business and
discusses OD skills. Case studies in organization
development are on Polaroid Corporation, General
Motors, Saab-Scania Corporation, and U.S.
Department of Energy.

RELEVANCE: This is a good introduction to
the practice of organization development.

                    <<<<<<>>>>>>

ORGANIZATIONAL CHANGE AND THE THIRD WORLD
Designs for the Twenty-First Century
1987
First
Jedlicka, Allen
141
0-2759-2317-7
Praeger Publishers
One Madison Avenue
New York, NY 10010-3603
(212) 685-5300

Excellent
Book; guide

INCLUSIONS: Index; case examples; chapter
notes

DESCRIPTORS: Organizational change;
organization development; training; international
business; cross-cultural relations; global
economy; futurism; international development;
third world; cross-cultural training; women; Japan

SUMMARY: This book applies concepts of

anthropology, training and organizational
development/change to the third world and whole
world. The author talks about the "window of
opportunity" now for moving toward a Walden II
metaphor where "the behavior of group members was
shaped so they would function smoothly for the
benefit of all." The approach emphasized for
doing this is trained, participative involvement
of change beneficiaries in the Third World as well
as change agents from the First World, having the
aim of integrating the world. Jedlicka points out
that top-down decision making by autocrats,
consultants, or managers has limited awareness
and efficacy. He discusses the need for
culturally sensitive training techniques and the
development of indigenous staff, and provides
training guidelines and specific training
exercises addressing five problem areas. Case
examples of China, India, and the Philippines are
used to illustrate facilitating conditions and
processes leading to success and failure
strategies and outcomes. The author views women
as superior, if under-recognized change agents,
and encourages their increased role. The author
believes that democratic individualist based
systems are demonstrating superiority over
communistic, collective forms.

RELEVANCE: This book integrates cultural
anthropological and organization training and
development approaches to third world and world
development issues. It is especially recommended
for persons working in the international arena of
development.

                    <<<<<<>>>>>>

ORGANIZATIONAL TRANSFORMATION
Approaches, Strategies, Theories
1986
First
Levy, Amir - Merry, Uri
347
0-275-92147-6
Praeger Publishers
521 Fifth Avenue
New York, NY 10175

(212) 685-5300
$42.95

Excellent
Book

INCLUSIONS: Index by subject; bibliography;
case studies; tables

DESCRIPTORS: Organizational change;
organization development; organizational
transformation; planned change

SUMMARY: This book deals with
organizational, transformational change. The
first chapter reviews theories and defines first-
and second-order change. Subsequent chapters
present these approaches to creating change:
paradigm change; "high performance" and
"excellence" creation in organizations;
transformation of myths and rituals; reframing;
re-channeling energy; and consciousness-raising
and changing. The second part of the book
compares transition and transformation strategies,
organizational renewal and starting over, and top-
down and bottom-up strategies. Part three deals
with research and theories on organizational
change and transformation. Part four, the
Summary, is on models of second-order change and
the integration of theory and practice.

RELEVANCE: This is a systematic, theory
book, which gives an overview of work in
organizational transformation. Many questions are
relegated to the results of further research.
This book is sophisticated and best recommended
for the scholar, consultant and organization
development expert.

                    <<<<<<>>>>>>

RE-INVENTING THE CORPORATION
Transforming Your Job and Your Company for the
New Information Society
1985
First

Naisbitt, John - Aburdene, Patricia
308
Warner Books
666 Fifth Avenue
New York, NY 10103
(800) 638-6460
$17.50

Excellent
Book; guide

INCLUSIONS: Index; notes; case examples

DESCRIPTORS: Organizational change;
organization development; lifework planning;
education; corporate training; lifelong learning;
career development; Japanese-style management;
participative management; flexible work; quality
of work; occupational health; wellness programs;
information age society; computerization;
corporations; management; entrepreneurship;
workers; women; comparable worth; child care;
networking

SUMMARY: The authors show how, driven by
new values and economic necessity, the time for
transforming our work lives is now. Corporation
is broadly defined and inclusive of profits and
non-profits, employees and proprietors, and is
viewed wholistically. The authors believe work
should be fun and related to other aspects of life
-- family, health, education. Separate chapters
are devoted to education, health, and women.
People are seen as "the strategic resource" within
a context of changing demography. Ten trends
impacting the corporation are identified: 1) the
shift to an information society; 2) the coming
seller's market and competition for employees; 3)
the replacement of middle management by computers;
4) entrepreneurial development; 5) diverse work
force; 6) working women; 7) intuition and vision;
8) the toll of education; 9) corporate health
programs; and 10) the values of baby boomers.

RELEVANCE: This book professes to apply
the changes described in Naisbitt's Megatrends and
this book to what to do about them. It talks
about the re-invention of a corporation which "is

equally pro-profits and pro-people." This book is
more conceptual than how-to. It is good reading
for reconceptualizing and noticing trends and how
they apply to one's life and work. Selected
boldfaced sentences throughout the text offer a
quick, easy way of moving through it.

<<<<<<>>>>>>

RUNNING CONVENTIONS, CONFERENCES, AND MEETINGS
1981
Lord, Robert
192
0-317-20407-6
Books on Demand
UMI
Division of University Microfilms, International
300 N. Zeeb Road
Ann Arbor, MI 48106
(800) 521-0600
$26.00

Good
Guide

INCLUSIONS: Index by subject; cross-
referenced

DESCRIPTORS: Conferences; conventions;
meetings

SUMMARY: This guide for running any type
of meeting or convention begins with advance
decisions and planning, such issues as whether to
have the meeting in the first place, theme, site,
length, price, committee work, program, speakers,
convention bureaus, hotels, advance registration,
badges and signs, kits and spouses. Other
chapters are devoted to promotion and publicity,
the meeting itself, post meeting activity, small
and special meetings, additional subjects, the
participant, and travel tips.

RELEVANCE: This is a handy, easy-to-read
overview for the initiate involved in running a
meeting.

THE SCHUSTER REPORT
The Proven Connection Between People and
Profits
1986
First
Schuster, Frederick
200
0-471-83293-6
John Wiley & Sons
605 Third Avenue
New York, NY 10158
(212) 850-6418
$19.95

Very good
Book; research report

INCLUSIONS: Index; appendix; bibliography;
tables

DESCRIPTORS: Productivity; Organization
development; human resource development;
management theory; employee participation

SUMMARY: Author Schuster researched 1300
major U.S. firms and presents his findings in this
book. He formulates "Strategy A" for "improving
productivity through attention to employees." The
seven-step, Strategy A process discussed is: 1)
measure the human organization; 2) act on key
opportunities for improvement; 3) pay executives
and managers for effective human resource
management; 4) break down barriers to
participation, communication, and contribution; 5)
involve employees in planning and implementing
changes; 6) remeasure the climate and condition of
the human organization annually; and 7) reinforce
Strategy A. Case examples presented of successful
organizations using Strategy A principles are IBM
and Donnelly Mirrors. Schuster discusses key
ideas of management theorists. The appendix
contains the methods, results, discussion and
conclusions of the Schuster research study.

RELEVANCE: This is a scientifically
oriented approach to the study of what kinds of
people management works to create increased
productivity. It is directed to executives and
managers.

THE SEMINAR MARKET
1980
First
Schrello, Dominick
123
Schrello Enterprises
555 East Ocean Blvd., 4th Floor
Long Beach, CA 90802
(213) 435-1789
$95.00

Excellent
Research report

INCLUSIONS: Appendix: List of Major Seminar
Suppliers; tables; charts; bibliography

DESCRIPTORS: Seminar market; training;
courses

IDENTIFIER: Short Courses and Business
Seminars in North America

SUMMARY: This report examines the $350
million dollar seminar industry. This (1980)
study reports that the market is growing at the
rate of 15% a year, with a million to two million
attendees a year. The report examines these
subjects: 1) the nature and structure of the
industry; 2) industry size and growth; 3) major
suppliers/competitors; 4) industry price
structure; 5) the customer; 6) the make-up of a
seminar; 7) sales promotion; and 8) the future.
Narrative is accompanied by statistical charts and
tables.

RELEVANCE: This is a highly readable
report of the seminar industry sure to interest
individuals and organizations that present them as
well as suppliers involved in support services,
e.g. travel, printing, advertising, hotels.

<<<<<<>>>>>>

SWEAT EQUITY
What It Really Takes to Build America's Best
Small Companies - By the Guys Who Did It

1986
First
Smith, Geoffrey - Brown, Paul
254
0-671-55210-4
Simon and Schuster
1230 Avenue of the Americas
New York, NY 10020
(800) 223-2336
$17.95

Good
Guide

INCLUSIONS: Index; case examples

DESCRIPTORS: Entrepreneurship; small
business; success; marketing; management

SUMMARY: Financial criteria were loosely
used to identify "the best" small companies. The
book is organized into four basics or stages of
development: idea, marketing, management, and
encore. Some of the topics discussed are: 1)
idea -- having a vision, readapting another idea,
competing by doing something differently,
identifying a market need, and having the
entrepreneurial motivation and nerve to carry out
an idea; 2) marketing -- convincing the venture
capitalist with a business plan, timeliness, being
ready to produce before involving a distributor,
quickly going public to find out what the
competition's customers want, having an
alternative when a market is skimmed, learning
from history, avoiding the "grass looks greener"
illusion, knowing how long a fad will likely last,
having patience in establishing a niche, seeing
opportunity in "an industry's dirty work," i.e.
cleaning up and unpleasant work, being big enough
in logistical support (land, plants), enlisting
an ally and having a superior product to break out
of a specialty niche into national competition,
and looking in limited markets for a competitive
edge; 3) management -- concentrating on your idea
and not trying to do everything yourself,
delegating and not getting bogged down in the
details, expecting to spend time on people
problems, bringing in new people who can do new

jobs, and leaving when you leave the company; 4)
encore -- leveraging with someone else's idea if
it will work better than yours, growing by
acquisition, getting the technical genius to focus
on the market, and passing the business on to new
leaders when the time comes.

RELEVANCE: This is written in a down-to-
earth, anecdotal style, providing tips and food
for thought along the way. It can be worthwhile
reading for entrepreneurs, business
owners/operators, and consultants.

<<<<<<>>>>>>

TRAINING AND DEVELOPMENT HANDBOOK
A Guide to Human Resource Development
1987 (The 1976 edition was abstracted.)
Third
Craigt, Robert
864
American Society for Training and Development
(ASTD)
0-07-013353-0
McGraw Hill, Inc.
1221 Avenue of the Americas
New York, NY 10020
(800) 262-4729
Cost not set

Very Good
Guide; handbook; sourcebook

INCLUSION: Index

DESCRIPTORS: Computer-assisted instruction;
training packages; correspondence study; training
needs assessment; training evaluation; career
planning; performance evaluation; instructional
systems; job enrichment; executive development;
vocational training; technical training;
continuing education; training; training and
development; program development; sales training;
health care training; computer-related training;
training methods; human resource development;
organization development

SUMMARY: This is a compilation of 59
contributors in 47 chapter essays on human
resource development organized in these five
sections: the training and development function;
program development; applications in training;
media and methods; and training and development
resources. This represents a massive effort to
bring together the many aspects of an ever-growing
field.

RELEVANCE: ASTD is one of the foremost,
national, professional associations for training
and development professionals. However, there has
not been an update in the Handbook for over ten
years.

<<<<<<>>>>>>

THE TRANSFORMATIONAL LEADER
Molding Tomorrow's Corporate Winners
1986
First
Tichy, Noel   - Devanna, Mary
306
0-471-82259-0
John Wiley & Sons
605 Third Avenue
New York, NY 10158
(212) 850-6418
$19.95

Very good
Book

INCLUSIONS: Index; references; chapter
notes; tables; diagrams; case studies

DESCRIPTORS: Leadership; organizational
change; organization development; human resource
development; organizational transformation

SUMMARY: This book focuses on leadership
capable of creating transformational change in
organizations. It is divided into three themes
and parts: recognizing the need for
revitalization, creating a new vision, and

institutionalizing change.   The authors
distinguish between leaders and managers, the
former committed toward change, the latter toward
maintenance.   They characterize transformational
leaders.   They talk about motivation, vision,
mission, strategy, structure, culture, and
transitional process.   Transformational leaders
and organizations discussed are: Michael
Blumenthal, Burroughs; J. Jeffrey Campbell, Burger
King; several, General Motors; Frederick Hammer,
Chase Manhattan; John Harvey-Jones, Imperial
Chemical Industries; Lee Iacocca, Chrysler; Mary
Ann Lawlor, Drake Business Schools; Don Mackinnon,
CIBA-Geigy; James Renier, Honeywell; Jack Sparks,
Whirlpool; Edward Thompson, Schneider Transport;
and Jack Welch, General Electric.

RELEVANCE: This is intended for persons
studying leadership and looking for leadership
role models.

CHAPTER 19

LAW, LEGAL, AND REGULATORY

This chapter contains:

- basic planning - legal
  considerations

- labor law and law of contracts

- law and education

- law of businesses and corporations

- insurance law

- law and accounting

- real estate law

- how to use a law library

- employee rights

- compensation

- employee protection

- affirmative action

- staying out of legal difficulties

- use of legal advisors

THE COMPLETE LEGAL GUIDE FOR YOUR SMALL BUSINESS
1982
First
Adams, Paul
218
0-471-09436-6
John Wiley & Sons
605 Third Avenue
New York, NY 10158
(212) 850-6418
$24.95

Excellent
Self-help guide

INCLUSIONS: Index by subject; bibliography;
appendix: employment agreement; forms; samples

DESCRIPTORS: Business law; small business
law; agreements; consulting law; licensing;
employment law; marketing law; purchasing law;
sales contract

SUMMARY: This book discusses contracts
briefly, then moves into the actual writing: the
format from beginning to end, and standard terms
and provisions or "boilerplate." Chapter four
deals with an agreement for consulting. Chapter
five on marketing presents a sample agreement for
distributors and for sales representatives.
Chapters six and seven deal with the purchase and
sale of goods, with recommended forms for purchase
orders and sales orders. Chapter eight presents
an employment contract. Chapter nine deals with
licensing -- patents, trade secrets, copyrights,
and trademarks. The concluding chapter cautions
careful analysis of each situation and to keep it
simple...if it's too complicated, see a lawyer.

RELEVANCE: This self-help book is intended
to help the non-lawyer, small business person,
especially manufacturer with a proprietary product
line and continuous product development, analyze
and draw up legal agreements. It is also intended
for the manager of a larger business. It explains
terms and encourages substitution of appropriate
material. This can help save attorney's fees. It
does not contain exhaustive legal details.

HOW TO FIND THE LAW
1983
Eighth
Cohen, Morris   -   Berring, Robert
790
0-314-25369-6
West Publishing Company
P.O. Box 64526
St. Paul, MN 55164-0526
(800) 328-2209
$8.95

Excellent
Guide; legal bibliography

INCLUSIONS: Indexes by name, subject;
appendices: legal bibliography in the states;
primary legal sources for the states; West
Regional Reporters and their state coverage;
sources of Federal Regulatory Agency rules,
regulations, and adjudications; exhibits; detailed
chapter tables of contents; chapter references;
footnotes

DESCRIPTORS: Law; legal research; legal
resources; legal bibliography

IDENTIFIER: American Casebook Series

SUMMARY: This is intended as "a
comprehensive approach to the basic elements of
legal bibliography." It contains footnotes and
suggested readings for further topical
exploration. The twenty-two chapters cover: the
nature of legal research; court reports; published
cases; annotated law reports; case finding;
constitutions; statutes; court rules; citators;
legislative history; administrative and executive
publications; research approaches and strategies;
loose-leaf services; legal encyclopedias and
research tools; treatises, restatements,
dictionaries; legal periodicals; general research
and reference sources; research in the social
sciences; English and Canadian materials; foreign
and comparative law; international law; and new
media in legal research. Each chapter is broken
down into subheadings and sub-subheadings. For
example, the chapter on new media covers:

computerized research (LEXIS, WESTLAW, JURIS,
FLITE, etc.); litigation support systems
(evidenciary, analytical, case management);
foreign and international systems, microforms, and
facsimile transmission.

RELEVANCE: This source is relevant for the
student of law and more advanced legal research.
An introductory source on legal research is
Cohen's Legal Research in a Nutshell.

<<<<<<>>>>>>

HOW TO FORM YOUR OWN CORPORATION WITHOUT A
LAWYER FOR UNDER $50.00
1982 (The 1981 edition was abstracted.)
Tenth
Nicholas, Ted
73
0-913864-69-2
Enterprise Publishing, Inc.
725 Market Street
Wilmington, DE 19801
(302) 368-4177
$19.95

Very good
Handbook

INCLUSIONS: Appendices (advertisements,
order form); annotated bibliographies; checklists;
directory (Delaware service firms); geographic
listings (incorporation fees, by states); sample
forms (articles of incorporation, bylaws,
minutes); tables

DESCRIPTORS: Corporations; new corporations;
nonprofit corporations; incorporation

SUMMARY: This is a complete legal guide
showing the most economical way to incorporate new
and existing firms. It covers advantages,
disadvantages and tax benefits of incorporating,
and procedures for incorporating different types
of corporations--close, subchapter "S", nonprofit,
professional, partnerships, proprietorships). It

shows how to determine if incorporation is
advisable and lists sources of help and gives
samples of necessary legal documents.

RELEVANCE: This work will help the
entrepreneur decide which form of business
organization is best for him/her. If
incorporation is the preferable type of business
form, then this work will allow you to incorporate
legally without the costly fees charged by
attorneys. Starting up a business can require
significant funds. What better way to save on
start-up costs than to handle the required
paperwork yourself.

                    <<<<<<>>>>>>

INTRODUCTION TO THE STUDY AND PRACTICE OF LAW
IN A NUTSHELL
1983
First
Hegland, Kenney
418
0-314-73632-8
West Publishing Company
P.O. Box 64526
St. Paul, MN 55164-0526
(800) 328-2209
$10.95

Very good
Guide

INCLUSION: Index by subject

DESCRIPTORS: Law; legal education

SUMMARY: Part one deals with what
lawyers do (3 chapters), part two with skills
needed in law school (4 chapters), and part three
with human issues in attending law school (4
chapters). Topics covered include: learning
lawyering skills, the trial process, legal
writing, moot court, exams, "fear and loathing,"
how to cope, ethics, and career choices -- e.g.
private practice, big firms, small firms, legal

aid, government jobs, teaching law, corporate
counsel, law publishing companies, and law
librarianship. The last chapter consists of 18
lawyers variously employed in law professions
discussing their jobs from personal, daily, and
philosophic perspectives.

RELEVANCE: This is written for the law
student or potential law student, and for those
seeking or exploring a law career. It may have
limited usefulness for consultants.

<<<<<<>>>>>>

LABOR LAW IN CONTRACTOR'S LANGUAGE
1979
First
Stokes, McNeill
434
0-07-061650-7
McGraw-Hill
1221 Avenue of the Americas
New York, NY 10020
(800) 262-4729
$42.50

Very good
Textbook

INCLUSIONS: Index by subject; case studies

DESCRIPTORS: Labor law; construction
industry; labor relations contracts; bargaining;
unions; employment discrimination; employment
standards

SUMMARY: This book clarifies labor laws
for those in the construction industry. It
outlines bargaining tactics and contract clauses,
explains how to legally resist union attempts to
undercut supervisors, discusses employment
discrimination and contractors' requirements under
federal employment standards, and explains the ins
and outs of national agreements, project
agreements, etc.

RELEVANCE: This is designed to help the
contractor avoid legal problems in hiring, firing,
and collective bargaining. It is a
straightforward account of contemporary labor laws
of special significance to building contractors.
It is written in simple, non-technical language
with illustrative cases to help the reader
understand how the National Labor Relations Board
has interpreted the law.

                    <<<<<<>>>>>

LAW BOOKS IN PRINT
Books in English Published Throughout the
World and In Print Through 1986
1987
Fifth
Triffin, Nicholas
6 volumes
0-87802-025-X
Glanville Publishers, Inc.
75 Main Street
Dobbs Ferry, NY 10522
(914) 693-1733
$600.00

Excellent
Bibliography

INCLUSION: Guide to subject headings

DESCRIPTORS: Law bibliography; law books

SUMMARY: Law Books in Print provides
bibliographic information on all kinds of law
books, as well as other sources having legal
contents. It is alphabetically arranged in the
following volumes: author/title (vols. 1-3);
series listing (vol. 3); subjects (vols. 4, 5),
and publishers (vol. 6). Entries include the
following information: author(s), title, edition,
publisher, date (original date if reprint), pages,
price, Library of Congress card number, ISBN
number, series, and subjects.

RELEVANCE: This is almost comprehensive
and it is the resource to use for finding
information on legal publications. It is
comparable to Books in Print, except focused on
the legal area. A lot of law book publishers do
not list in Books in Print. Law Books in Print
should be available in a university law library.

<<<<<<>>>>>

THE LAW OF BUYING AND SELLING
1978
Second
The first edition was in 1968.
White, Bertha
113
0-379-11112-8
Oceana Publications, Inc.
75 Main Street
Dobbs Ferry, NY 10522
(914) 693-1733
$5.95

Good
Handbook

INCLUSIONS: Index by subject; appendices on
charts, legislative act; sample forms; checklists

DESCRIPTORS: Commercial law; law of buying;
law of selling; sales; marketing

SUMMARY: This Handbook introduces and
discusses: 1) basic legal principles applying to
sellers and buyers of goods and services within
the general marketplace; and 2) the buyer's
and seller's fundamental rights and liabilities
under commercial law. It covers these and other
topics: what constitutes a sale; parties to a
sale; express and implied warranties; buyer's
right to examine goods; buyer's risk of loss or
damage; wrongfully delivered goods; non-payment
situations; seller's security for payment; oral
contracts; and breach of contract.

RELEVANCE: This is a basic introduction to
the laws of buying and selling.

<<<<<<>>>>>>

THE LAW OF COMPUTER TECHNOLOGY
1985, 1988 Supplement
First
Nimmer, Raymond
One volume (various pagings) plus 1988
cumulative supplement no.1
0-88712-355-4
Warren, Gorham, & Lamont
210 South Street
Boston, MA 02111
(800) 922-0066
$84.00

Excellent
Legal Treatise

INCLUSIONS: Index by subject and
paragraph; glossary; table of cases

DESCRIPTORS: Computer law; computer
contracts; video games law; videotext law;
electronic transactions; computer crime;
electronic publishing; computer privacy; computer
crime

SUMMARY: This book deals with law in
relation to computers and information technology.
It includes the application of the law of
contracts to computer software and hardware
transactions. Other new aspects of law are also
discussed. The author predicts better software
and increased use of computers in law beyond
WESTLAW and LEXIS search routines. The book is
organized into three main areas with subtopics and
sub-subtopics. The topics and subtopics are: 1)
Innovation incentives - copyright and computer
technology; patent law: software and systems;
trade secrets and confidentiality; research,
development and ownership; 2) Transactions and
Third-Party Liability - technology licensing;
computer contracts: leases and sales agreements;

computer-related torts; international trade
considerations; and 3) Information Age Issues -
computer crime; the electronic transaction
environment; electronic publishing and data
communications; computer privacy and data
disclosure.

RELEVANCE: This book is written for the
non-technical specialist. Each of the three parts
has an introductory narrative followed by well-
organized, indexed and specific subject
narratives. The 1986 Supplement provides up-to-
date developments and cases and is organized in
the same fashion as the main volume. This is a
highly usable resource.

                    <<<<<<>>>>>>

THE LAW OF CORPORATIONS IN A NUTSHELL
1987
Second
Hamilton, Robert
515
0-8299-2108-7
West Publishing Company
P.O. Box 64526
St. Paul, MN 55164-0526
(800) 328-2209
$9.95

Excellent
Legal guide

INCLUSIONS: Index by subject; glossary;
tables of cases

DESCRIPTORS: Corporate law; corporations

SUMMARY: This is an overview of law
regarding corporations. The author defines and
presents a perspective on corporations, discusses
choosing a corporate form of business and
corporate formation. Other chapters cover: the
doctrine of ultra vires; preincorporation
transactions; "piercing the corporate veil;"
financing; the closely-held corporation; the

publicly-held corporation; shares and
shareholders; directors and officers; inspection
of books and records; dividends, distributions and
redemptions; shareholder's suits; and amendments,
mergers and dissolution. Each of these areas is
further broken out into topical sections. Case
citations are included in the text. The question
of corporate social responsibility is briefly
discussed.

RELEVANCE: This is a good overview of
corporate law. The subject area may not inspire
exciting writing. Something to keep in mind is
that the Nutshell series is inexpensive and
readily available.

                    <<<<<<>>>>>>

THE LAW OF SCHOOLS, STUDENTS, AND TEACHERS IN
A NUTSHELL
1984
First
Alexander, David
409
0-314-80555-9
West Publishing Co.
50 West Kellogg Boulevard
P.O. Box 43526
St. Paul, MN 55164
(800) 328-9352
$11.95

Excellent
Handbook

INCLUSIONS: Index by subject; table of
cases; appendices: selected constitutional
provisions and federal statutes

DESCRIPTORS: Law; law education

SUMMARY: This book covers the following
subject areas: public school; instructional
program; freedom of speech and expression;
religious activities in public schools; student
publications; search and seizure; student

discipline; racial segregation; education of the
handicapped; sex discrimination; civil liability;
student records; defamation and privacy; student
testing; terms and conditions of teacher
employment; constitutional rights of teachers;
teacher dismissal; and employment discrimination.
Each of these subject areas is subdivided into
specific subject headings.

RELEVANCE: This is a good, manageable
overview of the field of law and education which
is very readable by the non-lawyer. It is well
organized and written in simple, non-technical
language.

                    <<<<<<>>>>>>

LEGAL RESEARCH IN A NUTSHELL
1985
Fourth
Cohen, Morris
452
0-314-83243-2
West Publishing Company
P.O. Box 64526
St. Paul, MN 55164-0526
(800) 328-2209
$10.95

Excellent
Guide; information sourcebook; legal bibliography

INCLUSIONS: Index by subject; appendices:
state research guides; content of reporters of
National Reporter System; current status of major
official state reports; loose-leaf services;
exhibits

DESCRIPTORS: Law; legal research; legal
resources; legal bibliography

SUMMARY: This book is an introduction to
and overview of legal research. It provides
bibliographic information on primary and secondary
legal resources and research tools. Primary
sources include legislative statutes, court

decisions, executive orders and decrees, and
administrative regulations. Secondary sources
include textbooks, manuals, treatises,
commentaries, restatements and periodicals.
Research tools include computerized databases,
LEXIS and WESTLAW, digests of decisions, citators,
encyclopedias, loose-leaf services, and indexes.
Cohen also cites "aids to research:" Dictionary
of Legal Abbreviations, Current American Legal
Citations, The Legal Citation Directory, and Index
to Legal Citations and Abbreviations. Chapters
cover the following: 1) judicial reports; 2)
case-finding; 3) statutes; 4) legislative history;
5) administrative law; 6) loose-leaf services; 7)
U.S. treatises; 8) secondary materials; 9) English
law; 10) civil law; and 11) international law.

RELEVANCE: This is an excellent place to
gain an overview of law and to start a search for
legal knowledge. We may at some time benefit by
knowing how to research a legal question without
using a lawyer. A more detailed, comprehensive
source for the student of law is Cohen and
Berring's How to Find the Law (see abstract).

                    <<<<<<>>>>>>

ORGANIZING CORPORATE AND OTHER BUSINESS
ENTERPRISES
1975
Fifth, revised
Annual
Rohrlich, Chester
Bender's Editorial Staff
595
Matthew Bender and Company, Inc.
235 East 45th Street
New York, NY 10017
(800) 821-2232
$90.00

Good
Reference

INCLUSION: Index by subject

DESCRIPTORS: Law; business law; taxes;
business; corporations; entrepreneurship

IDENTIFIER: There is a 1985 Supplement

SUMMARY: This is a compendium of facts
on various tax and legal consequences to be
considered in launching any new business. It
presents the various types of business entities -
proprietorship, partnership and its variants, and
corporation and its variants - and their
advantages and disadvantages. It emphasizes the
federal tax laws as they affect each type and the
need to consult state laws pertaining to business
activity within its jurisdiction. It advises on
the legal consequences of purchasing a business by
acquiring property or securities, or by
consolidation or merger. It covers the legalities
of raising funds by selling stock in a corporation
and the securities law. It discusses the
difference between a division and subsidiary of a
corporation. It explains the tax and insurance
considerations in coping with the death of a
business owner.

RELEVANCE: This book is good for lawyers,
schools, and the business person on business tax
and legal aspects. Copious footnotes referring to
court cases and documents such as the Internal
Revenue Code allow the reader to research any
topic in further depth. The chapters on selling
stock and the securities law aid in marketing
one's corporate stock in a legal manner.
Awareness of tax laws and the record keeping
requirements can help you select a good
accountant. Application of the advice included
will build business credibility in the community,
thereby enhancing marketability.

<<<<<<>>>>>>

SEX DISCRIMINATION IN A NUTSHELL
1982
First
Thomas, Claire
399

0-314-65663-4
West Publishing Company
P.O. Box 64526
St. Paul, MN 55164-0526
(800) 328-2209
$9.95

Excellent
Legal guide

INCLUSIONS: Index by subject; table of
cases; appendices: states with Equal Rights
Amendments; supplementary case readings

DESCRIPTORS: Sex discrimination; affirmative
action; preferential programs; constitutional
rights; reproductive rights; Equal Rights
Amendment; anti-discrimination laws; legal
remedies

SUMMARY: This book looks at sex
discrimination law. Thomas distinguishes right
from remedy, and states that rather than rendering
the right indefensible, "the resolution is to give
it a remedy under law." The book is divided into
parts on reproductive rights and health care;
historical development of constitutional and case
law; contemporary issues of constitutional and
case law; remedial legislation and case
development; criminal law; and state activity --
Equal Rights Amendments. Specific topics covered
include: contraception, abortion, sterilization,
health product liability, artificial insemination,
employment, marriage, child custody and support,
child abuse, sexual harassment, rape, fundamental
rights, finance, public accommodations, education,
affirmative action, and preferential programs.
The author discusses background history and
factors, such as the women's movement; provides
the rationale for theory and legal decisions; and
cites cases, e.g. Craig v. Boren, and Reed v.
Reed.

RELEVANCE: While this book is intended for
undergraduate and graduate students, it can be
useful for general edification of us all...female
and male...and especially female. Know your
rights and how to maintain them.

UNIFORM COMMERCIAL CODE IN A NUTSHELL
1984
Second
Stone, Bradford
516
0-314-84695-6
West Publishing Company
P.O. Box 64526
St. Paul, MN 55164-0526
(800) 328-2209
$11.95

Excellent
Legal guide

INCLUSIONS: Index by subject; table of
citations

DESCRIPTORS: Uniform Commercial Code;
commercial transactions; sale of goods; payment
for goods; legal remedies

SUMMARY: This is based on the over 700
pages of text of the (1978) Uniform Commercial
Text. The book is divided into these parts:
introduction; the process of selling goods; the
process of paying for goods with commercial paper;
the process of shipping and storing goods covered
by documents of title (warehouse receipts, bills
of lading); the process of financing the sale of
goods: the secured transaction; and the entire
commercial transaction made pursuant to a letter
of credit. Specific topics include: the contract
for sale, seller's warranty obligations,
performance of the contract for sale, remedies,
rights of third parties, bulk sales and transfers,
sale of investment securities, negotiability,
liabilities, the relationship between payor bank
and customer, the bank collection process, the
relationship between payor and presenter, and
altered and forged instruments.

RELEVANCE: This could be relevant to
anyone in the business of buying and selling.

WILLS AND TRUSTS IN A NUTSHELL
1979
First
Mennel, Robert
392
0-8299-2042-0
West Publishing Company
P.O. Box 64526
St. Paul, MN 55164-0526
(800) 328-2209
$9.95

Excellent
Legal guide

INCLUSION: Index by subject

DESCRIPTORS: Wills; trusts; estates

SUMMARY: This book covers the following:
1) wills -- intestacy, superseding rights of
spouse and issue, statue of wills, revoking and
changing wills, beneficiaries, changes in items
bequeathed, interpretation; 2) estate
administration; 3) creation of trusts; and 4)
trust administration -- powers and duties,
problems. Subheadings further organize chapters.

RELEVANCE: This book is clearly written.
Although it is intended for the law student, it
can be useful to non-lawyers dealing with wills
and trusts as well. It does not cover the writing
of wills. It should be kept in mind when reading
this and other Nutshell series books, that laws
change and details differ situationally.
Therefore it is recommended that actual, current
laws and a lawyer be consulted as is appropriate.

                    <<<<<<>>>>>>

WORKERS' COMPENSATION AND EMPLOYEE PROTECTION
LAWS IN A NUTSHELL
1983
First
Hood, Jack   - Hardy , Benjamin
274

0-314-78064-3
West Publishing Company
P.O. Box 64526
St. Paul, MN 55164-0526
(800) 328-2209
$9.95

Excellent
Legal guide

INCLUSIONS: Index by subject; appendix:
proposed National Workers' Compensation Standards
Act; table of cases

DESCRIPTORS: Employee rights; employee
protection laws; workmen's compensation;
unemployment compensation; fair labor standards;
occupational safety and health law; social
security; anti-discrimination laws; legal remedies

SUMMARY: This is an overview of laws
concerning employees. The book is divided into
parts on: 1) historical background on
compensation legislation (1 chapter); 2) the law
of workers' compensation (10 chapters); and 3)
employee protection legislation (7 chapters).
Specific topics covered include: the law of
torts; the employee-employer relationship; the
coverage formula; death; medical expenses,
disabilities, and benefits; administration;
extraterritorial problems and overlapping
coverages; third party actions; future of workers'
compensation; unemployment compensation; Fair
Labor Standards Act; Occupational Safety and
Health Act; retirement and survivors insurance;
disability insurance; medicare; supplemental
security income; federal and state anti-
discrimination laws; and miscellaneous employee
protection laws. Background information,
rationale, and cases are provided.

RELEVANCE: This is an introduction to the
field. Other recommended books for further
exploration are the Workers' Compensation and
Employment Rights Casebook by Malone, Plant, and
Little, and the Law of Workmen's Compensation by
Larson.

CHAPTER 20

LIBRARY AND INFORMATION SCIENCE

This chapter contains:

- library and book trade information

- major markets and information
  sources

- how to use a library

- basic skills in information research

- professional associations and
  resources

- library training and education
  opportunities

ANNUAL REVIEW OF INFORMATION SCIENCE AND
TECHNOLOGY
1987
Annual
Volume 22
Williams, Martha
Variable
0-4447-0302-0
0066-4200
Elsevier Science Publishing Company Inc.
52 Vanderbilt Avenue
New York, NY 10017
(212) 370-5520
$798.00

Very good
State of the art review

INCLUSIONS: Indexes: main; author and
keyword for volumes 1 through 22

DESCRIPTORS: Information science; computers;
communications; computers and publishing

SUMMARY: Each annual volume is made up
of several scholarly state of the art reviews
written by various authors. The review includes
opinions of the expert author as well as facts,
which provide the reader with a bibliography from
which to select additional, related reading.
Topics for each volume are selected on the basis
of timeliness and current reader interest. The
keyword and author index to previous volumes
allows the reader to determine which volumes
contain a review of interest.

RELEVANCE: This serial publication is
intended to help the reader begin to grasp the
state of the art on subjects discussed. The
bibliography provided at the end of each chapter
serves to guide the reader to other sources of
information.

BOOKS IN PRINT
1987
Annual
R.R. Bowker Company Staff
7 volumes
0-8352-2370-1
R.R. Bowker Company
245 West 17th Street
New York, NY 10011
(800) 521-8110
$625.00

Excellent
Bibliography

DESCRIPTOR: Books in print

SUMMARY: Books In Print contains
bibliographic information on in-print books.
Volumes one through three are organized
alphabetically by author. Volumes four through
six are organized alphabetically by title. Volume
seven has publishers information, and is organized
in these parts: key to abbreviations index, name
index, publishers' and distributors' toll-free
numbers, distributors and wholesalers index,
geographic index to wholesalers and distributors,
new publishers, and inactive and out-of-business
publishers.

RELEVANCE: Books In Print is a key library
resource useful to librarians and users alike. It
is fairly comprehensive. Books may not be
included due to the failure of the publisher to
make contact with R.R. Bowker to list a book.
Sometimes books will appear in either the author
or title volumes rather than in both, so that a
reference may have to be looked up in more than
one way. Related resources are R.R. Bowker's
Paperbound Books In Print, and Forthcoming Books,
which have what their titles say. For law books,
see the abstract for Law Books In Print.

BOOKS IN SERIES IN THE U.S.
Original, Reprinted, In-Print, and
Out-of-Print Books, Published or Distributed
in the U.S. in Popular, Scholarly and
Professional Series
1985 (The 1979 edition was abstracted.)
Fourth
9945, 6 volumes
0-8352-1938-0
R. R. Bowker Company
245 W 17th Street
New York, NY 10011
(800) 521-8110
$325.00

Very good
Bibliography

INCLUSIONS: Indexes by series, author,
title, subject index to series; key to
abbreviations; key to publishers' and
distributors' abbreviations

DESCRIPTORS: Books; Series

SUMMARY: This lists books published in
series in the U.S., including original, reprinted,
in-print, and out-of-print series. It contains
four main sections: series index, author index,
title index, subject index to series. It defines
inclusive and exclusive criteria for "series" and
excludes series for children, elementary and high
school textbooks, government publications,
imprints, series with numbers used for stock
control, series with common format only, series of
promotional material, and series which "represent
the major portion of a publisher's output." The
status of research did not permit inclusion of all
titles of all series, and some information, such
as prices for old publications may be missing.

RELEVANCE: This is an invaluable aid to
identification of series publications, well
organized and with adequate user information. It
enables the user to identify series publications
and the series market. Information on series can
tell the market researcher or publisher the nature
of successful series in the past.

BOWKER ANNUAL OF LIBRARY AND BOOK TRADE
INFORMATION
1988
Annual
33rd
Spier, Margaret
743
0-8352-2468-6
0068-0540
R. R. Bowker
245 W 17th Street
New York, NY 10011
(800) 521-8110
$89.95

Excellent
Directory; handbook

INCLUSIONS: Index, cross-referenced;
calendar of association meetings and promotional
events of national and international scope;
bibliographies; tables

DESCRIPTORS: Libraries; book trade industry;
information industry; publishing

IDENTIFIER: Sponsor: The Council of
National Library and Information Associations Inc.

SUMMARY: This contains authored articles
on a range of subjects and state of the art
reports pertinent to the library and book trade
industry and information industry. Major parts
are: reports from the field; legislation, funding
and grants; library/information science education,
placement and salaries; research and statistics;
reference information; and directory of
organizations.

RELEVANCE: This is most useful for
librarians and booksellers. It provides
information to librarians on job opportunities,
funding and professional support systems.

GALE DIRECTORY OF PUBLICATIONS: 1988
1988
120th
Annual
Gill, Kay
2345, 2 volumes; Supplement; Updating Service
0-8103-2544-6
0892-1636
Gale Research Company
Book Tower
Detroit, MI 48226
800 223-4253
$145.00; $95.00 Supplement; $95.00 updating
service

Excellent
Directory; bibliography

INCLUSIONS: Indexes by newspaper feature
editor, geographic arranged by state,
title/keyword; 18 specialized indexes organized by
type or frequency of publication; maps

DESCRIPTORS: Publications; periodicals;
serials

SUMMARY: The first volume is the
geographic list of publications. The second
volume consists of indexes and maps.This provides
directory information to over 25,000 publications
in the United States and Canada. The word
"publications" refers to newspapers, magazines,
and journals. Each entry includes publisher name,
address, telephone number, descriptive annotation,
subscription rates, advertising rates, circulation
rate and publication ownership.

RELEVANCE: This is an invaluable tool once
you have identified your market and are ready to
reach that market.

                    <<<<<<>>>>>>

GUIDE TO AMERICAN DIRECTORIES
1982 (The 1978 edition was abstracted.)
Eleventh

Klein, Bernard
580
0-87340-000-3
B. Klein Publications
P.O. Box 8503
Coral Springs, FL 33065
(305) 752-1708
$55.00

Very good
Directory

INCLUSION: Index

DESCRIPTOR: Directories

IDENTIFIER: Former title: Directory of
Directories

SUMMARY: This is a comprehensive
directory of directories categorized into
information fields. Directories listed are
published by business, book, reference book, and
magazine publishers trade associations, chambers
of commerce, and government agencies. Over 6000
directories are listed in this edition. The
directories are listed under some 300 industrial,
technical, mercantile, scientific and professional
headings, such as accounting, bibliographies,
business management, civil rights, and
consultants. The Guide lists manufacturers by
state as well as has sections on miscellaneous
manufacturers and manufacturers' representatives.
One section lists directories on marketing.

RELEVANCE: This source helps consultants
and business people find new markets for products
and services. For over twenty years Guide to
American Directories was known as Directory of
Directories.

                        <<<<<<>>>>>

GUIDE TO REFERENCE BOOKS
1986 (The 1976 edition was abstracted.)
Tenth

Irregular
Sheehy, Eugene
1586
0-8389-0390-8
American Library Association
50 East Huron Street
Chicago, IL 60611
(800) 545-2433
$50.00

Very Good
Guide

INCLUSION: Index

DESCRIPTOR: Reference works

IDENTIFIER: Formerly titled Mudge

SUMMARY: This lists and describes
reference works by subject area.   Information is
categorized under sub-topics and subheadings.
Major subject areas are general reference,
humanities, social sciences, history and area
studies, pure and applied sciences.   Some emphasis
is given to reference tools for scholarly
research.   It provides introductory notes for many
sections.   It covers reference materials
including: bibliography, library sources;
encyclopedias; language dictionaries; periodicals;
newspapers; government publications;
dissertations; biography; genealogy; philosophy;
linguistics; literature; fine, applied, and
theatre arts; education; sociology; statistics;
economics; political science; law; history; Africa
(and other areas); astronomy (and other sciences);
mathematics; psychology; medical sciences, etc.

RELEVANCE: Useful for librarians and
business persons or professionals, this is a
widely used guide to reference materials.
However, descriptions of reference works are
unsystematic and vary in length, content, and
quality.

HOW TO USE THE BUSINESS LIBRARY, WITH SOURCES
OF BUSINESS INFORMATION
1984   (The 1972 edition was abstracted.)
Fifth
Johnson, Herbert
267
0-538-05750-5
South-Western Publishing Company
5101 Madison Road
Cincinnati, Ohio 45227
(800) 543-0487
$8.95

Excellent
Guide

INCLUSION: Index

DESCRIPTORS: Business library; library;
business information; information sources

SUMMARY: This explanation of the
business library familiarizes readers with
information sources and research methods on a wide
range of topics. It presents basic library usage
information. It includes discussion of types of
publications, including handouts, yearbooks,
pamphlets, periodicals, reports, directories,
business directories, government publications,
almanacs, dictionaries and encyclopedias. Other
areas covered are: research foundations;
commercial, industrial, technical and trade
organizations; aids for small business; audio-
visual aids; business research and reports; data
processing; and business and marketing
forecasting.

RELEVANCE: This is an easy to use, concise
training guide for using the business library.

                    <<<<<<>>>>>>

HOW TO WIN WITH INFORMATION OR LOSE WITHOUT IT
The Indispensable Executive Guide to
Information: How to Get It, How to Use It -
And How to Make It Work for You

1983
Updated, revised
Garvin, Andrew   -   Bermont, Hubert
185
0-93068-608-X
The Consultant's Library
815 15th Street N.W.
Washington, D.C. 20005
$26.00

Excellent
Guide

INCLUSIONS: Index; appendices: information
sources; databases and vendors; information
retrieval services; how-to bibliography;
information science organizing sources; and
generalist source list (bibliography, publishers,
firms); examples; case example

DESCRIPTORS: Information science;
information retrieval; databases; information
gathering; libraries

SUMMARY: This book's aim is to raise its
readers' "information consciousness." The authors
begin by showing the necessity for executive and
professional knowledge as a solution to business
problems and basis for success. They point out
that information is the key ingredient of our
changed, information-oriented society. They
distinguish information from assumption. They
discuss the importance of asking the right
questions, and the value and cost of information -
- information costs (even time is money) -- but
it's worth having and paying for it. They state
that successful information interpretation is
based on the reliability of the source, the way in
which the information is presented, and the
perception of the receiver. Today's technology --
the computer database and telecommunications --
lie at the heart of the "new information
environment." The authors discuss types of
database sources, e.g. general, financial, legal,
company, market research, industry specific, etc.
They also discuss remedies for "information
paralysis:" 1) examining types of information
sources to turn to -- government; associations;

commercial publishers, services and sources; and
libraries; and 2) suggesting "information
categories" to pursue: competition, markets, the
world, management practice, and government
regulations. One chapter is devoted to examining
a case example of information needed on a
particular industry. Finally the authors discuss
appropriate information-gathering systems, moving
from the individual to large-scale organizations,
from the use of the professional information
retrieval specialist and service to the in-house
information center respectively.

RELEVANCE: This is a thoughtful,
authoritative approach to the business of getting
informed. It also contains helpful lists of
sources. While this book can be useful to just
about anyone, its particular focus is the business
world.

<<<<<<>>>>>>

PUBLISHERS' TRADE LIST ANNUAL 1986
1987
Annual
Spier, Margaret
8000
0-8352-2386-8
0079-7855
R. R. Bowker Company
245 West 17th Street
New York, NY 10011
(800) 521-8110
$165.00

Very good
Directory; bibliography; catalog

INCLUSIONS: Indexes by publishers, subject,
publishers' series

DESCRIPTORS: Publishers; book trade;
publications; book lists

SUMMARY: This lists titles and related
bibliographic information about in-print books

classified by publishing source. In addition to
books, it includes related products, such as
periodicals, prints, posters, games, maps, crds,
software, etc. Publishers choose inclusions and
provide catalogs of their book lists, which are
bound together. A supplement, yellow pages (front
of volume one) has small and specialist publishers
with less than four pages of publications, and
publishers who do not supply printed catalogs.
The scope of publishers extends from trade book
publishers to textbook, law, and medicine. The
subject index to publishers has 67 subject fields
including: bibliography; business, economics,
finance, directories, education; foreign affairs;
government, political science; health
science/service; journalism and writing; law;
library science; macropublishing; motion pictures,
radio, television; periodicals; programmed
learning and multimedia; reference; scholarly;
science, technology; social science; travel; and
women studies.

RELEVANCE: This work is good to maintain
current awareness. It lists publications for the
current year.

                    <<<<<<>>>>>>

REFERENCE SOURCES
1983
Annual (to 1983)
Seventh
Silver, Terry
374
0-87650-165-X
Pierian Press
P.O. Box 1808
Ann Arbor, MI 48106
(800) 443-5915
$75.00   Reference Service Review: $42.50
per year for institutions, $22.50 per year for
individuals

Very good
Sourcebook

INCLUSIONS: Indexes by author, title; list
of abbreviations; periodicals list

DESCRIPTORS: Reference sources; periodicals;
book reviews

SUMMARY: This sourcebook to reference
materials provides an alphabetical index to 80
periodicals in this edition. It is an index of
book reviews of reference sources. The Research
Services Review reviews reference publications
relevant to general, academic, and special
libraries.

RELEVANCE: This is a simply organized, easy
to use sourcebook written for the librarian as an
aid in the selection and use of reference sources.

                    <<<<<<>>>>>>

STANDARD PERIODICAL DIRECTORY
1988
Eleventh
Annual
Hagood, Patricia
1594
0-917460-12-X
Oxbridge Communications, Inc.
150 Fifth Avenue, Suite 301
New York, NY 10011
$325.00

Excellent
Directory

INCLUSIONS: Index by subject, cross
referenced to publication titles; user's guide

DESCRIPTOR: Periodicals directory

SUMMARY: This is a comprehensive current
directory of 65,000 periodicals in the U.S. and
Canada. It includes consumer magazines; trade
journals; newsletters; government publications;
house organs; directories; transactions and
proceedings of scientific societies; yearbooks;

museum, religious, ethnic, literary and social
group publications, etc. Computer lists and
printouts of contents are available. The 230
subject fields include: accounting, advertising
and marketing, advertising shopping guides,
economics, education, employment, fund raising,
international trade, journalism, library,
management, public management and planning, radio
and television, U.S. government - organization,
and women's liberation. Entry information is very
complete.

RELEVANCE: This is one of the best sources
on periodicals. It lists periodicals dealing with
advertising and marketing and identifies resources
for advertising and marketing which reach specific
readerships.

<<<<<<>>>>>>

YOUR LIBRARY
A Reference Guide
1984
Second
Katz, William
242
0-03-063011-8
Holt, Rinehart and Winston, Inc.
383 Madison Avenue
New York, NY 10017
(212) 750-1330
$22.95

Very good
Guide

INCLUSION: Index publication

DESCRIPTORS: Library research; libraries

SUMMARY: This book shows how to find
answers to questions on any subject by utilizing a
library and librarians. It introduces the reader
to the library card catalog; identifies the
various types of general reference works and what
distinguishes them from each other; shows how to

use periodical indexes, encyclopedias, almanacs,
yearbooks, directories, dictionaries, manuals and
atlases.   It provides lists of sources in specific
subject areas -- humanities, sciences, Afro-
Americans, business, economics, education,
history, current events, political science,
psychology, sociology, and women.

RELEVANCE: This is written for the
inexperienced library user who wants to learn how
to exploit the wealth of information on products,
marketing, service delivery, small business,
management, problem solving, and much more
available in public libraries.

CHAPTER 21

MARKETING, INTERNATIONAL MARKET, AND SALES

This chapter contains:

- planning, strategizing and
  conducting of marketing

- market research and analysis

- decision making

- direct marketing methods --
  mail/mail order, telemarketing, and
  media

- marketing yourself

- international market

BUSINESS MAILER'S HANDBOOK
1977
Foster, Robert
280
0-13105-106-7
Prentice Hall, Inc.
Rt. 9 West
Englewood Cliffs, NJ 07632
(201) 767-5049
Order: 200 Old Tappan Road
Old Tappan, NJ 07676
(201) 592-2000

Very good
Handbook

INCLUSIONS: Index by subject; bibliography
(booklets, brochures); case histories; charts;
checklists; data (postal costs and rates); guides
(classes of mail; mail routing); guidelines
(mailing; management; training); photographs;
regulations (postal); tables

DESCRIPTORS: Business mail; mail management;
mailing operations; postal services mailing costs;
mailroom operations; mail services; parcel post

SUMMARY: This is filled with scores of
practical suggestions for cutting mailing costs
and developing an efficient mailing operation.
For examples, it shows how to: 1) handle domestic
and international mailing tasks; 2) properly
classify mail; 3) determine and use lowest
available rates; 4) use special postal services
and alternative delivery services; 5) avoid
commonly made errors; 6) evaluate one's mailing
operation; 7) train mailroom personnel; and 8)
develop a mail routing guide.

RELEVANCE: This can be helpful for anyone
in business handling their own mail and for mail
personnel in larger companies. Most of us could
benefit from knowing mail practices. However,
policies and rates change, so check with the
postal service for current information.

THE DARTNELL DIRECT MAIL AND MAIL ORDER
HANDBOOK
1980
Third
Past issues were in 1964 and 1977.
Hodgson, Richard
1538
Dartnell Corporation
4660 North Ravenswood Avenue
Chicago, IL 60640
(800) 521-8110   (800) 537-8416 (Canada)

Excellent
Handbook; manual

INCLUSIONS: Index; appendices; bibliography
(annotated: business directories, books);
checklists; evaluation-selection aids; forms;
glossary; illustrations; aids; regulations;
samples; tables

DESCRIPTORS: Direct mail; direct mail
advertising; direct marketing; mail order

SUMMARY: This is a comprehensive,
definitive, practitioner's guide. It covers
proven, effective, strategies, methods and
techniques. It contains hundreds of practical
"how to" suggestions, in 49 chapters, guides and
guidelines, data on costs, standards, and
statistics, legal information on copyright
law, management and marketing aids, postal
information, code of ethics, and case histories.

RELEVANCE: This is a storehouse of
knowledge on direct mail techniques useful for
both the beginner and experienced practitioner.

                    <<<<<<>>>>>

DATA SOURCES FOR BUSINESS AND MARKET ANALYSIS
1983
Third
Irregular
Frank, Nathalie   -   Ganly, John
484

0-8108-1618-0
The Scarecrow Press, Inc.
52 Liberty Street
P.O. Box 4167
Metuchen, NJ 08840
(201) 548-8600
$35.00

Very good
Sourcebook

INCLUSIONS: Index, cross-referenced;
tables; appendix of state statistical abstracts

DESCRIPTORS: Marketing; information services

SUMMARY: This is an annotated guide to
information sources arranged by type of source:
compendia, federal statistical program, Bureau of
the Census, other federal sources, regional and
local sources, foreign sources, university
programs, research institutions, professional and
trade associations, services, advertising media,
business firms, directories and mailing lists,
periodicals, abstracts and indexes, information
centers and specialists, and research aids.
Emphasis is on statistical serials and continuing
series.

RELEVANCE: This is a useful source for
librarians. Some may have found topical
arrangement a preferable organization of material.
The third edition attempts to keep up to date,
especially with the inclusion of databases,
although other sources have naturally come into
being since its publication. Another edition is
planned and may be available when this comes
to press.

                    <<<<<<>>>>>>

DIRECT MARKETING MARKETPLACE
The Directory of the Direct Marketing Industry
1988
Ninth
Annual

Stern, Edward
714
0-934464-04-9-X
Hillary House Publishers
1033 Channel Drive
Hewlett Harbor, NY 11557
(516) 295-2376
$85.00 (1987)

Excellent
Directory; resources guide

INCLUSIONS: Advertisements; annotated
bibliography; calendar; classified listings;
consultant firms; directories (associations and
organizations, firms, individuals, telephone);
geographic listings; index to advertisers

DESCRIPTORS: Direct marketing; consulting
services; direct mail; direct marketers; marketing
suppliers

SUMMARY: This is a complete directory
and guide to firms, services and agencies,
organizations, individuals, products and other
resources within the direct marketing industry.
Much of it is annotated.   It includes direct
marketers; service firms and suppliers of direct
marketers; creative, direct mail and consulting
services; direct marketing associations, clubs and
organizations in the U.S. and Canadian and foreign
firms and organizations.   It contains profiles of
businesses and consultants, training suggestions
and statistics, meetings and events, prizes and
awards; and company names, addresses, and phone
numbers.

RELEVANCE: This is a useful resource for
anyone seeking to find marketing resources in a
variety of fields and locations, and marketing
support services and organizations.

<<<<<<>>>>>

DO-IT-YOURSELF MARKETING RESEARCH
1982

Second
Irregular
Breen, George - Blankenship, A.
303
0-07-007446-1
McGraw-Hill Book Co.
1221 Avenue of the Americas
New York, NY 10020
(800) 262-4729
$32.95

Very good
Guide

INCLUSION: Index by subject

DESCRIPTORS: Marketing research; marketing

SUMMARY: This Handbook shows how to do
quick and low cost marketing research. It
discusses items one should consider before
implementing a marketing research effort.
Thereafter, the rest of the book shows how to do
the research and write a report. Topics covered
in the book include manufacturers' and retailers'
research methods, media research, data collection
methods, sampling, questionnaire design and
testing, and data processing, as well as finding
and working with a research firm when necessary.
The text is accompanied by humorous illustrative
drawings.

RELEVANCE: This is written for the
nonprofessional interested in doing semi-
professional marketing research. It's good for
owners, managers, consultants and others in small
business. It treats a subject which can be
ponderous and droll in a humorous, folksy style.

                    <<<<<<>>>>>>

FOREIGN TRADE MARKETPLACE
1977
First
Schultz, George
662

0-8103-0981-5
Gale Research Company
Book Tower
Detroit, MI 48226
(800) 223-4253
$130.00

Good
Directory

INCLUSION: Index, cross-referenced

DESCRIPTORS: International trade; foreign
markets

SUMMARY: This source provides
information on U.S. firms doing international
business. It identifies published sources of
information on these firms and selected references
on in-depth economics of foreign markets. It
excludes coverage of U.S. import merchants or
agents, freight forwarders, and custom house
brokers.

RELEVANCE: This source can be an aid in
international marketing efforts, providing
information, ground rules, and resources for
operating in this marketplace. It provides direct
trade contacts, lists shipping lines and airlines
for cargo, and lists banks and other institutions
that facilitate transactions. An updated edition
is called for.

                    <<<<<<>>>>>>

HANDBOOK OF INTERNATIONAL BUSINESS
1982
Walter, Ingo - Murray, Tracy
1312
0-471-07949-9
John Wiley and Sons
605 Third Avenue
New York, NY 10158
(212) 850-6418
$74.95

Excellent
Handbook

INCLUSIONS: Index, cross-referenced, chapter
bibliographies; appendices on sources of
information on international business and
bibliography of international business

DESCRIPTORS: International business;
international trade; international finance;
international marketing

SUMMARY: This is a comprehensive,
concise work on international business organized
into 42 chapters in the following major parts:
the environment of international business;
international trade; international finance; legal
aspects of international business; international
marketing; and management of international
operations. The 44 contributors are of
authoritative stature.

RELEVANCE: The Handbook is intended for
the non-specialist executive, accountant, banker
or lawyer, and we will add, consultant.

                    <<<<<<>>>>>>

INCREASING SALES EFFECTIVENESS
A Complete Guide to a Successful Selling
Program
1987
Sanchez, Joseph
204
0-94135-14-2
Feris-Lee Press
P.O. Box 560
97A Mary Street
Lodi, NJ 07644-0560
(201) 778-4163
$21.00

Good
Guide

INCLUSIONS: Footnotes; appendices:

telemarketing assistance; government publications;
sources of new products

DESCRIPTORS: Sales; selling; direct mail;
telemarketing

SUMMARY: This sales guide discusses the
significance of sales and aspects of sales. The
book is organized into these parts: 1) economics
of selling -- including product sales report,
contribution accounting, payback; 2) sales staff -
- training, performance, drugs and alcoholism; 3)
sales management -- market segmentation,
leadership, motivation, delegation, control,
productivity, benefits, problem solving; 4)
selling program -- prospecting, principles and
practices, imaginative approaches, meetings; and
5) specialized sales programs -- independent
agents, telemarketing, direct mail.

RELEVANCE: This guide can be used as an
overview of sales. However, it suffers from very
poor print quality and some lack of organizational
clarity within parts, an example being discussion
of prospecting in parts one and four.

<<<<<<>>>>>>

THE INSURANCE MARKET PLACE
A Guide to Non-Standard Coverages
and Specialty Lines
1987 (The 1980-81 edition was abstracted.)
Eighteenth
Annual
Clapp, Wallace
178
Rough Notes Company
1200 North Meridian
Indianapolis, IN 46204
(317) 634-1541

Very good
Guide

INCLUSION: Index of advertisers

DESCRIPTORS: Insurance; insurance market

SUMMARY: This lists companies which
provide various non-standard and specialty lines
of insurance coverage. It explains each type of
insurance. It provides a company home office
directory. It provides a directory of companies
with countrywide operations for excess and surplus
or specialty lines. Information is based on
mailed questionnaires. It covers many types of
insurance: abstracters professional liability,
accountants credit bureau errors and omissions,
data processors errors, employee benefit plans --
overseas, excess fidelity bonds, excess liability,
film and television producers indemnity, financial
institutions, home warranty programs, insurance
agents and brokers errors and omissions,
investment counselors errors and omissions, life
underwriters, medical personnel service
organizations, oil drilling, public official
liability, psychiatrists professional liability,
publishers liability, real estate agents errors
and omissions, unemployment compensation, etc.

RELEVANCE: This is a useful reference for
finding insurance coverage and companies for
specialty insurance.

                    <<<<<<>>>>>>

MANAGEMENT OF THE SALES FORCE
1987
Seventh
Irregular
Stanton, William   -   Buskirk, Richard
704
0-256-03635-7
Richard D. Irwin, Inc.
1818 Ridge Rd.
Homewood, IL 60430
(312) 798-6000
$35.95

Excellent
Textbook

INCLUSIONS: Index; case examples; diagrams;
chapter summaries; questions and problems

DESCRIPTORS: Sales force management; sale
training; sales planning; sales performance;
marketing

SUMMARY: This book provides an overview
of the management of the sales force. It is
divided into these parts: 1) introduction to
sales-force management; 2) sales-force staffing
and operations; 3) sales planning; 4) evaluation
of sales performance; and 5) a forward look.
Topics covered include strategic marketing and
planning, sales administration, sales job
selection and recruitment, sales training,
leadership and motivation, compensation, expenses
and transportation, supervision, morale,
forecasting, budgeting, territories and routing,
sales quotas, sales volume, cost and
profitability, performance evaluation, ethics and
careers.

RELEVANCE: This is intended for the
student of sales and is directed to companies with
an outside sales force. It is well-organized and
has many case examples.

                    <<<<<<>>>>>>

MARKETING DECISION MAKING
Concepts and Strategy
1980 (The 1976 edition was abstracted.)
Second
Irregular
Cravens, David - Hills, Gerald - Woodruff,
Robert
781
0-256-023484
Richard D. Irwin Inc.
1818 Ridge Road
Homewood, IL 60430
(800) 323-4560
$34.95

Very good
Textbook; how-to guide

INCLUSIONS: Index; tables; figures;
suggested exercises; discussion and review
questions

DESCRIPTORS: Marketing; marketing
management; marketing environment; market
segmentation; new product management; distribution
channel; advertising; sales force

SUMMARY: This contains a conceptual
presentation focused on how marketing management
decisions should be made, and provides an
operational framework for decision analysis,
strategy design, and management control. It
treats these subjects: 1) the marketing process;
2) managerial analysis of marketing environment;
3) market opportunity analysis; 4) marketing
strategy and decision making; 5) marketing
decision areas; and 6) marketing, a broader
perspective. It treats these topics in
successive chapters: 1) the macro-marketing
perspective; 2) the marketing environment, the
technological environment, societal change and the
consumer, the governmental environment; 3)
analysis of market opportunities; market
segmentation strategy; buyer decision processes;
4) corporate and marketing strategy, decision-
making concepts and models, marketing information
planning, planning the marketing program, managing
new products, evaluating new product
opportunities; channel of distribution strategy,
channel design, implementation and control; 5)
price decisions, advertising decisions, evaluating
advertising effectiveness, sales force decisions;
and 6) managing the sales force, controlling the
marketing program; and non-business marketing.

RELEVANCE: This marketing training tool
enables the user to focus on the decision making
process. It teaches basic marketing concepts and
processes and details steps involved in managing
one's marketing efforts. It covers applications
of marketing management principles and practices
within both business and non-business worlds.

MARKETING INFORMATION
A Professional Reference Guide
1987 (The 1982 edition was abstracted.)
Second
Goldstucker, Jac
425
0-88406-195-7
George State University
University Plaza
Atlanta, GA 30303
(404) 658-4253
$85.00

Excellent
Directory; bibliography

INCLUSIONS: Indexes by title, publisher

DESCRIPTOR: Marketing information

SUMMARY: This is a multi-purpose guide
to marketing information divided into two parts.
Part one is a directory of marketing associations
and organizations, including marketing research
and consulting organizations, largest 300
advertising agencies, special libraries, research
centers, continuing education courses, and
government agencies. Part two is an annotated
bibliography organized into 20 subject fields,
such as advertising, sales, retailing, packaging,
statistics, and specialized areas of marketing.

RELEVANCE: This is useful for the
marketing executive and for locating consultants
with industry specializations.

                   <<<<<<>>>>>>

PROFESSIONAL'S GUIDE TO PUBLICITY
1982 (The 1978 edition was abstracted.)
Third revised
Irregular
Weiner, Richard
176
Public Relations Publishing Co., Inc.
888 Seventh Ave.

New York, NY 10106
(212) 315-8250
$9.50

Very good
Handbook; primer

INCLUSIONS: Index by subject; appendices;
bibliographies (annotated: periodicals, reference
materials); glossaries (film and media terms);
guidelines; illustrations; reviews (reference
materials); samples (letters, news releases, tip
sheets)

DESCRIPTORS: News media; news releases;
publicity; public relations; press relations

SUMMARY: This is a practitioner's guide
to planning and executing public relations and
publicity efforts. It shows how to: 1) prepare
and distribute public service announcements, news
features, and "exclusives," different types of
news releases and contact letters; 2) work with
news bureaus/syndicates, newspapers, magazines,
trade publications, and related media personnel;
3) use press kits and photographs; and 4)
publicize products, personnel and special events.
It is loaded with practical "how to" suggestions
and advice.

RELEVANCE: This can be helpful to profit
and non-profit organizations in identifying and
describing a varity of publicity techniques.

                    <<<<<<>>>>>

STRATEGIC SELLING
The Unique Sales System Proven Successful By
America's Best Companies
1985
Miller, Robert   -   Heiman, Stephen
319
0-688-04313-5
Miller Heiman & Associates, Inc.
2150 Shattuck Avenue, Suite 400
Berkeley, CA 94704

William Morrow and Company, Inc.
105 Madison Avenue
New York, NY 10016
(800) 631-1199
$19.95

Good
Guide

INCLUSION: Index

DESCRIPTORS: Sales; selling; strategic
selling

SUMMARY: This book is based on a sales
training developed for Hewlett-Packard and carried
out with many other companies. It presents the
workshops and "key elements" developed in this
sales program: "buying influences," "red flag for
danger - or opportunity," "buyer level of
receptivity," "the four response modes," "win-
results," "the sales funnel," and "ideal
customer." The last chapter is on developing an
action plan. The emphasis of the book is on
developing a strategy for the long-term and
replacing the negatively stereotyped salesperson
as one of pushy person, to the positive
perspective of meeting customer needs.

RELEVANCE: The approach to selling used
here may work. It is supposedly practical, but
comes off as a lot of conceptual discussion. The
"key elements" and concepts are not immediately
clear, so this book takes some wading through.

                <<<<<<>>>>>>

SUCCESSFUL DIRECT MARKETING METHODS
The Bob Stone Direct Marketing Book
1984
Third
Irregular
Stone, Robert
496
0-8442-3086-3
Crain Books

740 Rush Street
Chicago, IL 60611
(800) 621-6877
$29.95

Excellent
Textbook; handbook; guide

INCLUSIONS: Index: alphabetical by subject;
glossary; lists; checklists; chapter self-quizzes
and pilot projects

DESCRIPTORS: Marketing; direct mail
advertising; marketing-media; telemarketing

SUMMARY: This provides detailed
information on how to get started - the scope of
direct marketing; strategic business planning; the
offer; choosing media - mailing lists, magazines,
newspapers, electronic media, co-ops,
telemarketing; techniques of creating and
producing direct marketing - direct mail packages,
catalogs, print advertising; and managing the
direct marketing operation - lead generation,
mathematics of direct marketing; idea development
and testing; research; and direct marketing in the
marketing mix.

RELEVANCE: Coverage is comprehensive and
sophisticated. This source is full of specific
pointers consultants can use in developing and
carrying out direct marketing.

<<<<<<>>>>>

TELEPHONE MARKETING
How to Build Your Business by Telephone
1976
First
Roman, Murray
218
0-07-053595-7
McGraw-Hill Book Company
1221 Avenue of the Americas
New York, NY 10020
(800) 262-4729
$46.95

Excellent
Book

INCLUSIONS: Index; appendices (14); facts;
tables; examples; case studies

DESCRIPTORS: Telemarketing; marketing;
business communications

SUMMARY: This book does the following:
1) explains how you can successfully use telephone
marketing in your business; 2) examines the unique
aspects of telephone communication, e.g. its
personal, voice only characteristics; 3) tells
how to identify your market, promote your message,
recruit and train communicators, set up a work
environment; 4) outlines dos and don'ts of
telephone communication and ethics; and 5)
discusses future prospects of telephone marketing.
This covers the broad spectrum of information and
issues pertinent to telephone marketing. It
instructs how to: develop a telephone marketing
plan; structure systems for sales programs;
utilize support materials, e.g. taped messages,
scripts, and communicator response modules; design
controls, record-keeping; and cost accountability
procedures; evaluate programs, costs, techniques;
pretext scripts, operator norms, response feedback
and cost per order. The appendices are: total
expenditures for media in the U.S.; identification
of audience criteria; demographics,
psychographics, and census tracts; using zip code
data; list brokers and compilers; voices on tape;
legal aspects; direct marketing agencies; direct
marketing consultants; cost calculation;
bibliography; directories; data on telephone
usage; and alternative telephone marketing
systems.

RELEVANCE: This book is written for
marketing professionals and can be useful for any
consultant who uses telemarketing, which most of
us do or will.

CHAPTER 22

PRODUCT DEVELOPMENT, SAFETY, PACKAGING AND DISTRIBUTION

This chapter contains:

- product planning and management

- safety and liability

- product-line strategies

- packaging for the marketplace

- packaging sources

- repositioning old brands

DEVELOPING NEW PRODUCTS AND REPOSITIONING
MATURE BRANDS
A Risk Reduction System That Produces
Investment Alternatives
1980
First
Cafarelli, Eugene
253
0-471-04634-5
John Wiley & Sons
605 Third Avenue
New York, NY 10158
(212) 850-6418
$41.95

Very good
Guide

INCLUSIONS: Index; bibliography; marketing;
case study; tools

DESCRIPTORS: Product development; product
pricing; industrial products; risk management

IDENTIFIER: Ronald Series on Marketing
Management

SUMMARY: This guide covers the following
material: the rationale for new product
development, steps to take, organizational and CEO
considerations, product concept generation and
development, product evaluation; product
definition refinement, product testing,
development and pretesting the advertising and
communications package, pricing, the marketing
plan, and test market simulation and real test. A
chapter is devoted to repositioning the mature
product as distinguished from creating a new
product. Repositioning may involve selecting a
new segment of the current market or restatement
about the product to the current market.
Repositioning involves identifying the market
segment(s), understanding the consumer, and
testing the new positioning. The last chapter is
about applying the system discussed to industrial
products.

RELEVANCE: This is an easily read book
intended for the general manager, student or
practitioner.

<<<<<<>>>>>>

THE DISTRIBUTION HANDBOOK
1985
Robeson, James
1000
0-02-923700-3
The Free Press
866 Third Avenue
New York, NY 10022
(800) 257-5755
$75.00

Excellent
Handbook; textbook

INCLUSIONS: Index, cross-referenced;
bibliography; appendices: associations and
organizations in distribution, publications and
organizations that frequently publish material on
distribution, depositor-warehouse agreements

DESCRIPTOR: Distribution of goods

SUMMARY: Written by educators,
practitioners and consultants in the field of
distribution, this book covers conceptual and
practical aspects of distribution. The book has
14 sections and 32 chapters. The sections are:
perspectives on distribution management,
distribution planning, distribution system
components and design, financial analysis and
productivity measurement, the computer and
quantitative analysis, demand forecasting,
purchasing, transportation, facilities, inventory
management, packaging, international distribution,
distribution organization, and distribution
personnel.

RELEVANCE: This is a good, authoritative,
single source on all aspects of distribution.

MANAGING NEW PRODUCTS
Competing Through Excellence
1988
First
Kuczmarski, Thomas
304
0-13-550716-2
Prentice-Hall
Rt. 9 West
Englewood Cliffs, NJ 07632
(201) 592-2000
Order: 200 Old Tappan Road
Old Tappan, NJ 07675
(201) 767-5054
$24.95

Very good
Book; guide

INCLUSIONS: Index; chapter summaries;
diagrams; tables

DESCRIPTORS: Product development; innovation

SUMMARY: This book is about how to go
about developing and managing new products. The
author identifies the following ten key "success
factors:" 1) new product blueprint; 2) new
product strategy; 3) consistent execution process;
4) enough up-front homework; 5) tracking system;
6) clear accountability; 7) teamwork and
communication; 8) motivation and rewards; 9)
tenure and experience; and 10) commitment. Other
chapter topics discussed are: conducting a
diagnostic audit, managing new products, structure
and leadership in an organization, rewards and
motivation, and innovation.

RELEVANCE: This is another book in the new
way of business thinking, which goes beyond left
brain approaches and talks about the people factor
-- risk-taking, motivation, and commitment.
Structural considerations are discussed as well.
The book is conceptually oriented and intended for
top management and product managers, though it
could also be used by consultants and in business
schools.

PACKAGING MARKETPLACE
The Practical Guide to Packaging Sources
1978
First
Hanlon, Joseph
288
0-8103-0989-0
Gale Research Company
Book Tower
Detroit, MI 48226
(800) 223-4253
$120.00

Excellent
Directory; resource guide; marketplace guide

INCLUSIONS: Glossaries; resource lists

DESCRIPTORS: Packaging; manufacturers;
distributors; suppliers

SUMMARY: This a comprehensive list of
packaging services materials, equipment, and
related information. It enables the user to find
the nearest manufacturer. It notes areas of
specialization for each supplier. Each of the
four sections has brief descriptions of trade
practices and terminology. It lists distributors
of packaging materials, who provide small lots of
products. The information sources section
includes associations, government agencies, honors
and awards, publications, and schools. The
section on services includes consulting, contract
packaging, decorating, and designing. The
section on materials includes adhesives, bottles,
carboys, displays, envelopes, and film. The
section on equipment includes aerosol equipment,
bag making, code marking, filling, labeling,
typing, weighing, and wrapping.

RELEVANCE: This resource provides unique
coverage of sources on packaging with clear
presentation. It enables one to: 1) research
market segments; 2) find related materials,
equipment, information sources; and 3) identify
competitive services, suppliers and products.

PRODUCT LIABILITY
A Multibillion Dollar Dilemma
1984
First
Settle, Stephen   -   Spigelmeyer, Sharon
64
0-81442-308-6
AMA Membership Publications Division
135 West 50th Street
New York, NY 10020
(212) 903-8087
$7.50 (members), $10.00 (non-members), $3.75
(students)

Very good
Guide

DESCRIPTORS: Product liability; risk
management; quality control

SUMMARY: The authors discuss: the rising
problem and costs of product liability suits; the
legal theories of product liability; product
liability prevention -- minimizing defects, design
safety reviews, labeling, warning and
instructions, advertising and marketing,
minimizing errors; organizing liability
prevention; documents management; insurance
shopping; lawsuit defense; wholesalers'/
distributors' liability problems; and legislative
solutions.

RELEVANCE: This is a very short, easy,
good overview of product liability recommended for
any business selling a product. The specialist
will require additional, detailed reading.

                <<<<<<>>>>>

PRODUCT-LINE STRATEGIES
1982
First
Bailey, Earl
76
0-8237-0253-7

The Conference Board, Inc.
845 Third Avenue
New York, NY 10022
(212) 759-0900
$50.00

Very good
Guide

INCLUSIONS: Examples; graphs; tables

DESCRIPTORS: Product marketing; strategic
planning; marketing management; consumer product
line; industrial product line

SUMMARY: A group of fourteen chapter
contributors discuss factors in strategic planning
of product marketing. The book is divided into
major sections on basic product-line strategy, and
planning for products for consumer markets and
industrial markets. A sampling of chapters
includes: "The Broader Determinates of Market
Strategy," "Identifying New Competitive
Opportunities," "The Line vs. the Brand,"
"Successful Market Positioning," "Critical Trade-
Offs," "Market Leverage," "Pricing New Industrial
Products."

RELEVANCE: This Guide can be helpful to
strategic planners, marketing managers and general
managers.

                    <<<<<<>>>>>>

PRODUCT MANAGEMENT
Marketing in a Changing Environment
1984
First
Hehman, Raymond
1200
0-8709-4562-9
Dow Jones-Irwin
1818 Ridge Road
Homewood, IL 60430
(800) 323-4566
$29.50

Very good
Guide

INCLUSIONS: Index; charts; appendix case
example of marketing plan

DESCRIPTOR: Product management

SUMMARY: This book grew out of a
continuing education course at New York
University. It has chapters on the concept of
product management, product positioning, sales
forecasting, promotion planning, the product
manager and the agency, marketing research,
product budgeting and control, and marketing
plans. A chapter on the use of the computer for
product management is intended as a mathematical
presentation of other chapter contents.

RELEVANCE: This book is intended to help
the product manager perform the job. It is easy
to read with how-to examples. The chapter on how
to use the personal computer for product
management is a good inclusion but is poorly
explained and needs more explicit narration.

                    <<<<<<>>>>>>

PRODUCT SAFETY AND LIABILITY
A Desk Reference
1980
First
Robinson, Jeremy - Weine, Ruth
Kolb, John - Ross, Steven
688
0-07-035380-8
McGraw-Hill Book Company
1221 Avenue of the Americas
New York, NY 10020
(800) 262-4729
$46.75

Excellent
Handbook

INCLUSIONS: Index by subject; bibliography;
appendices (10 includes bibliography; glossary);
index of standards for specific products and
practices; checklists; photograph; illustrations;
tables; graphs

DESCRIPTORS: Product liability; product
safety; loss control; risk management; consumer
safety; occupational safety; liability insurance;
consumer protection; safety regulation; insurance
management

SUMMARY: This reference traces in order
of process the considerations in planning,
developing, producing, marketing, distribution and
servicing of products. Separate chapters are
devoted to chemical products, going to court, and
insurance. Appendices include: checklists for
designers and installers, toxic substances,
hazardous materials handling, American National
Standards for Safety and Health, index of Consumer
Product Safety Commission Standards, federal
record-retention requirements related to product-
safety and liability, standards-setting and
safety-information organizations, and information
sources.

RELEVANCE: This volume is relevant to
small and large company personnel in an
environment of increasing safety problems.
Unfortunately the authors' concerns about safety
have not been reflected in the atmosphere during
the Reagan administration. Prosecutors have not
been adverse to stepping in where government
regulation has fallen off.

CHAPTER 23

PUBLISHING AND WRITING

This chapter includes books, periodicals, directories, microform, and art sources. It contains:

- getting published and working with publishers and writers

- writing style manuals and editing

- creation and production of print materials

- use and marketing of print resources -- books and magazines.

- publishing support resources -- typesetting, printing, and copying

- graphics and illustrating

- writing guides and manuals

- self-publishing, self-help guides for books and directories

BOOK MARKETING HANDBOOK
Tips and Techniques for the Sale and Promotion
of Scientific, Technical, Professional, and
Scholarly Books and Journals
1983 (The 1980 edition was abstracted.)
Second
Bodian, Nat
607
0-8352-1685-3
R.R. Bowker Company
205 E. 42nd Street
New York, NY 10017
(800) 521-8110   (800) 537-8416 (Canada)
$59.95

Excellent
Handbook; resources guide

INCLUSIONS: Indexes; appendices (4);
annotated bibliographies; checklists; calendar;
directories (associations, organizations,
outlets); glossary; illustrations; samples; tables

DESCRIPTORS: Book marketing; books;
marketing handbooks; sales promotion

SUMMARY: This is a complete, step-by-
step guide to marketing, promoting and selling
books and reference works to professional and
scholarly markets. It covers proven, effective,
marketing strategies, channels, methods and
outlets. It gives hundreds of practical
suggestions and ideas and contains case histories,
statistics, research data, marketing and sales
guidelines, subject guides, and direct mail,
marketing, and review media guides.

RELEVANCE: This is a useful guide to
professionals and consultants in marketing their
books.

<<<<<<>>>>>

BOOK PUBLISHERS DIRECTORY
A Guide to New and Established Private and
Special Interest, Avant-Garde and Alternative,

Organization and Association, Government and
Institution Presses
1984 (The 1979 edition was abstracted.)
Second
Brewer, Annie   -   Geiser, Elizabeth
668
Gale Research Company
Book Tower
Detroit, MI 48226
(313) 961-2242
$110.00

Excellent
Directory

INCLUSIONS: Indexes by publishers; subject;
geography

DESCRIPTORS: Book publishers; publishers;
alternative publishers; small publishers;
specialized publishers; women and minority
publishers

SUMMARY: This Directory contains all the
publishers you were unable to find in Writer's
Market and Literary Market Place. The 1979
edition covers over 3,400 publishing houses.
Major headings in the subject index include:
accounting, advertising, alternative lifestyle,
alternative technology, American Indian, bible,
bibliography, bilingual books, Black studies,
broadcasting, careers, computers, consumer
research, cooperative societies, environment,
energy, education (adult, legal, sex, special),
finance, graphics, health care, labor, Marxism,
nutrition, occult, politics, pollution, religion,
self-help, social change, urban affairs, and
women.

RELEVANCE: This Directory is especially
relevant for the writer whose work would be a
likely candidate for alternative presses. It is
easy to use, with its alphabetic listing and
wonderful indexes. It is available in most public
libraries, in case buying it seems expensive to
you too.

THE COMPLETE GUIDE TO SELF PUBLISHING
Everything You Need to Know to Write, Publish,
Promote, and Sell Your Own Book
1985
Second
Ross, Tom - Ross, Marilyn
399
0-89879-167-7
Writer's Digest Books
9933 Alliance Road
Cincinnati, OH 45242
(800) 543-4644
$19.95

Excellent
Guide; resources guide

INCLUSIONS: Index; glossary; bibliography;
appendices (4): organizations and other
information sources, federal information sources,
selected book manufacturers, marketing contacts;
publishing timetable; samples

DESCRIPTORS: Self-publishing; book
promotion; book distribution; book publishing;
book production; book publicity; book marketing;
trade publishing; subsidy publishing

IDENTIFIER: Revision of earlier work, The
Encyclopedia of Self Publishing, published by
Communication Creativity

SUMMARY: This is probably the best guide to
self-publishing available. It includes 21
chapters on all the essential aspects of self-
publishing, including chapters on: assessing self-
publishing itself, choosing a subject, product
development, business aspects and operating
procedures; use of personal computers; early
activities; design and production; book
manufacturing; advertising; mail-order ads; direct
marketing; publicity; promotion; distribution;
talks and author tours; subsidiary rights;
attracting a trade publisher; agents; and a
critical evaluation of subsidy publishers.

RELEVANCE: This cookbook is chock full of
helpful information, creative ideas and tips for
making a self-publishing venture successful. It

is recommended reading for any self publisher. It
can be followed selectively in one's publishing
process from start to finish.

                    <<<<<<>>>>>>

DIRECTORY OF AMERICAN BOOK PUBLISHING, FROM
FOUNDING FATHERS TO TODAY'S CONGLOMERATES
1975
First
Kurian, George
397
0-67118-745-7
Simon and Schuster, Inc.
1230 Avenue of the Americas
New York, NY 10020
(212) 245-6400
$25.00

Very good
Reference

INCLUSIONS: Index; bibliography; glossary;
appendices;   commonly used publishing
abbreviations; glossary of publishing terms;
company addresses; bibliographies on general
reference, biographies and memoirs and on company
histories

DESCRIPTORS: Book publishing; publishing;
publishers

SUMMARY: This Directory describes
publishing houses in the U.S. The largest section
is on today's publishing houses. Other sections
are on founding fathers and their enterprises;
conglomerates; multiple publishing houses; book
trade associations; and major prizes, awards and
events. The Directory is not all inclusive. It
includes all major publishing houses founded
before 1968 and all university presses. Entries
cover founding information, legal form, history,
publishing program interests, samples of important
publications, and information on primary persons.

RELEVANCE: This source can help authors
and editors become familiar with the character and
interests of major publishing houses.

                    <<<<<<>>>>>>

DIRECTORY OF PUBLISHING OPPORTUNITIES IN
JOURNALS AND PERIODICALS
1981
Fifth
Irregular
844
Marquis Academic Media
Marquis Who's Who, Inc.
200 East Ohio Street
Chicago, IL 60611
(800) 621-9669
$52.50

Excellent
Directory

INCLUSIONS: Indexes by periodical title;
subject; cross-references; sponsoring
organization; editorial staff

DESCRIPTORS: Publishing; journals;
publications; periodicals

IDENTIFIER: Fomerly titled Third Volume:
Directory of Publishing Opportunities

SUMMARY: This Directory provides
detailed information on academic and professional
journals, technical journals, and publications by
business firms, unions, and associations. The
information was obtained from questionnaires.
Major categories are humanities, area studies,
social sciences, science and technology, medical
and health sciences, trades, manufacturing and
industry. It contains an Introduction,
"Ruminations on Becoming Published" with a helpful
discussion of author motivations in relation to
publishing strategy and publication selection. It
lists over 3900 journals, with 450 new ones in
this edition. It contains 73 specific interest

fields, including art; library science and
services; African, Asian, Pacific, European, Latin
American, Middle and Near Eastern, and North
American studies; accounting; business and
economics; finance and banking; labor studies;
management and personnel; communications
(journalism and publishing, radio and television,
speech); education (administrative, elementary,
secondary,higher); social and human services;
minority studies (Native American, Black,
Hispanic, Women); etc.

RELEVANCE: This volume is indispensable
for the author looking for appropriate journals
and for learning relevant information about them.

                    <<<<<<>>>>>>

DIRECTORY PUBLISHING
A Practical Guide
1985
First
Perkins, Russell
160
0-91306-101-8
Morgan-Rand Company
2200 Sansom Street
Philadelphia, PA 19103
(800) 354-8673
$19.95

Very good
Guide

INCLUSIONS: Index by subject; bibliography;
worksheets; samples

DESCRIPTORS: Book publishing; directory
publishing

SUMMARY: This publication provides
information on directory publishing. The
directory market is large, with over $30 billion
annually and an estimated 800 U.S. directory
publishers producing fifteen to eighteen thousand
directories. Perhaps 600 new directories come

into being each year for a growth rate of 18.5%.
Topics covered are: the directory publishing
industry; the nature of different types of
directories; market research and definition;
financial analyses; editorial form and style; the
editorial package to potential listees; computer-
based publishing, on-line databases and compact
disks; production; advertising; circulation; sales
promotion; fulfillment; legal considerations
surrounding copyright, trademark, disclaimer,
contracts, etc.; and additional sources of revenue
-- literature fulfillment, package inserts,
discount coupons, mailing lists, etc.

RELEVANCE: This is the first publication to
focus on directory publishing. It is a valuable
guide for directory publishers, especially
potential ones. The author points out that with
the aid of microcomputer technology, small and new
directory publishers can successfully compete with
large publishers in the production aspect and in
markets which are not "owned" (a subject area
successfully dominated by a particular publisher).
Large publishers have the advantage in
distribution networks. Capital requirements are
at least $5000 to get into the business and
preferably more. However, a good marketing
strategy and mailing lists can help to solve this
problem. Directory publishing has a higher profit
margin than book and magazine publishing.

                     <<<<<<>>>>>>

GREGG REFERENCE MANUAL
1984 (The 1977 edition was abstracted.)
Sixth
Tinervia, Joseph   -   Sabin, William
456
0-07-054399-2
McGraw-Hill Book Company
1221 Avenue of the Americas
New York, NY 10020
(800) 262-4729
$18.00

Very good
Manual

INCLUSIONS: Index; examples; illustrations

DESCRIPTORS: English language; writing

SUMMARY: This is a guide to the English
language and formal usage in writing. Part one
deals with grammar, usage, and style. Part two
deals with techniques and procedures. Part three
deals with references and resources. Eighteen
sections cover the following topical areas:
punctuation, capitalization, numbers,
abbreviations, plurals and possessives, spelling,
compound words, word division, grammar and usage;
dictation, transcription and typing techniques,
letters and memos, reports and manuscripts,
tables, forms of address, glossary of grammatical
terms, and reference books.

RELEVANCE: This is an easy-to-use
reference for anyone seeking answers to English
language usage and writing.

<<<<<<>>>>>

HOW TO GET PUBLISHED IN BUSINESS-PROFESSIONAL
JOURNALS
1980
First
Shulman, Joel
256
0-81445-555-7
AMACOM
135 West 50th Street
New York, NY 10020
(212) 586-8100
$14.95

Very good
Guide

INCLUSION: Index by subject, cross-
referenced

DESCRIPTORS: Business report writing;
authorship; writing

SUMMARY: This work is about the nature
of the business and professional press, its
readership and specific techniques pertinent to
getting published. It discusses the need for
becoming informed of relevant publications and
finding out if the editor is interested in your
idea. Topics discussed are types of articles,
exclusives, data sources, organization, research
and documentation, matters of style, visuals,
manuscript preparation and methods of querying
editors. It stresses the importance of written
approval from all sources involved, e.g. company,
individual, about what is being written and
mentions publisher request to get author approval
on typeset copy to ensure accuracy. It discusses
payment/non-payment for writing in journals,
magazines, for a company, and tips for getting
paid, e.g. division of topic and market.

RELEVANCE: This informs prospective
writers for business and professional presses what
editors look for and how to proceed. Its approach
is one of reasoned advice.

                    <<<<<<>>>>>>

HOW TO PUBLISH YOUR OWN BOOK
A Guide for Authors Who Plan to Publish A Book
at Their Own Expense
1976
First
Mueller, Lothar
184
0-8187-0019-X
Harlo Press
50 Victor Avenue
Detroit, MI 48203
(313) 883-3600
$6.95

Excellent
Book; guide

INCLUSIONS: Glossary; important magazine
addresses; bibliography

DESCRIPTORS: Publishing; self-publishing;
printing

SUMMARY: This book advises on why and how
to self publish. It discusses manuscript
preparation, print quantity and size, book
pricing, preparation of jacket cover, artwork and
illustrations, proofreading, promotion before
publication, sales after printing, discounts and
returns, invoicing and shipping, copyright law,
how to obtain Library of Congress catalog card
number and ISBN number, how long printing and
binding takes, the parts of a book, what to do
with unsold books, and vanity publishing as an
unsavory alternative.

RELEVANCE: This is a well-written guide
for consultants interested in self publishing.

                <<<<<<>>>>>

INTERNATIONAL LITERARY MARKET PLACE
1987 (The 1980 edition was abstracted.)
Seventeenth
Biennial
587
0-8352-2341-8
R. R. Bowker Company
245 West 17th Street
New York, NY 10011
(800) 521-8110   (800) 537-8416 (Canada)
$110.00

Excellent
Guide

INCLUSIONS: Index; book trade calendar

DESCRIPTORS: Book trade; publishers;
literary market; literary agents, remainder
dealers; booksellers; libraries; translation; book
clubs; library associations; literary awards

SUMMARY: This is a guide to publishers,
agents, publications, book trade organizations,
etc. by country (49). Subheadings under each
country are: general information, book trade
organizations, book trade reference books and
journals, publishers, remainder dealers (UK only),
literary agents, book clubs, major booksellers,
major libraries, library associations and
societies, literary periodicals, literary prizes,
translation agencies and associations. The
following information is provided under "general
information" on each country: language, religion,
population, literacy rate, bank hours, shop hours,
currency, export/import information, and
copyright. Information under "publishers,"
usually includes contact information, personnel,
subsidiary company and bookshop, subjects, number
of titles, founding date, and ISBN publishers
prefixes.

RELEVANCE: This Guide enables users to
identify international book markets and pertinent
organizations and individuals.

<<<<<<>>>>>>

INTERNATIONAL WRITERS' & ARTISTS' YEARBOOK 1988
1988
81st
Annual
528
Writer's Digest Books
1507 Dana Avenue
Cincinnati, OH 45207
(800) 543-4644
$14.95

Good
Directory; sourcebook

INCLUSIONS: Index by subject; complete
sample of all marks used in marking-up copy for
composition and for the correction of printers'
proofs

DESCRIPTORS: Writing; art; publishing

IDENTIFIER: Title varied in past years:
Writer's Yearbook; International Writers' and
Artists' Yearbook

SUMMARY: This work is divided into two
main parts. Part one provides the names of
companies to contact for writers or photographers
who want to market their creations. Part two
includes information about financial and legal
matters, preparation of manuscripts, resource
list of writer associations, and literary awards
and prizes. It is international in scope, including the United Kingdom, Africa, Australia,
Canada, Republic of Ireland and Northern Ireland,
New Zealand, South Africa, and the United States.
Markets are identified by type of artistic work,
such as articles, books, scripts, poetry,
illustrations, photographs, picture research, and
music.

RELEVANCE: This source helps users locate
literary and art markets internationally, gives
practical advice to writers, and lists resource
organizations and awards.

                   <<<<<<>>>>>>

LAW (IN PLAIN ENGLISH) FOR WRITERS
1987
First
Duboff, Leonard
274
0-88089-016-9
Madrona Publishers
P.O. Box 22667
Seattle, WA 98122
(206) 325-3973
$9.95

Excellent
Guide

INCLUSIONS: Index by subject; glossary;
notes; organizations offering help (Volunteer
Lawyers for the Arts chapters); writers'
organizations

DESCRIPTORS: Writing; publishing; law;
copyright; legal considerations for writers;
contracts; agents

SUMMARY: This book provides publishing
and legal information for the writer. Chapters
contents include the following subjects:
organizing a form of business (sole
proprietorship, partnership, corporation); taxes
(income, estate, gift); considerations in seeking
a publisher; finding an agent; alternatives to
large publishers (university presses, small
presses, writers' cooperatives, vanity presses,
self-publishing, copublishing, subsidy
publishing); copyright law; censorship and
obscenity; defamation and libel; the right of
privacy; and finding a lawyer. It covers basic
elements of contracts, author-publisher aspects,
and magazine contracts. Specific aspects of
author-publisher contracts discussed include:
royalties, the manuscript (format, content,
changes, publication time, revisions), copyright,
subsidiary rights, warranty and indemnity, non-
competition covenant, termination and reversion,
arbitration, authorship rights (credit, free
copies, author purchase), agency, waiver or
breach, etc.

RELEVANCE: This book details important
considerations for writers seeking and negotiating
publication. It is highly recommended reading
whether or not you have a lawyer or agent for
help.

                    <<<<<<>>>>>>

LITERARY MARKET PLACE WITH NAMES AND NUMBERS
1988 (The 1985 edition was abstracted.)
48th
900
0-8352-2391-X
R. R. Bowker Company
205 East 42nd Street
New York, NY 10017
(800) 521-8110   (800) 537-8416 (Canada)
$85.00

Very good
Directory

INCLUSIONS: Indexes by sections, advertisers

DESCRIPTORS: Literary market; publishing;
book clubs; book trade; literary awards

SUMMARY: This is a buyer's guide and
register of personnel in the publishing industry.
Major subjects are book publishing; book clubs;
rights and representatives; associations and other
organizations; book trade events, conferences and
courses; literary awards, contests and grants;
services and suppliers; direct mail promotion;
book review, selection and reference; radio and
television; wholesale, export and import; book
manufacturing; and magazine and newspaper
publishing. It contains a large section on names
and numbers of publishers, firms, organizations,
and individuals. It also lists agents, agencies,
manufacturers, reviewers, sales representatives,
consultants, personnel agencies, printers,
photographers, proofreaders, advertisers,
stenographers, typists, typesetters, suppliers,
lettershop, duplicating and mailing services.

RELEVANCE: This enables users to find
detailed information about many aspects of the
literary marketplace. It's very useful for
writers and publishers.

                    <<<<<<>>>>>>

MAGAZINE INDUSTRY MARKET PLACE
1987 (The 1984 edition was abstracted.)
Annual
975 (1987 edition)
0-8352-2269-1
R. R. Bowker Company
245 West 17th Street
New York, NY 10011
(800) 521-8110
$59.95 (1987)

Excellent

Serial; catalog; classified directory; marketplace
resource guide; marketing guide

INCLUSIONS: Indexes(10); advertisements;
annotated bibliographies; directories(40);
reference bibliography; free listings; consultant
listings; consulting firm profiles (annotated);
consulting organization profiles (annotated);
annotated resource descriptions (suppliers,
service firms, publishers, magazines, periodic
publications, organizations, agents, agencies,
syndicates, mailing list sources); illustrations
(graphics, photographs); calendars (trade
conferences and exhibits); market statistics;
resource lists (awards, contests and prizes);
suggested readings (reference publications)

DESCRIPTORS: Magazine industry; periodical
publishers; journals; periodicals; magazines;
trade publications; publications - personnel and
organizations serving ; service firms; suppliers

SUMMARY: This lists and describes
publishers, consultants, vendors, service firms,
key company personnel, organizations and allied
groups serving the magazine and periodic
publications industry. It gives annotated
descriptions of the kinds of services and products
supplied by each. It includes newsletters,
magazines, reference books and national
associations of the trade; names, addresses and
phone numbers; new publications; and
vendors/services. It includes these general types
of firms/services: back date periodical dealers,
color separators, distributors, lettershops,
multiple periodical publishers (four or more
periodicals annually), micropublishers, paper
merchants, paper mills, publication printers,
syndicates; artistic, data processing, exhibit,
fulfillment, duplicating, mailing, marketing
research, mailing list, illustration, messenger,
personnel and recruiting, photography, public
relations, shipping, subscription, translation,
and typesetting. It lists about 125 consulting
firms with these specializations: advertising and
promotion, circulation and distribution, direct
mail, editorial, financial, library, management,
marketing, paper/paper products, pictorial,
printing, and publishing.

RELEVANCE: MIMP is patterned after Literary
Marketplace. It is useful for persons interested
in the creation, production, selection, use and/or
sale of magazines, periodicals, and periodic
reference publications and non-periodicals as
well.

<<<<<<>>>>>>

MANUAL OF STYLE
1969
Twelfth, revised
546
University of Chicago Press
Chicago, IL 60637
568-1550
$10.00

Excellent
Manual

INCLUSIONS: Index; bibliography

DESCRIPTORS: Writing; book preparation

SUMMARY: This Manual presents the
elements and rules of style (used by the
University of Chicago Press). Major parts are:
bookmaking, style, and production and printing.
It covers the complete process of book
preparation, including sections on: parts of a
book; manuscript preparation, proofs; rights and
permissions; punctuation; spelling and distinctive
treatment of words; names and terms; numbers;
foreign languages in type; quotations;
illustrations; captions and legends; tables;
mathematics in type; abbreviations; notes and
footnotes; bibliographies; the citation of public
documents; indexes; design and typography; and
glossary of technical terms.

RELEVANCE: This is a good reference for
authors, editors, and copywriters. It enables the
user to prepare books in accepted, marketable
style.

MICROFORM MARKET PLACE 1986-87
An International Directory of Micropublishing
1986
Second
Maxen-Berneir, Roberta
250
0-88736-073-4
Meckler Publication Corporation
11 Ferry Lane West
Westport, CT 06880
(203) 226-6967
$39.95

Very good
Directory

INCLUSIONS: Indexes by subject, geography;
advertisers; annotated bibliography; calendar
(conferences, meetings, seminars)

DESCRIPTORS: Micropublishers;
micropublications

SUMMARY: This Directory presents
comprehensive information about micropublishers.
It provides information on commercial and non-
commercial micropublishers worldwide. It includes
publishers which market micropublications and
reprographic centers (university and national
library centers). It excludes micrographics
equipment and supply manufacturers. It contains a
section on mergers and acquisitions, which has
been added since the previous edition. It
contains microform jobbers, which market
micropublications for micropublishers; and
organizations concerned with educational use of
microforms in the library.

RELEVANCE: This is written for purchasers
and librarians. It is the most detailed listing
of micropublishers available. The calendar of
conferences, meetings, and seminars will be of
interest to purchasers of micropublications.

PUBLISHERS DIRECTORY
A Guide to Approximately 15,000 New and
Established, Commercial, Private, Alternative, and
Nonprofit Corporate and Association, Government
and Institution Publishing Programs and Their
Distributors
1987; 1988 Supplement
Eighth
Hubbard, Linda
2200 (2 volumes); 250 (Supplement)
0-8103-2513-6
0-8103-2516-0 Supplement
Gale Research Company
(800) 223-4253
$275.00 set; $250.00 (1987); $155.00
(Supplement)

Excellent
Directory

INCLUSIONS: Indexes by publishers; imprints
and distributors; geography; subject; sample
entry; publisher and distributor listings

DESCRIPTORS: Publishers; book publishers;
alternative publishers; small presses; specialized
publishers; women and minority publishers;
distributors

IDENTIFIER: Formerly titled Book Publishers
Directory

SUMMARY: This Directory contains
publishers you were unable to find in Writer's
Market and Literary Market Place. It lists
publishers and distributors of the U.S. and
Canada. It includes "sources of non-periodical
materials of all kinds, including producers of
books, classroom materials, databases, reports,
calendars, product guides, chapbooks, and other
kinds of publications." It excludes only vanity
presses and publishers listed in Literary Market
Place. Entries are arranged alphabetically.
Examples of headings in the subject index are:
accounting, advertising, alternative lifestyle,
alternative technology, American Indians, Bible,
bibliography, bilingual books, careers, computers,
consumer affairs, databases, environment, graphic

arts, health, labor, political science, religion,
social issues, Soviet Union, textbooks, and women.

RELEVANCE: This Directory is especially
relevant for the writer whose work would be a
likely candidate for alternative and small
presses. It is easy to use, with its alphabetic
listing and wonderful indexes.

                    <<<<<<>>>>>

PUBLISHERS, DISTRIBUTORS, AND WHOLESALERS OF
THE UNITED STATES 1987-1988
A Directory of Publishers, Distributors,
Associations, Wholesalers, Software Producers
and Manufacturers Listing Editorial and
Ordering Addresses, and an ISBN Publisher
Prefix Index
1986
Irregular
1986-87 edition
R. R. Bowker Company's
Database Publishing Group
1689
0-8352-2384-1
R. R. Bowker Company
245 West 17th Street
New York, NY 10017
(800) 521-8110
$85.00

Excellent
Directory

INCLUSIONS: Indexes: name, wholesaler,
distributor, inactive and out-of-business
publishers, publishers by fields of activity,
subsidiaries, imprints and divisions, geographic
index to publishers, publishers and distributors'
toll-free numbers, ISBN prefix, and key to
abbreviations of publishers

DESCRIPTORS: Publishers; book distributors;
book wholesalers; book associations; small
publishers

SUMMARY: This volume lists 57,000
publisher and publisher-related companies and
organizations. It includes small publishers and
covers maps, posters, audio-visual materials,
computer software not covered in Books in Print,
and over 13,500 associations that may publish
print and non-print materials.

RELEVANCE: This is a high-quality Bowker
reference to publishers useful libraries,
individuals and organizations. You should find
the publisher you're looking for here.

                    <<<<<<>>>>>>

PUBLISHERS' INTERNATIONAL DIRECTORY WITH ISBN
INDEX
1987 (The 1985 edition was abstracted.)
Thirteenth
Irregular
Verrel, Barbara
2192
3-598-20535-X
K. G. Saur, Inc
175 Fifth Avenue
New York, NY 10010
(212) 982-1302
$215.00

Excellent
Directory

INCLUSIONS: Abbreviations; area of
specialization codes; list of countries with
relevant page numbers

DESCRIPTORS: Publishers; international
publishing

IDENTIFIER: This work is also the Handbook
of International Documentation and Information,
volume 7

SUMMARY: Volume one is an alphabetical
listing of international publishers with a second
volume containing a numerical ISBN index.   There

are over 160,000 entries and over 93,000 have an
ISBN prefix. The ISBN prefixes listed in volume
one are arranged numerically in volume two. The
entry includes the firm name and country. Entries
include: firm name, local and mailing address,
telephone and telex numbers, cable address,
telecopier number and system, branch addresses,
member firms or distributors, and areas of
specialization.

RELEVANCE: This is a useful information
source on international publishers.

                    <<<<<<>>>>>>

THE SELF-PUBLISHING MANUAL
How to Write, Print & Sell Your Own Book
1986 (The 1984 edition was abstracted.)
Fourth
Poynter, Dan
352
Para Publishing
P.O. Box 4232-R
Santa Barbara, CA 93140-4232
(805) 968-7277
$14.95

Excellent
Guide

INCLUSIONS: Index by subject; planning
calendar; resources: print, organizations, book
dealers, printers, reviewers, publicists,
supplies, maillists, book fairs

DESCRIPTORS: Book publishing; self-
publishing; book promotion; writing; publishing

SUMMARY: This covers self-publishing
from start to finish. It begins with a discussion
of publishing options, self-publishing and
writing. It discusses: 1) going into business and
specific information, things to do, and issues in
a publishing business, including name, place,
equipment, supplies, legalities, and finances; 2)
printing materials, design, and details of putting

a book together, selecting a typesetter and
printer; 3) announcing a book, including getting
ISBN, SAN, and CIP numbers and contacting
directories of publishers; 4) financing - setting
prices, discounts, estimating sales, rates for
retail bookstores, college bookstores,
wholesalers, libraries, shipping, accounts
receivable, consignments, credit, and collections;
5) promoting - analysis, contacts, materials,
testimonials, news releases, reviews, radio and
TV, author tours, magazine articles, seminars,
book promotion services, etc.; 6) marketing - to
whom, when, what, rights, wholesalers,
distributors, bookstores, libraries, government,
book fairs, etc.; 7) advertising - ads,
advertorials, brochures, catalogs, agencies,
direct-mail, co-op, radio and TV, commissioned
sales reps, telemarketing, etc.; 8) distributing -
mail order, order processing, dealer order,
complimentary copies, inventory control, packing
and shipping, returns, fulfillment houses, etc.;
11) computing and book publishing - writing,
editing, producing, fulfillments, promotion,
market research, financial management; and 12)
coping with being an author and doing articles,
consulting, speaking, etc.

RELEVANCE: Along with Tom and Marilyn
Ross' book on self publishing abstracted in this
volume, this is a "must read" for the new self-
publisher. It contains much information and many
handy tips, spiced up with numerous pithy quotes
and one-liner advice.

<<<<<<<>>>>>>

THE WRITERS' AND ARTISTS' YEARBOOK
1988
78th
Annual
528
(0480) 212666
Black, Adam -   Black, Charles
35 Bedford Row
London WC1R4JH
Distributed in the U.S. by Writer's Digest Books
$7.50 (1985)

Good
Directory; sourcebook

INCLUSION: Index

DESCRIPTORS: Writing; art; publishing

IDENTIFIERS: Title varies in past editions:
Writers' Yearbook; International Writers' and
Artists' Yearbook. Subtitle varies: A Directory
for Writers, Artists, Playwrights, Writers for
Film Radio and Television, Photographers and
Composers

SUMMARY: This work mostly contains
listings of publishers, print media sources, and
markets for writers, artists, photographers and
composers, with some narrative articles and tips
on a variety of subjects. It is international in
scope, including in parts, the United States,
United Kingdom, Australia, New Zealand, Canada,
India, Ireland, and South Africa. Sections are:
newspapers and magazines; book publishers;
theatre, television, radio, agents; art, music
prizes, clubs; and copyright, tax, and services.
The section on newspapers and magazines includes
journals; syndicates, news and press agencies; and
a discussion of markets for verse. The section on
book publishers includes publishers, book
packagers, book clubs, and vanity publishing.

RELEVANCE: This provides an overall though
not exhaustive information source for various
creative professions in the mostly English-
speaking world. It is somewhat uneven in
treatment and organization and is inexpensive.

CHAPTER 24

TELECOMMUNICATIONS

This chapter contains:

- telecommunications industry and
  market

- telephone, satellites and networks

- computer telecommunications

- databases

- government regulation

- telecommunications and economic
  development in less-industrialized
  countries

- teleconferencing

- future developments

CHANGING MARKET STRUCTURES IN TELECOMMUNICATIONS
Proceedings of an OECD Conference Held 13-15
December 1982
1984
First
Ergas, Henry   -   Okayama, Jun
451
0-444-86855-0
OECD (Organization for Economic Cooperation
and Development)
2, rue Andre
75775 Paris - Pascal Decdex 16, France
(212) 370-5520
$67.50

Excellent
Compilation

INCLUSION: List of participants

DESCRIPTORS: Telecommunications;
international telecommunications

SUMMARY: This compilation of articles
presented by authorities and organizations
examines developments in national
telecommunications services in OECD member
countries and international implications. Two
conclusions from the discussion were: 1) The
question is neither monopoly nor competition but
how to best combine them; and 2) No single
objective can be used to evaluate market
organization in telecommunications. While
national diversity is recognized, international
cooperation and integration is desired. Part one
contains sections with articles on the issues,
policy developments, expert points of view,
perspective of international organizations, user
standpoint, and overview. Part two discusses
telecommunications services in Australia, Austria,
Belgium, Canada, Denmark, Finland, France,
Germany, Ireland, Italy, Japan, Luxembourg, The
Netherlands, New Zealand, Norway, Portugal, Spain,
Sweden, Switzerland, Turkey, United Kingdom, and
United States.

RELEVANCE: This is must reading for anyone
seeking to understand the facts and issues

involved in international telecommunications
markets as well as related issues of international
cooperation.

<<<<<<>>>>>>

COMPUTER-READABLE DATABASES
A Directory and Data Sourcebook
1985
Irregular
Fourth
Williams, Martha
2 volumes
0-444-87613-8 Vol: Science, Technology and
Medicine
0-444-87614-6 Vol: Business, Law, Humanities
& Social Sciences
American Library Association
50 East Huron Street
Chicago, IL 60611
(312) 944-6780
$157.50 set; $139.00 separately

Very good
Directory; sourcebook

INCLUSIONS: Indexes by name, processor,
producer, subject

DESCRIPTORS: Databases; bibliographic
databases

IDENTIFIER: Formerly titled: Computer-
Readable Bibliographic Data Bases - A Directory
and Data Sourcebook

SUMMARY: This source consists of two
volumes: Science, Tehnology and Medicine, and
Business, Law, Humanities & Social Sciences. The
directory covers 2805 databases and 2509 separate
entries. The information was obtained from
database producers based on returned
questionnaires. Criteria for inclusion of a
database is that it be computer readable and
publicly available. Databases are alphabetically
arranged. Entries include basic information,

subject matter and scope of data in database,
indexing/coding/classification, data elements
present, and user aids available.

RELEVANCE: This is a good source for
bibliographic databases. Elsevier publishes the
separate volumes, while the American Library
Association publishes the set.

                    <<<<<<>>>>>>

DATAPRO MANAGEMENT OF DATA COMMUNICATIONS
1988; monthly report; monthly newsletter
Annual, monthly update
Peck, Richard
2 volumes
Datapro Research
1805 Underwood Blvd.
Delran, NJ 08075
(800) 328-2776
$640.00

Excellent
Loose-leaf information service; current awareness
service

INCLUSIONS: Index; glossary; user's guide;
directory of communications consultants

DESCRIPTORS: Telecommunications; data
communications management

IDENTIFIER: Formerly titled: Datapro
Communications Solutions

SUMMARY: These volumes contain
approximately 200 reports and 2000 pages. The
reports discuss problems and solutions in the
process-oriented organization of planning,
designing and managing data communications. The
tabbed sections, each with a topic index cover:
basic concepts, system components, planning,
system design, selection and acquisition,
installation and maintenance, operations
management, systems management, future systems,
and standards and protocols.

RELEVANCE: This work contains a wealth of
information for the data management professional.
The directory of communications consultants is a
welcome feature.

                    <<<<<<>>>>>>

DIRECTORY OF ONLINE DATABASES
1988
Quarterly, two complete issues and two update
supplements a year
Volume 9, Number 3
Variable
0193-6840
Cuadra/Elsevier
52 Vanderbilt Avenue
New York, NY 10017
(212) 916-1180
$150.00

Excellent
Directory; current awareness service

INCLUSIONS: Indexes by subject; vendor
geographic; producer; online service/gateway;
telecommunications; master; user information

DESCRIPTORS: Databases; online databases

SUMMARY: This source contains
information on 3893 databases available through
576 online services internationally. The
Directory distinguishes these databases types:
reference -- bibliographic, referral; source --
numeric, textual-numeric, full text, and software.
Criteria for inclusion are that the database be
online, and available to the public through an
online service organization connected to
international telecommunications systems, although
also included are databases available through
leased lines or direct long-distance call. The
bulk of the Directory contains the database
entries, including fields: name, type, subject,
producer, online service, conditions, content,
language, coverage, time span, and updating.

RELEVANCE: This directory has the advantage of keeping up-to-date in what is a changeable market. This can be of use to anyone who uses databases, such as librarians, researchers, business people, and consultants.

`<<<<<<>>>>>`

FUTURE DEVELOPMENTS IN TELECOMMUNICATIONS
1977
Second
Martin, James
624
0-13-345850-4
Prentice-Hall, Inc.
Rt. 9 West
Englewood Cliffs, NJ 07632
(201) 592-2000
200 Old Tappan Road
Old Tappan, NJ 07675
(201) 767-5054
$60.67

Good
State of the art review; textbook

INCLUSIONS: Index by subject; bibliographies (articles; publication list; technical reports); data (costs; equation); glossary; illustrations; statistics; specifications; tables

DESCRIPTORS: Telecommunications; telecommunications technology; communications media; forecasts

SUMMARY: This has descriptions of: 1) emerging media and telecommunications technologies, which will be used in businesses, corporations, the home and broader community; and 2) the major inventions, technological developments and hardware components upon which they are based. It covers applications and uses of computer, electronic and laser technologies; audio and voice systems; communications satellites; data banks; cable TV, interactive

television, video telephone, radio, and other
systems.

RELEVANCE: This is perhaps one of the
easier books on telecommunications though it is
still technical. It also needs to be updated,
especially since it's supposed to be dealing with
the future.

<<<<<<>>>>>>

HOW TO CUT COSTS AND IMPROVE SERVICE OF YOUR
TELEPHONE, TELEX, TWX AND OTHER TELECOMMUNICATIONS
1982 (The 1974 edition was abstracted.)
Second
Griesinger, Frank
310
0-07024-760-9
McGraw-Hill Book Company
1221 Avenue of the Americas
New York, NY 10020
(800) 262-4729

Good
Handbook

INCLUSIONS: Index by subject; annotated
bibliographies (books; magazines; newsletters);
cost data; evaluation-selection aids; guidelines
(user); illustrations (figures; photographs)

DESCRIPTORS: Telecommunications equipment;
telecommunications services; telegraph services;
telephone communications systems; telephone
services

IDENTIFIERS: Centrex; TELEX, TWX and WATS
services

SUMMARY: This is a practical consumer's
guide to services and equipment supplied by
telecommunications utilities and private vendors.
It shows how to select, effectively manage and use
basic, interconnected and supplemental systems.
It discusses commonly used systems and services --
Foreign Exchange; local and long distance;

mailgram; postal; teleprinter exchange; Western
Union; and others.

RELEVANCE: Good in concept, this is
somewhat technically outdated.

                    <<<<<<>>>>>>

OMNI ONLINE DATABASE DIRECTORY 1985
1984
Davies, Owen   -   Edelhart, Mike
384
Omni Publications International, Ltd.
0-02-079920-9
Macmillan Publishing Company
(800) 257-5755
$19.95

Very good
Directory; sourcebook

INCLUSION: Index of databases

DESCRIPTORS: On-line data processing;
information storage and retrieval systems;
computer networks; data libraries; databases

SUMMARY: This reference is divided into
three parts. The first part is text and answers
such questions as how to use a database, select an
appropriate service, and analyze costs. The
second part is an alphabetical directory and
review of over 1000 services. Each database
description includes the title, contexts, user's
comment, access (names of online service vendors
who make the database available), suppliers (the
organizations that produced the information in the
database), and cross-references (to other
databases). It describes major online vendors:
the Source, CompuServe, Delphi, and NewsNet. The
third part consists of three appendices: the
online directory of service vendors with at least
four databases; the telecommunications directory
of telephone numbers for local access to the three
largest U.S. telecommunications networks, Tymnet,
Telenet, and Uninet; and an index of databases

reviewed.   Criteria for inclusion of databases
were that they be online and available to the
public.

RELEVANCE: This is a very useful reference
for anyone considering or using online databases.
It could use a subject index.   Another, similar,
and equally good source is put out by Cuadra
Associates.

                    <<<<<<>>>>>>

TELECOMMUNICATIONS AMERICA
Markets Without Boundaries
1984
First
Irwin, Manley
147
0-89930-029-4, IIsl Quorum
Greenwood Press
88 Post Road West
P.O. Box 5007
Westport, CT 06881
(203) 226-3571
$35.00

Excellent
Book

INCLUSIONS: Index, cross-referenced;
bibliography; tables; figures

DESCRIPTORS: Telecommunications; telephone;
AT&T; Bell

IDENTIFIER: Quorum Books

SUMMARY: This is an examination of the
conflicting forces of technology and government
regulation.   While regulation is based in
traditional boundary lines, technology breaks them
down.   Irwin traces the development of
telecommunications, and the history of AT&T and
Bell operating companies.   He notes the
dissolution of market boundaries and evolving
competition between previously distant industries.

He asks whether federal (FCC) or state governments
or the market will be the arbiter of the emerging
information infrastructure in an environment of
intensified competition nationally and
internationally.

RELEVANCE: This book is recommended for
anyone seeking to gain insight into our new world
of telecommunications, corporate development, and
government regulation. The author seems to think
that government regulation is getting in the way
of a dynamic market that can result in
technological growth and consumer benefit.

                    <<<<<<>>>>>>

TELECOMMUNICATIONS AND ECONOMIC DEVELOPMENT
1983
First
Hitchcock, Virginia
Saunders, Robert   -   Warford, Jeremy   -
Wellenius, Bjorn
395
The World Bank
0-8018-2829-5
Johns Hopkins University Press
701 W 40th Street, Suite 275
Baltimore, MD 21211
(301) 338-7864
$14.95

Very good
Book

INCLUSIONS: Index, cross-referenced;
chapter notes; bibliography; appendices (4)

DESCRIPTORS: Telecommunications; telephone;
underdeveloped countries

SUMMARY: This book focuses on telephone
use in underdeveloped countries. Its purposes are
to review the evidence on the role of
telecommunications in development, and to provide
policymakers with information on the use of
economic analysis for resource allocation and

policies. The book explores the questions as to
what the barriers are to the development of
telecommunications and how to use economic
analysis to help determine appropriate investment.
Cost benefit and microeconomic analyses are seen
as unsatisfactory in judging benefits. Several
chapters provide examples of international
telecommunications usage. The focus of the book
is on common carrier communication and
broadcasting and on telephone service.

RELEVANCE: This book takes an academic and
technical approach and is more appropriate for the
specialist than for the general reader.

                    <<<<<<>>>>>>

TELECOMMUNICATIONS FOR MANAGEMENT
1984
First
Meadow, Charles   - Tedesco, Albert
400
0-07-04198-0
McGraw-Hill Book Company
1221 Avenue of the Americas
New York, NY 10020
(800) 262-4729
$37.95

Excellent
Textbook

INCLUSIONS: Index; chapter bibliographies;
case histories; illustrations

DESCRIPTORS: Telecommunications;
telecommunications management; communication;
telephone; videotext; teleconferencing;
electronic-mail; networks; local area networks;
digital communication networks; television;
transmission; mobile communication

IDENTIFIER: McGraw-Hill Series in
Management Information Systems, Gordon Davis,
Consulting Editor

SUMMARY: The individually authored (by
company experts, consultants, and professors) 19
chapters are grouped into six major subject areas:
1) elements of Communication, on communication
fundamentals; 2) basic Technology, on
telecommunications technology, including chapters
on transmission systems, the telephone system,
digital communication networks, and local area
networks; 3) applications, including chapters on
television in the corporate environment,
electronic mail, teleconferencing, mobile
communication, and videotext; 4) management of
telecommunications, including chapters on cost-
benefit analysis, regulation, international
telecommunications, and managing a
telecommunications facility; 5) case histories on
the Insurance Company of North America (INA),
which merged with Connecticut General to form
CIGNA Corporation, and the Washington Post; and
6) the future.

RELEVANCE: The chapter contributions are
high quality, technical, historical, and
contribute to a well-integrated theme.   They
explain not only what but how the various
technologies work.

                    <<<<<<>>>>>>

THE TELECOMMUNICATIONS INDUSTRY
The Dynamics of Market Structure
1981
First
Brock, Gerald
336
0-674-87285-1
Harvard University Press
79 Garden Street
Cambridge, MA 02138
(617) 495-2471
$25.00

Good
Book; Study; Sourcebook

INCLUSIONS: Index; notes

DESCRIPTORS: Telecommunication - Europe;
telecommunications industry; telecommunications -
law and legislation; telecommunication policy -
United States

SUMMARY: This provides an overview of
the development of the telecommunications
industry. Its purported purposes are to "clarify
the causes of change in industry structures," to
"examine the competitive uses of regulation and of
systems effects," and to "provide an organized
account of the development and current conditions
in the telecommunications industry." It compiles
facts from histories and regulatory proceedings
within an economic framework and from a
methodology of industrial organization in
economics. It is divided into 11 chapters
covering such topics as the telegraph and the
telephone in the United States and Europe;
monopoly, competition, and regulation; the long-
distance market; new competition in terminal
equipment and changing industry boundaries,
including computers, electronic mail, and
satellites; and public policy.

RELEVANCE: This takes an academic and
historical approach to the development of the
telecommunications industry for interested
readers.

<<<<<<>>>>>>

TELECONFERENCING
Linking People Together Electronically
1985
First
Cross, Thomas
300
0-08-028597-X
Pergamon Press Inc.
Maxwell House
Fairview Park
Elmsford, NY 10523
(914) 592-7700
$350.00

Excellent
Book

INCLUSIONS: Index by subject; resource
references; glossary; communications inventory
checklists; audience checklist; illustrations

DESCRIPTORS: Teleconferencing; audiographic
teleconferencing; audio teleconferencing;
telecommunications; computer teleconferencing;
productivity; human resources management;
strategic planning; consulting process; video;
quality of work life; consultant role

SUMMARY: This provides an overview of
what teleconferencing is, which is defined as "the
use of an electronic medium to communicate
interactively by individuals or groups who are
located remotely from one another for the purpose
of conferring with one another." Teleconferencing
is shown to be particularly appropriate for the
post-industrial, information society for areas of
increased communication, participation,
production, and quality of work life. The authors
show that teleconferencing can do the following:
1) substitute for many meetings, and meetings
constitute half of the white collar workers' work
time; 2) enhance human resources management and
training functions; 3) facilitate and support
strategic planning, and decision making; and 4)
provide tools for management. A detailed
discussion of the process of introducing and
integrating teleconferencing into an organization
is presented. The consultant role in planning and
implementing a system is discussed. Variant
formats for optimal communications presented are
broadcast/presentation, panel, round-table
discussion, interview, embedded teleconference,
and multi-topic. Type of teleconferencing system
options are discussed: audio, audiographic,
video, and computer.

RELEVANCE: This is an excellent source for
anyone wanting to know about teleconferencing, its
technology, and applications. It is particularly
relevant for business owners, managers,
consultants, trainers, information systems
professionals, and others who may be or become
involved with teleconferencing applications.

THE TELECONFERENCING RESOURCE BOOK
A Guide to Applications and Planning
1984
First
Parker, Lorne - Olgren, Christine
452
0-444-86887-9
Elsevier Science Publishing Company, Inc. B.V.
52 Vanderbilt Avenue
New York, NY 10017
(212) 370-5520
$50.00

Good
Resource book

INCLUSIONS: Tables; illustrations

DESCRIPTORS: Teleconferencing; audio
teleconferencing; audiographic teleconferencing;
video teleconferencing; computer teleconferencing;
international teleconferencing

SUMMARY: This volume contains 54 papers
written by company experts and professors on a
variety of teleconferencing applications for
meetings, training and marketing in business,
education, health care, and government. The
volume is organized into sections on audio,
audiographic and freeze-frame video,
videoconferencing and computer teleconferencing;
teleconferencing technologies; system planning,
evaluation and research; and training and program
design.

RELEVANCE: This is a good source for
generating ideas for teleconferencing
applications. While articles have headings and
subheadings, the book as a whole could benefit
from being better organized and the inclusion of
an index. The copy is uneven and difficult to
read in parts.

VIDEOTEXT, THE COMING REVOLUTION IN
HOME/OFFICE INFORMATION RETRIEVAL
1980
Second
Sigel, Effrem
Sigel, Effrem - Roizen, Joseph - McIntyre,
Colin - Wilkinson, Max
154
0-9142-3641-5
Knowledge Industry Publications, Inc.
701 Westchester Avenue
White Plains, NY 10604
(800) 248-5474
$27.95

Very good
Report

INCLUSIONS: Index by subject; directories
(2); illustrations (photographs, graphics,
computer graphics, charts); resource descriptions
(videotext systems)

DESCRIPTORS: Information retrieval;
information systems; information services;
information technology research; videotext
systems; video transmission systems; data
transmission systems; broadcast reception
equipment; telecommunications research; television
research

IDENTIFIERS: Prestel; CEEFAX; Teletext;
Viewdata; Telidon; ANTIOPE VIDEOTEX; ORACLE;
TIFAX; QUBE; TITAN

SUMMARY: This describes promising
videotext systems -- electronic information
transmission systems which display textural
information in a video display screen in the form
of words and/or numbers. It describes various
systems (broadcast and telephone) in stages of
research, development, testing and application in
Great Britain, France, Canada, Japan, the United
States, and other countries. It explains what
videotext technology is all about -- how it was
developed, who developed it, how it works, how it
can be used, and for what purposes. After a brief
introduction the following topics are

treated in successive chapters: 1) the technology
of Teletext and Viewdata; 2) Teletext in Britain -
the CEEFAX story; 3) Viewdata -- the Prestel
System; and 4) videotext in other countries. The
concluding chapter treats some of the major
factors expected to impede/foster future use of
videotext systems and competitive technologies.
It discusses issues and considerations expected
to impact upon the marketing and sales of emerging
videotext services and products.

RELEVANCE: This is somewhat technical,
but written for the lay reader and it is important
reading for persons who: 1) plan to publish and
deliver their expertise in printed or electronic
form; 2) must supply clients with current, timely
information; 3) regularly use computer based
information retrieval services; and/or 4) work in
the news media, publishing, mass media, computer
applications, telecommunications or information
services industries.

CHAPTER 25

WOMEN AND MINORITIES

This chapter contains:

- going into business

- doing business with minority market

- women planning and conducting
  business

- success characteristics

- managers

- financial management

- networking

- biographical dictionary of women
  managers and administrators

- minorities bibliography

- directory of minority business firms

- ethnic sources, newspapers and
  periodicals

THE AMBITIOUS WOMAN'S GUIDE TO A SUCCESSFUL
CAREER
1980 (The 1975 edition was abstracted.)
Second
Higginson, Margaret - Quick, Thomas
240
0-317-27306-X
Books on Demand
UMI
Division of University Microfilms,
International
300 North Zeeb Road
Ann Arbor, MI 48106
(800) 521-0600
$72.00

Good
Book; guide

INCLUSIONS: Index, cross-referenced;
resource list; employment; bibliography

DESCRIPTORS: Women in business; career

SUMMARY: This book is on women in the
work place. It discusses ways to overcome
personal obstacles, focus on objectives,
determinants of success, plan one's life and
career, move through the educational process,
skills development, deal with financial matters,
career choice, assess and improve personal
appearance and image. Other topics include career
paths in traditional, non-traditional,
professional and non-professional occupations,
organizational and entrepreneurial approaches, job
hunting, the fast track, interpersonal skills, the
boss, peers, and subordinates. It advises on
resume preparation, job interviewing and
promotion.

RELEVANCE: This book is intended for the woman
beginning, resuming or working at a career. It
offers orientation, perspective and suggestions to
help women get ahead. Its statistics are dated.

AMERICAN WOMEN MANAGERS AND ADMINISTRATORS
A Selective Biographical Dictionary of
Twentieth-Century Leaders in Business,
Education, and Government
1985
First
Leavitt, Judith
317
0-313-23748-4
Greenwood Press
P.O. Box 5007
88 Post Road West
Westport, CT 06881
(203) 226-3571
$45.00

Very good
Biographical dictionary

INCLUSIONS: Index; bibliography; appendix

DESCRIPTORS: Women; women in business; women
in management; women in education; women in
administration; biography of women

SUMMARY: This work lists 226 living and
deceased women managers and administrators of the
2,986,000 of them listed by the Women's Bureau of
the U.S. Department of Labor in 1981. Almost half
of those listed were "firsts" in their areas of
achievement. Women earn less than men as managers
and administrators and very few reach the top
echelons. Women do better in academe, and the
number of women in government office is low but
increasing rapidly. Entries contain biographical
information followed by bibliography about and/or
by the woman.

RELEVANCE: This volume is included
(generally biographies are not included) due to
the rarity of women in top managerial and
administrative positions, to honor some American
women who have made it into leadership positions,
and because it may be helpful to women aspiring to
emulate and/or contact these women.

BE YOUR OWN BOSS
A Woman's Guide to Planning and Running Her
Business
1980
First
McCaslin, Barbara - McNamara, Patricia
352
0-13072-207-3
Prentice-Hall, Inc.
Rt. 9 West
Englewood Cliffs, NJ 07632
(201) 592-2352
Order: 200 Old Tappan Road
Old Tappan, NJ 07675
(201) 767-5049
$16.95

Very good
Book; guide

INCLUSIONS: Index by subject; glossary;
chapter bibliographies; worksheets

DESCRIPTORS: Women in business;
entrepreneurship; small business; business
planning

IDENTIFIER: Women Entrepreneur's Project
funded by the Division of Vocational Education
Research, U.S. Office of Education

SUMMARY: This book covers areas needed
to start and run a business: marketing research,
marketing plan, legal structure, financing,
purchasing, inventory, employees, etc. It is
based on the experience of over 300 women business
owners and experts and the materials were tested
by over 50 women in workshops. The book is geared
and addressed to women while covering basic and
"how to" information.

RELEVANCE: It is written for women who
think they want to start a business; those who
want to and don't know how, and those who have a
business and could use some help.

THE BLACK MANAGER
Making It in the Corporate World
1982
Dickens, Floyd   -   Dickens, Jaqueline
333
0-8144-5678-2
AMACOM
135 West 50th Street
New York, NY 10020
(212) 903-8087
$24.95

Excellent
Guide

INCLUSIONS: Index; appendix - The Research
Method; bibliography

DESCRIPTORS: Blacks; minorities; management

SUMMARY: This Guide identifies common
experiences, attitudes and behaviors, presents a
predictive model, and successful strategies and
role models for black managers. It is based on
research data from a "number of black managers."
Part I presents the four-phased development model
for the "way to success:" entry, adaptation,
planned growth, and success. Part II has chapters
for each phase organized by: 1) critical issues;
2) analysis of critical issues; 3) development of
how-to solutions; and 4) summary of basic
concepts. Part III consists of three chapters,
each focused on critical guidelines for success,
organized into three chapters -- internal,
external, and environmental. Internal struggles
are: effective style, management of rage, getting
the new job together, resisting power, self-
evaluation, setting your sights higher, and
resisting black self-hate. External strategies
are: management of subordinates, using resources,
reading cues, and successful confrontation.
Environmental strategies are: using strategic
management, using the grapevine, using power, and
using black development. Part IV is Learning for
Success, with chapters on Personal Planning and
Corporate and Institutional Planning.

RELEVANCE: This Guide helps business
people become aware of problems blacks have in
white corporations. It offers practical solutions
to management problems faced by black managers and
success strategies. It deals with how culture
impacts the work place and can be useful for other
minorities as well as blacks.

                    <<<<<<>>>>>>

A COMPREHENSIVE BIBLIOGRAPHY FOR THE STUDY OF
AMERICAN MINORITIES
1976
First
Miller, Wayne
1183 in 2 Volumes
0-8147-5373-6
New York University Press
70 Washington Square
New York, NY 10012
(212) 598-2886
$150.00

Very good
Bibliography

INCLUSIONS: Indexes by author, title

DESCRIPTORS: American minorities; ethnic
groups; ethnic group literature

SUMMARY: This bibliography has the
following sections: "From Africa and the Middle
East," "From Europe," "From Eastern Europe and the
Balkans," "From Asia," "From the Islands," and
"Native Americans." Each of these has an
introductory, historical bibliographical essay
describing the group and useful sources. It also
has a selective list of general sources. Sources
are listed by category, such as bibliography,
encyclopedia, dictionary, scholarly journal,
biography and autobiography, history and culture,
education, economics, health, literature, etc.

RELEVANCE: This is the most comprehensive
bibliography of its type. It does need to be
updated by over a decade.

ENCYCLOPEDIC DIRECTORY OF ETHNIC NEWSPAPERS AND
PERIODICALS IN THE UNITED STATES
1976
Second
Wynar, Lubomyr - Wynar, Anna
248
0-8728-7154-1
Libraries Unlimited, Inc.
P.O. Box 263
Littleton, CO 80120
(303) 770-1220
$15.00

Excellent
Directory; resource guide

INCLUSIONS: Index by periodical title;
appendix

DESCRIPTORS: Ethnic periodicals; American
minorities; ethnic groups; ethnic press

SUMMARY: This volume contains the
following: 1) an introductory chapter on the
methodology, scope, arrangement, entries, etc. of
the volume; 2) a chapter discussing the
terminology, history, role, and present status of
the ethnic press; 3) the multi-ethnic press; 4)
the ethnic press of 63 ethnic groups in 51
sections; 5) an appendix of statistical analyses
of individual ethnic presses, including frequency
publication in relation to language and
circulation; and 6) a title index. Directory
entries include title and translation, year of
origin, editorial address, telephone number,
editor's name, language(s) used; sponsoring
organization; circulation; frequency; annual
subscription rate; and annotation.

RELEVANCE: The coverage, narrative and
organization of this work is excellent. Ethnic
presses go largely unnoticed, yet are an important
research tool and expression of the fabric of
American life.

ETHNIC INFORMATION SOURCES OF THE UNITED STATES:
A Guide to Organizations, Agencies,
Foundations, Institutions, Media, Commercial
and Trade Bodies, Government Programs,
Research Institutes, Libraries and Museums,
Religious Organizations, Banking Firms,
Festivals and Fairs, Travel and Tourist
Offices, Airlines and Ship Lines, Bookdealer
and Publishers' Representatives, and Books,
Pamphlets and Audio-visuals on Specific Ethnic
Groups
1983 (The 1976 edition was abstracted.)
First
Wasserman, Paul - Morgan, Jean
751
Gale Research Company
Book Tower
Detroit, MI 48226
(800) 223-4253

Very good
Sourcebook

INCLUSIONS: Indexes by organization,
publication; guide to ethnic arrangement

DESCRIPTORS: Ethnic groups; ethnic
information

SUMMARY: This is alphabetically arranged
by ethnic group and then by topic within each
group. It excludes Blacks, Native Americans and
Eskimos based on other coverage on them. Topics
are broad, including embassy and consulate,
mission to the United Nations, organizations,
publications, audio-visual materials, etc. It
sometimes misses the mark, for examples, in
classifying some Jewish fraternal organizations
under religious organizations and in missing
newer, progressive, Jewish organizations and
publications formed since publication.

RELEVANCE: This source would have been rated
excellent except for the fact that it is not
comprehensive. It brings together many
types of information and resources on each ethnic
group, and can be useful to individuals,
organizations, government and business.

MARKETING YOURSELF
The Catalyst Women's Guide to Successful
Resumes and Interviews
1981 (The 1980 edition was abstracted.)
Second
Catalyst Editors
185
0-553-23751-9
Bantam Books Inc.
666 Fifth Avenue
New York, NY 10019
(800) 323-9872
$3.55

Very good
Guide

INCLUSIONS: Sample letters; forms

DESCRIPTORS: Marketing yourself; women;
resumes; interviews

SUMMARY: This is a step-by-step aid for
women job hunters based on the experience of
Catalyst, an organization dedicated to helping
women to develop successful careers. It counsels
women in knowing and marketing themselves. Part
I, resume preparation, is from the Catalyst
manual. Part II is an interview guide. It treats
the how to's of writing a resume, interviewing,
record and evaluative rating forms, preparatory
questions to ask oneself, and role plays. It
breaks down the job hunting process into steps:
analyzing one's achievements, determining job
targets, developing one's personal biography,
choosing a resume format, etc. The interview
process treats these steps: getting ready,
handling final preparations, and handling the
interview.

RELEVANCE: This source presents a clear-
cut approach to job hunting.

                    <<<<<<>>>>>>

NETWORKING
The Great Way for Women to Get Ahead

1981
Welch, Mary
304
0-446-30556-1
Warner Books
666 Fifth Avenue
New York, NY 10103
(800) 638-6460
$3.50

Good
Book

INCLUSIONS: Index; appendices (4),
including state by state network directory, and
bibliography

DESCRIPTORS: Women; career; networking

SUMMARY: This book shows women how to do
what the "old boys" have been doing for decades.
"Networking" is defined as the "process of
developing and using your contacts for
information, advice, and moral support as you
pursue your career." The emphasis is on women's
networks and it can also be done with men.
Networks can be in-house, issue oriented,
"overground groups," which are autonomous and use
company facilities, "underground groups," which
are secret and across company lines, and "multi-
nets," for the woman who joins more than one
network. Separate chapters are devoted to city-
wide and internal company networking. Twenty-five
success stories and some "unsuccess" stories
illustrate how networking works or could have
worked. Another section is entitled "Getting
Organized" and covers fourteen basic questions.

RELEVANCE: This is a helpful book for the
new and aspiring career woman.

                    <<<<<<>>>>>>

NEW BUSINESSES WOMEN CAN START AND
SUCCESSFULLY OPERATE
1977

Leslie, Mary - Seltz, David
244
0-87863-129-1
Longman Financial Services Publishing
500 N Dearborn Street
Chicago, IL 60610
(312) 836-0466
$9.95

Good
Book; guide

INCLUSIONS: Appendix of information
sources; checklists; self evaluation questionnaire

DESCRIPTORS: Women in business; women-
careers

SUMMARY: This book is on various
businesses a woman might have. It starts with
some basics about women's changing role and women
in business; how to raise capital; image making
through marketing--advertising, public relations,
direct mail, special projects; location; and
appearance. It provides information on twelve
major and many specific areas of business
women might pursue, including research, art,
handicrafts, food, writing, management consultant,
bookkeeper, promotion, sales, animals specialties,
storekeeper, and childcare.

RELEVANCE: This is an easy-to-read, well-
organized and written book for the prospective
woman entrepreneur looking for business ideas.

<<<<<<>>>>>>

NEW CAREER OPTIONS
A Woman's Guide
1977
First
Farmer, Helen - Backer, Thomas
60
Human Interaction Research Institute
10889 Wilshire Boulevard
Los Angeles, CA

0-87705-272-7
Human Sciences Press
72 Fifth Avenue
New York, NY 10011
(212) 243-6000

Good
Guide

INCLUSION: Lists of information sources

DESCRIPTORS: Career; women

IDENTIFIER: National Institute of Education
funded

SUMMARY: The authors discuss the
problems and opportunities for women at work in
the U.S., provide some statistics on women in the
crafts, management, and professions, and discuss
the chances for women in these fields. They cover
issues of marriage, family and career, career
planning and where to turn for help, how to look
for a job, and where to get information, including
government and non-government publications,
publishing houses with materials on women,
Catalyst and its national network of local
resource centers, and women's units in 67
organizations.

RELEVANCE: This is a handy little pamphlet
intended for the 1970's, so it is somewhat
outdated, yet it contains some useful information.
A companion work for counselors is New Career
Options for Women: A Counselor's Sourcebook.

                    <<<<<<>>>>>

SEVENTY BILLION IN THE BLACK
America's Black Consumers
1978
First, revised
Gibson, Parke
230
0-0254-3160-9
MacMillan

Front and Brown Streets
Riverside, NJ 08370
(212) 935-2000
$10.95

Very good
Book

INCLUSIONS: Index; bibliography; appendix
on consumer expenditures and income; case
histories

DESCRIPTORS: Blacks; minorities; black
consume market; Hispanic market

IDENTIFIER: D. Parke Gibson International

SUMMARY: This book offers insights about
the need for recognition of the Black consumer
market, and related marketing considerations. It
is based on the author's proven and observed
experience. Sections treat understanding the black
consumer, marketing planning and market
development. It gives case histories of how some
companies developed black-oriented campaigns. It
notes that the nation's 24.1 million blacks and
3.2 million other non-white minorities comprise
the ninth largest U.S. consumer market and
annually buy $70 billion of goods and services.
It describes market characteristics useful in
developing better marketing programs, introducing
new products, and establishing brand position. It
focuses on segmented marketing approaches directed
to black and Hispanic populations. It discusses:
uses of media, "integrated" advertising methods
(using minorities in white-oriented media);
advertising strategies; sales promotion and
merchandising techniques; and public relations
practices. It also treats distributor
cooperation, corporate social responsibility, and
the potential of the black market for travel and
leisure oriented sales. It discusses developing
press relations and educating business personnel
about low-income consumers. It describes
effective marketing campaigns used by the Pepsi-
Cola, Publicker Distillers, Greyhound, Teacher's
Scotch, Carnation, and American Airlines firms.

RELEVANCE: This provides a wealth of
insights and suggestions about ways to
successfully relate to the needs and opportunities
of the black and other non-white markets.

                    <<<<<<>>>>>

SURVIVAL IN THE CORPORATE FISHBOWL
Making It Into Upper and Middle Management
1987
First
Fernandez, John
336
0-669-10336-5
Lexington Books
125 Spring Street
Lexington, MA 02173
(800) 235-3565
$24.95

Very good
Guide

INCLUSIONS: Index; bibliography; chapter
notes; appendix; case studies

DESCRIPTORS: Career advancement; women;
minorities; human resource development

SUMMARY: This presents a dog-eat-dog as
reality picture of an inequitable, bureaucratic
Corporate America. It looks at the realities of
competition as a white male, woman, and minority.
Chapters deal with career problems, advancement,
surviving corporate games and politics, racism and
sexism, career problems and solutions.   The
author advises men to forget about reverse
discrimination, deal with performance and the
reality of unfairness and discrimination against
women and minorities, and be prepared to work in
an heterogeneous environment. He advises women to
recognize their unique problems on the job,
develop "a repertoire of techniques," and "change
the system, not join it." He advises minorities
to develop a "positive self-concept, expert
technical skills, and more importantly written and

oral skills." Both women and minorities should
work together to win equal opportunity for all.
The author advises corporate leaders to confront
reality and make efforts to reduce inequality and
unfair treatment.

RELEVANCE: This is relevant for all
workers and management.

<<<<<<>>>>>

TRY US
National Minority Business Directory
1987 (The 1985 edition was abstracted.)
Sixteenth
383 (1985)
National Minority Business Directories
65 22nd Avenue N.E.
Minneapolis, MN 55418
(612) 781-6819
$32.00 (1985)

Very good
Directory

INCLUSIONS: Keyword index; alphabetical
listing of firms

DESCRIPTOR: Minority business

SUMMARY: This directory lists over 5000
ethnic minority firms. The firms are arranged in
83 subject categories, then by State in alphabetic
order. A 3000 keyword index helps locate products
and services. Subjects include: accounting,
advertising, banks, consultants, educational
materials, executive search agencies, information
processing, office supplies, unusual products and
services, etc. Each entry includes the firm name,
address, telephone number, principal officer(s),
and description of work. Each firm entry is
listed and indexed by number.

RELEVANCE: This is the most comprehensive
minority business directory and can be used to
locate firms by those wishing to do business with

minority firms and meet affirmative action sub-
contracting goals. A geographic index would be
helpful. The directory is computerized.

<<<<<<>>>>>>

WOMEN AT WORK
Overcoming the Obstacles
1979
Pinkstaff, Marline   -   Wilkinson, Anna
191
0-20105-720-2
Addison-Wesley Publishing Company
1 Jacob Way
Reading, MA 01867
(800) 447-2226
$8.95

Good
Book

DESCRIPTOR: Women-employment

SUMMARY: This book covers chapters on
self-image; guilt; sharing the work at home;
support systems; achievement;
power/politics/promotion; networks; sexism; sexual
harassment; resentment and other feelings. It
stimulates consciousness- raising and offers
advice and techniques for overcoming sexist and
detrimental attitudes in oneself and others. It
apprises women of their rights, for example, in
overcoming sexual harassment in the workplace.

RELEVANCE: The book concentrates on the
woman and emphasizes a psychological approach
rather than external barriers to success in the
work world.

<<<<<<>>>>>>

WOMEN'S HANDBOOK OF INDEPENDENT FINANCIAL
MANAGEMENT
1979

First
Lee, Steven   -   Hassay, Karen
182
Van Nostrand Reinhold Company
135 West 50th Street
New York, NY 10020
(212) 254-3232
$12.95

Good
Guide

INCLUSIONS: Index by subject; cast studies;
illustrations; worksheets; glossary; bibliography

DESCRIPTORS: Finance; personal finance; women

SUMMARY: This book briefly surveys the
various types of individual investments common in
this economy. It includes stocks, bonds, real
estate, collectibles, insurance, pensions, and
savings accounts. Ideas are presented at an
elementary level in regards to how to budget, use
credit, save, invest, estate plan, and income tax
planning. Since tax laws as well as other factors
in the economy change, some specific information
in this work is dated and no longer provides valid
details.

RELEVANCE: This is a tool for the person new
to investing, budgeting, and financial planning.
It's important that women know how to manage their
finances independently.

AUTHOR/EDITOR INDEX

Figgie
  Harry, 5
Figueroa
  Oscar, 53
Fish
  Edith, 250
Fisher
  John, 32
Flamholtz
  Eric, 296
Forhbieter-Mueller
  Jo, 65
Forrestal
  Dan, 24
Foster
  Robert, 352
Frailey
  Lester, 217
Frank
  Nathalie, 353
Fried
  Charles, 141
Friedman
  Jane, 141
Fryburger
  Vernon, 17
Fuori
  William, 102
Furman
  Amy, 39

Ganly
  John, 353
Garvin
  Andrew, 345
Geiser
  Elizabeth, 379
Gelatt
  Esther, 294
George
  Abraham, 202
Gibson
  Parke, 428
Giddy
  Ian, 202
Gill
  Kay, 341

Goehlert
  Robert, 232
Goldberg
  Philip, 207
Goldscheider
  Robert, 147
Goldstucker
  Jac, 363
Goodstein
  Leonard, 123
Gotsick
  Pricilla, 218
Gottfredson
  Gary, 74
Gottschall
  Edward, 43
Granick
  Lois, 278
Green
  James, 91
  JoAnn, 180
Griesinger
  Frank, 407
Gross
  Malvern, 7
Gruber
  Frank, 57
  Katherine 30
Grupenhoff
  John, 274
Gunderson
  Nels, 232
Guttman
  Daniel, 136

Hagood
  Patricia, 348
Hamilton
  Robert, 327
Hanlon
  Joseph, 372
Hardy
  Benjamin, 334
Harris
  Philip, 304
Hart
  Lois, 286

SUBJECT INDEX

Computer crime, 326
Computer distributors, 104
Computer graphics, 44
Computer languages, 93
Computer law, 326
Computer literature, 90
Computer mail-order houses, 104
Computer management, 96, 98
Computer manufacturers, 104
Computer networks, 408
Computer periodicals, 93, 104
Computer personnel, 104
Computer privacy, 326
Computer products, 42
Computer programming, 103
Computer resources, 93
Computer reviewers, 90
Computer services, 104
Computer software, 107, 108
Computer systems, 92, 104, 107
Computer technology, 97
Computer teleconferencing, 414, 415
Computer wholesalers, 104
Computer-aided management, 58
Computer-assisted instruction, 315
Computer-related training, 315
Computerization, 310
Computers, 91, 92, 97, 99, 101, 102, 103, 115, 337
Computers and publishing, 337
Computing reviews, 90
Conferences, 311
Conflicts of interest, 59
Congressional legislation, 229
Congressional publishing, 229
Constitutional rights, 332
Construction industry, 323
Consultant, 122
Consultant characteristics, 134
Consultant directories, 114, 124
Consultant role, 414
Consultants, 112, 114, 117, 119, 123, 124, 128,
  130, 132, 133, 136, 138
Consultation, 119, 120, 121
Consultation - mental health, 127
Consulting, 111, 112, 113, 115, 117, 123, 126,
  128, 129, 130, 133, 134, 135, 136
Consulting - legal issues, 113, 129
Consulting business, 129
Consulting contracts, 113, 129

TITLE INDEX